# REASONABLE CARE

## The Broker Oversight Playbook for Importers

*Broker Oversight, ACE Auditing, and 19 CFR Part 111*

James R. Ferry II, CCS, CES, CIT

Trade Underground Press

*First Edition*

**Reasonable Care: The Broker Oversight Playbook for Importers**



Published by Trade Underground Press.



The author writes from The Trade Underground. Ferry Trade Group (FTG) is the author's trade-compliance consultancy. The views in this book are the author's own.

This book is educational material and is not legal advice. See the Important Notice that follows for the full terms, including the limitation of liability, the note on the author's credentials, and the instruction to consult your own qualified counsel before relying on any model document, procedure, deadline, or figure in this book.

First Edition, 2026. Corrected printing, September 2026.

Law and agency guidance stated as of September 2026.

ISBN: 979-8-951909-05-3 (Ebook) · 979-8-951909-06-0 (Paperback)

*For my Love.*

# Important Notice: Please Read First

## This book is educational material, not legal advice

> This book is a practitioner's field manual written for general educational and informational purposes only. It is not legal advice, and it is not a substitute for the advice of a licensed attorney. The author is a working trade-compliance practitioner, not a lawyer; reading this book, using its materials, or contacting the author does not create an attorney-client relationship or any other professional-client relationship, and nothing here should be understood as an opinion about your specific situation. Customs and trade law changes constantly and applies differently to every company, every product, and every shipment. Any decision you make about your own imports is yours alone.

The frameworks, procedures, and enforcement summaries in this book reflect the author's operational experience and reading of public sources as of the date of writing. They are offered so that you can understand how the customs system works and ask better questions, not so that you can substitute this book for your own professional judgment or that of your advisors.

## How to use the model documents, checklists, and templates

The model Power-of-Attorney addendum, the Service Level Agreement, the prior-disclosure and audit language, the checklists, the scorecards, and the SQL and integration examples in this book are illustrative drafting starting points and teaching examples. They are not execution-ready legal instruments, and they are not tuned to your contracts, your jurisdiction, your counterparties, or your facts. Do not sign, send, file, or deploy any of them as written. Treat each as a first draft to hand to your own qualified customs or trade-law counsel, who should adapt it to your situation before you rely on it. Statutory citations, regulatory citations, case references, dollar figures, and deadlines are provided to orient you and should be confirmed against the current primary source before you act.

## No warranty, and no liability

This material is provided "as is," without any warranty of any kind, express or implied, including any warranty of accuracy, completeness, currency, or fitness for a particular purpose. To the fullest extent permitted by law, the author and publisher disclaim all liability for any loss, penalty, cost, or damage of any kind arising out of or connected to the use of, or reliance on, anything in this book. You are solely responsible for your own compliance decisions and assume all risk associated with them. By continuing to read and use this book, you accept these terms; if you do not accept them, do not use the materials in this book.

## On the 2026 enforcement changes

This book was written as Executive Order 14411, "Strengthening Customs Enforcement" (signed June 3, 2026), was taking effect. An executive order directs federal agencies to act; it is not, by itself, a change to the statute. Several of the changes described here (the mandatory penalty floor, the elimination of mitigation for repeat offenders, and the "good standing" importer registry) depend on rulemaking that CBP and DHS were directed to complete within 90 and 180 days of the order. Where the text describes those changes, read them as the enforcement regime the order builds toward, and confirm the final rules as published before relying on any specific mechanic or deadline.

## About the author's credentials

James R. Ferry II holds the Certified Customs Specialist (CCS), Certified Export Specialist (CES), and Certificate in International Trade (CIT) designations. These are professional trade-compliance certifications earned through the trade community; they are not a license to practice law. The author's perspective in this book is that of a working trade-compliance practitioner, not an attorney.

# Contents

# Start Here: How to Use This Book

This is a working manual for a single job: taking back control of the customs liability that is already yours, whether or not you have been exercising it. If your company's number sits in the Importer of Record box on a CBP entry summary, federal law already holds you, not your broker, responsible for the accuracy of everything filed under it. This book is about closing the gap between that legal reality and the way most importers actually operate.

## A word about your broker

This book is hard on the structure of modern customs brokerage: the volume economics, the remote entry desk, the one-sided standard contract. It is not a case against brokers. A good Customs Broker is one of the most valuable partners your supply chain has: a licensed professional who knows the ports, the rulings, and the traps you will never see coming. The purpose of everything that follows is not to fight your broker. It is to build the oversight structure that lets a good broker do their best work, leaves a careless one no room to hurt you, and protects both of you when CBP comes asking questions.

Oversight is not war. It is the scaffolding of an accountable partnership, and the best brokers welcome a client who finally knows what to ask for. If you take the tools in this book to your broker as an ultimatum, you will get the wrong result. Take them as the standard you both now work to.

## Who this book is for

You are most likely a trade-compliance manager or director, an in-house counsel, or a CFO or controller who has noticed how much of the company's cash leaves through the duty line. You may also be the owner-operator of a smaller importer who wears all of those hats before lunch. The book is written for every one of you, but not every part applies to every one of you at once, which is what the tiers below are for. And if you are a licensed Customs Broker: read it as a map of what your most sophisticated clients are about to ask for, and a head start on being the broker who already offers it.

## If you do only three things

The full program in this book is deep, and no one implements all of it on day one. If you read nothing else, do these three. They prevent the large majority of the damage, at any size, for a fraction of the effort.

1. Fix your Power of Attorney. The standard broker POA is written to protect the broker. Chapter 4 shows the addendum that rebalances it: a one-time legal task with a permanent payoff.
2. See what is actually filed under your number. Even a quarterly manual pull of your ACE entry data, checked against your own records (Chapter 1), will surface most broker errors while you can still fix them for free.
3. Know your clocks. The 300-day Post-Summary Correction window (Chapter 10) is your free-correction period; the response window on a CBP inquiry (Chapter 12) is measured in days; and, while it lasts, the IEEPA refund clock runs separately, through CAPE rather than a PSC (Chapter 14). Miss any of them and a fixable problem, or a large refund, becomes a loss.

## Find your tier

Match yourself to the description that fits your volume and staffing, then follow that path. You can always climb.

**Tier A: Small or occasional importer** (under roughly 500 entries a year; no dedicated compliance staff). Start with Chapter 1 (the twenty-minute quarterly check) and Chapters 2–3, then the

POA addendum in Chapter 4 and the AD/CVD and UFLPA basics in Chapter 11 if they touch your goods. Leave the SQL and API build, the formal SLA machinery, and the annual forensic audit for later.

**Tier B: Mid-market importer** (roughly 500–5,000 entries a year; a compliance manager, limited IT). Add the SLA in Chapter 5, monthly ACE spot-audits in Excel from Chapter 7, the CEE playbook in Chapter 12, and the PSC and prior-disclosure playbook in Chapter 10. Adopt the manual versions before the full system-to-system integration in Chapter 9.

**Tier C: Enterprise importer** (5,000+ entries a year; compliance plus IT and data resources). The full program is built for you: API master-data sync in Chapters 8–9, the SQL audit engine in Chapter 7, the annual audit and scorecard in Chapter 13, and the complete Broker Oversight Manual in Chapter 14. Use the appendix instruments as your starting templates.

## How to read it

The book has two kinds of chapters. Some are meant to be read front to back: Part I (the twenty-minute check, and why the liability is yours), Part IV (high-risk lines and CBP inquiries), and Part V (building a program that outlives any one employee). Others are reference: Part II (the model POA and SLA language) and Part III (the data-audit and software mechanics). Read the opening of each reference chapter to get the idea, then return to the SQL, schemas, and field maps when you are ready to build. The appendix collects the master instruments in ready-to-adapt form; treat it as your toolbox, not bedtime reading.

One thing to say plainly, because the book's page count hides it: Parts III and V are the enterprise build: the SQL, the API integration, the annual forensic audit, the full oversight manual. They exist for the Tier C reader. If you are Tier A or B, skim their openings and leave the machinery for later. A reader who does the twenty-minute check in Chapter 1 and fixes the POA in Chapter 4 has the core of the program already, and most of the protection with it.

## A note on the 2026 rules

The spine of this book is older than the current news cycle. Since the Customs Modernization Act of 1993, 19 U.S.C. § 1484 has placed a non-delegable duty of reasonable care on the importer of record, and the courts have enforced it for just as long. In United States v. Trek Leather the Federal Circuit reached a company's own officer personally in 2014, well before any 2026 rule. Executive Order 14411 does not create that liability. It sharpens the price of ignoring it. As the disclaimer notes, an executive order directs agencies to write rules. It is not, by itself, the rule. Where the book describes the penalty floors, the repeat-offender bar, or the good-standing registry, read them as the regime the order builds toward, and confirm the final published rules before you rely on a specific deadline or number. The direction is not in doubt. The details are still settling.

# PART I: THE ILLUSION OF DELEGATION & THE 2026 ENFORCEMENT PARADIGM

# Chapter 1: The Twenty-Minute Quarterly Check

The full program in this book is deep. This chapter is not part of it.

This chapter is for the importer who has no compliance department, no ERP integration, no SQL, and no realistic prospect of any of those this year: the owner-operator, the controller wearing four hats, the operations manager who inherited customs because nobody else would take it. If that is you, most of this book is aspirational. This part is not. It takes about twenty minutes a quarter, it requires nothing but a browser and a spreadsheet, and it will surface the large majority of what is going wrong under your number.

Do this and nothing else, and you will be ahead of most importers your size.

### Step zero: get your own ACE Portal account

This is the only part that takes longer than twenty minutes, you only do it once, and **you do not need your broker's permission or cooperation to do it.**

Apply for an ACE Secure Data Portal account at CBP's site as an importer. You designate an **Account Owner** (also called the Trade Account Owner, or TAO), who can be any employee you choose. CBP defines the Account Owner by function: the person who handles the account's day-to-day administration, and treats it as distinct from a company officer, so it need not be an officer.

Two reasons this matters more than it sounds.

**First, CBP's inquiries route through it.** The ACE Forms module: Forms 28, 29, and 4647, is available through the importer of record's own portal account, and the importer of record is the party responsible for responding. (CBP also sends the broker electronic courtesy copies where the broker's sub-account has a registered e-mail and Portal mode, but that is a copy to the broker, not a substitute for your own access, and you should not depend on it.) If you have no account, you find out that CBP asked you something when, and if, your broker forwards it. Chapter 12 explains how expensive that gap gets.

**Second, it is your independent copy of the record.** Everything in this chapter comes out of your portal account. None of it depends on a broker sending you anything, which means none of it stops working if the relationship does.

If your broker set up portal access for you, check whose account it actually is. If you have a user profile under *their* account, that access ends when the relationship does. You want an account in your own name with your own employee as Account Owner, and your broker holding a user profile under it, never the reverse.

**The twenty minutes**

Once a quarter, sit down and do the following.

**1. Pull the quarter's line-item data (3 minutes).** Run the entry summary line-item report: the ES-002/ES-003, for the quarter just ended. Export to CSV and open it in Excel.

**2. Sort by duty paid, largest first (1 minute).** You are not auditing everything. You are auditing where the money is. Take the top twenty lines and ignore the rest. On a typical small importer's book those twenty lines will be a third or more of the duty you paid.

**3. Run five checks against those twenty lines (10 minutes).**

- **Do you recognize the tariff number?** Keep a one-page list of the HTS codes your products should be entering under. A spreadsheet is fine, this is not a compliance system. Anything on your top-twenty that isn't on your list is a question. Not necessarily an error. A question.

- **Does the code end in `.90` or `.9000`?** These are basket provisions: "other: other." Sometimes they are correct. Often they are what a clerk picked because the invoice said "machine parts" and the clock was running. Every one of them on your list deserves a specific answer to "why this code and not a more specific one?"
- **Is the country of origin what you actually bought?** Compare against your purchase order, not against the vendor's invoice. Those are different documents and they disagree more often than you would think.
- **Does the entered value match your commercial invoice?** Look for decimal slips and currency conversion errors. A value that is off by exactly ten times, or off by roughly the exchange rate, is not a coincidence.
- **Are you claiming the trade preferences you are entitled to?** If you import from a USMCA country and the Special Program Indicator column is empty, you may be paying duty you do not owe.

**4. Run two structural checks on the whole file (5 minutes).** These are filters, not line-by-line reviews.

- **Filter for Entry Type 03.** These are your antidumping and countervailing duty entries, and they carry the highest penalty exposure in the book. For every one, confirm the non-reimbursement indicator is set to `Y`. If it is blank, read Chapter 11 before you do anything else. This is the error that can cost you the duty twice.
- **Filter for the Section 301 exclusion headings `9903.88.69` and `9903.88.70`.** Those two are the live exclusion claims. The rest of the `9903.88` series carries the Section 301 duties themselves, not exclusions, so filter for the two exclusion headings specifically rather than the whole series. Check that the exclusion is still live, and, as of this writing, that you know **all 178 remaining exclusions expire on November 9, 2026.** If your duty savings depend on one, you need that number in front of whoever runs your budget now, not in December.

**5. Write down what you found (1 minute).** A dated note in a file. Three columns: entry number, what looked wrong, what you did about it. That file is not busywork. It is the entire evidentiary record of your reasonable care, and it is the difference described in Chapter 14 between a company that can show its work and one that can only remember it.

### What to do with what you find

Take the questions to your broker in writing, and ask for an answer in writing. Most will have one. "That code is correct because the ruling on this commodity says X" is a fine answer and you should keep it. It becomes part of your list for next quarter.

Where there is a real error, you generally have **300 days from the date of entry, or until fifteen days before the entry's scheduled liquidation date, whichever comes first** (and longer where liquidation is suspended or extended: common on AD/CVD entries), to fix it through a Post-Summary Correction. For a good-faith error your own controls caught, that correction carries no penalty. But be clear on one thing the next chapters develop: a PSC is not a § 1592 safe harbor. Where the error is a material misstatement rather than an honest slip, only a prior disclosure limits penalty exposure, and that decision comes first. Chapter 10 covers both. The clock still frames it: inside the window a genuine mistake is an administrative correction; outside it, a mistake is a protest, a prior disclosure, or a penalty.

Which means the single most valuable feature of doing this quarterly is that you find things while they are still free to fix.

### What good looks like

You are not aiming for zero questions. You are aiming for a shrinking list, answers you can point to, and no surprises in the two structural filters.

If you run this four times and find nothing meaningful, that is real information: your broker is doing careful work, and you now have a documented basis for saying so. If you run it once and find four things, that is also real information, and Chapter 4 is where you go next.

**When to graduate**

Move up to the monthly Excel audit in Chapter 7 when any of these is true: you pass roughly five hundred entries a year; you start importing anything subject to an AD/CVD order or a forced-labor priority sector; you find errors two quarters running; or you hire someone whose job includes compliance.

Until then, twenty minutes a quarter is not a compromise. It is the highest return on time available anywhere in this book.

# Chapter 2: The Agency Trap: Why Your Broker Is an Agent, Not a Shield

### First, about your broker

This chapter is going to be hard on the structure of modern customs brokerage. Before it is, I want to be exact about what I am criticizing, because the distinction matters and it will get lost otherwise.

I am not criticizing brokers. I have worked alongside licensed Customs Brokers who are the best compliance professionals I know: people who refuse to guess a classification, who stop an entry rather than force it through on a vague invoice, who read the rulings, and who treat a national permit as something to protect rather than something to spend. If you have one of those, this book is not an indictment of them. It is the structure that lets them prove they are what they say they are.

What I am criticizing is an economic model. A brokerage that charges seventy-five dollars to file an entry summary cannot afford to spend forty-five minutes on it. That is not a moral failing on anyone's part. It is arithmetic. The entry clerk working under a fifty-file daily quota is not careless. They are doing exactly what the system pays them to do, at exactly the speed it pays them to do it. The problem is that the system's incentive is velocity, the law's requirement is accuracy, and the gap between those two lands on you.

So the argument of this chapter is narrow, and I want it stated plainly up front: **the liability is yours by statute, and the visibility is not yours by default.** Everything else in this book exists to close that gap.

Oversight is not war. Done right it is the scaffolding of an accountable partnership, and the good brokers welcome it, because a client who can finally see the work is a client who can finally tell the difference between good work and the low bid down the street. If you take the tools in this book to your broker as an ultimatum, you will get the wrong result and you will deserve it. Take them as the standard you both now work to.

Now, the law.

**The Legal Illusion: 19 U.S.C. § 1484 and 19 CFR Part 111**

In corporate legal departments and boardrooms, one belief about customs liability persists above all others, passing from one supply-chain vice president to the next as settled fact:

*"We hired a licensed Customs Broker, so our customs liability is covered."*

It is a misreading of how the federal statutory architecture is built, and it has cost importers real money under 19 U.S.C. § 1592.

To understand why this belief is a complete illusion, one must look at the stark, unyielding divide between two distinct bodies of federal law: 19 U.S.C. § 1484 and 19 CFR Part 111.

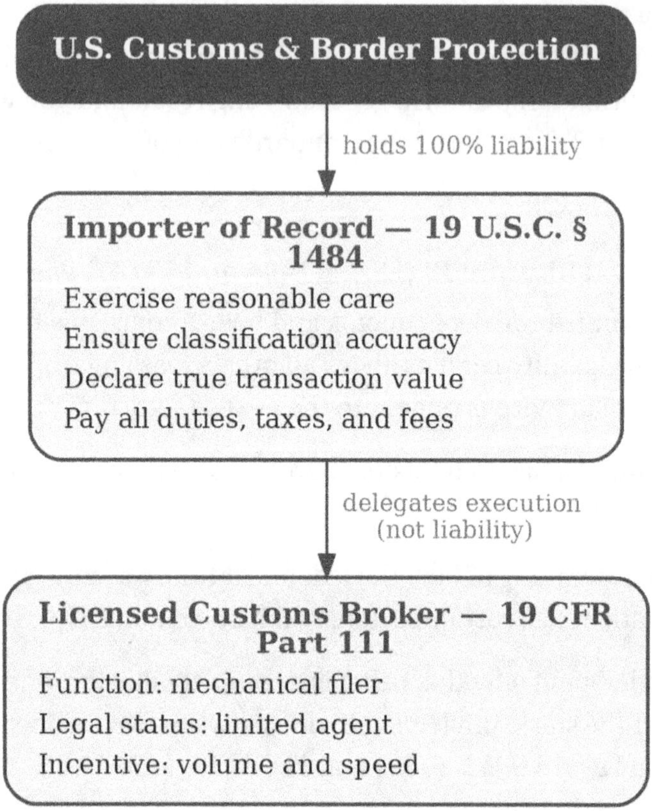


**The Statutory Anchor: 19 U.S.C. § 1484**

Enacted as part of the Tariff Act of 1930 and radically overhauled by the Customs Modernization Act ("Mod Act") of 1993, 19 U.S.C. § 1484 places the non-delegable duty of reasonable care on the Importer of Record (IOR). The statute is unambiguous:

> *"[The importer of record]... either in person or by an agent authorized by the party in writing, shall, using reasonable care, (A) make entry... by filing with the Customs Service... such documentation... as is necessary... and (B) complete the entry... by filing with the Customs Service the declared value, classification and rate of duty applicable to the merchandise." (19 U.S.C. § 1484(a)(1))*

Notice what the statute does not say. It does not state that a licensed Customs Broker must exercise reasonable care on your behalf. It does not state that delegating entry filing to a licensed professional satisfies the importer's statutory duty. What it does is place on you, the corporate entity holding the IOR number, the duty to exercise **reasonable care** in the information transmitted to U.S. Customs and Border Protection (CBP). Be precise about that standard, because the rest of the book depends on it: reasonable care is a care standard, not strict liability. You are not an insurer of absolute accuracy; you are responsible for the diligence a prudent importer would exercise. And § 1484(a)(1) expressly lets you enter "by an agent authorized ... in writing," so the *task* of filing is delegable. What is non-delegable is the *liability* for it. Hire the broker; you still own the duty.

When an entry summary (CBP Form 7501) is transmitted into the Automated Commercial Environment (ACE), the legal declaration being executed belongs to the importer. If the Harmonized Tariff Schedule (HTS) classification is wrong, if the declared transaction value omits a $500,000 tooling assist, if an Antidumping/Countervailing Duty (AD/CVD) case number is missing, or if a partner government agency (PGA) flag is bypassed, the importer is on the hook, and its exposure is not reduced by the broker's involvement. That is the point to hold onto; it is not that the importer is the *only* party who can be penalized. Section 1592(a) reaches "any person," brokers are separately disciplined under § 1641(d), and individuals can be reached in their own name (Chapter 3's discussion of Trek Leather is exactly that). Your liability stands on its own feet, whether or not anyone else shares it.

### The Operational Shell: 19 CFR Part 111

Conversely, 19 CFR Part 111 governs the licensing, conduct, and regulatory obligations of Customs Brokers. While Part 111 requires a broker to exercise "due diligence" in preparing and filing records relating to any customs business matter (19 CFR § 111.29(a)), this regulatory requirement creates zero statutory indemnity for the importer.

A Customs Broker operating under Part 111 is, in the eyes of federal administrative law, a limited agent executing mechanical filing tasks on behalf of a principal. Under foundational principles of common law agency, which govern the relationship between IORs and brokers, the acts of the agent performed within the scope of their authority are legally imputed to the principal.

When your broker's entry clerk fat-fingers an HTS code, converting a duty-free electronic subassembly into a 25% Section 301 tariff-eligible item (or worse, converting an AD/CVD-subject steel component into an un-flagged generic item), the law treats that mistake as if you personally typed it into ACE yourself.

The Divide Is Stark:

| 19 U.S.C. § 1484, The Importer | 19 CFR Part 111, The Broker |
|---|---|
| Non-delegable legal liability | Limited regulatory mandate for due diligence |
| Mandates "reasonable care" | Governs operational licensing and conduct |
| Liability not reduced by the broker's involvement | Separately exposed under § 1592 and disciplined under § 1641(d) |
| Non-delegable duty for valuation and HTS | Mechanical executor of client instructions |

### The Penalty Paradigm

When CBP detects a pattern of misclassification, undervaluation, or duty evasion, the civil enforcement mechanism utilized is 19 U.S.C. § 1592. Under Section 1592, penalties are assessed based on the degree of culpability:

- Negligence: Failure to exercise Reasonable Care. Penalties can reach the lesser of the domestic value of the merchandise or two times the lawful duties, taxes, and fees of which the government was deprived.

- Gross Negligence: Acted with actual knowledge of, or wanton disregard for, the relevant facts and statutory obligations. Penalties can reach the lesser of the domestic value or four times the lawful duties, taxes, and fees.
- Fraud: Voluntarily and intentionally committing a violation. Penalties equal the domestic value of the merchandise.

These maxima are the revenue-loss measures, and they are not the only cap. Where a violation deprives the government of no duty at all, a misstatement on a duty-free line, for instance, Section 1592(c) instead measures the penalty against the dutiable value of the merchandise: up to 20% of that value for negligence and up to 40% for gross negligence, with fraud still reaching the domestic value. A practitioner should not assume the duty-multiple is the only ceiling; a "no-loss" error still carries real exposure.

When an importer facing a Section 1592 penalty investigation attempts to mount a defense by claiming, "We relied on our broker to pick the right HTS code," CBP's consistent position, expressed across its Reasonable Care guidance and its penalty practice, and paraphrased here rather than quoted, comes to the same thing: reliance on a Customs Broker does not by itself establish reasonable care. The importer must be able to show it gave the broker complete, accurate, expert-vetted information and actively monitored the filings. The case law below, not any single CBP pronouncement, is what makes that position stick.

The courts have said the same thing, for decades. In United States v. Golden Ship Trading Co., 25 CIT 40 (2001), the Court of International Trade found an importer negligent under Section 1592 where she signed entry documents certifying their accuracy but made no independent effort to verify the country of origin her supplier had reported. Hiring a licensed broker did not, by itself, discharge her own duty of reasonable care. The individual who signed, Joanne Wu, was held personally liable alongside her company: the same personal-exposure principle Trek Leather later drove home.

Golden Ship shows what happens when an importer does nothing to verify. A second case shows something subtler and, for our purposes, more useful: what happens when the importer does something, but the wrong thing.

In United States v. Horizon Products International, Inc., 82 F. Supp. 3d 1350 (Ct. Int'l Trade 2015), the government sought both unpaid duties and a negligence penalty over misclassified plywood. The court split the two. On the duties it granted summary judgment for the government: the goods were misclassified, and the money was owed regardless of anyone's care. On the § 1592 negligence penalty it denied summary judgment and sent the question to trial.

Why it denied is the part worth sitting with. Horizon had used a licensed broker, and the court treated that fact as material, not as a defense, and not as nothing, but as evidence a factfinder would have to weigh, cutting in more than one direction. The court noted a factfinder could as easily conclude the broker shared responsibility, given brokers' own classification duties. What complicated the picture further was that Horizon had faxed its broker the wrong classifications. The record could support more than one inference about whose failure that was, and the penalty factors courts use in these cases required a trial to sort out.

Two lessons come out of that, and they point in opposite directions from each other.

The first is reassuring. Using a broker is not irrelevant to your reasonable-care posture. Courts do weigh it. What Golden Ship punishes is not delegation. It is delegation with no verification at all.

The second is not reassuring, and it is the one that should shape how you operate. The quality of what you send your broker is your exposure, not theirs. Horizon's broker filed what Horizon told it to file. That instruction, a fax with the wrong codes on it, became the centerpiece of a federal case. Every classification you push into your broker's system, every value you send on a commercial invoice, every origin you declare on a purchase order is a statement you are making to CBP through an intermediary. It carries your name.

That is why the master data work in Chapters 7 and 8 is not an IT project. It is the mechanism by which what you meant to declare and what actually got declared stay the same thing.

Note also what the split holding means practically: the duties and the penalty are separate fights. You can lose the first and still win the second, and the second is where the reasonable-care record does its work. An importer with documented controls may end up paying the duty it always owed and no penalty on top. An importer without them pays both.

There is no single codified test for what reasonable care requires; the courts weigh it on the totality of the circumstances. But the case law points consistently at three things you must be able to show before "I relied on my broker" carries any weight. Treat the following as a practical self-test, not a statute.

| What you must be able to show | Why it matters |
|---|---|
| Your expert was qualified for the specific question | A broker retained to file entries is not automatically qualified to opine on a novel classification or an AD/CVD scope question. Match the expert to the issue. |
| You gave the expert full and truthful facts | Reliance collapses if you handed the broker a lump-sum vendor invoice |

| What you must be able to show | Why it matters |
|---|---|
| | with no itemized freight, assists, or origin detail. You cannot rely on advice you starved of information. |
| You relied in good faith and verified the result | Signing whatever comes back is not reliance; it is abdication. Reasonable care includes independently reviewing what was actually transmitted under your number. |

Miss any one of these and the reliance defense does little to blunt a Section 1592 negligence case. Valuation is where importers most often fall short. If you buy under EXW or DDP and forward a single-figure vendor invoice to your broker without breaking out international freight, inland drayage, and origin charges, you have deprived the broker of the facts needed to declare value correctly, and the same reasoning that decided Golden Ship, that a signature without verification is not reasonable care, applies with equal force to value.

CBP's published guidance and its penalty practice both treat unexamined reliance on a broker as failing the reasonable-care standard rather than satisfying it. If you handed your broker a vague commercial invoice with a description like "Machine Parts" and allowed their entry desk to guess the 10-digit HTS code, you would have a hard time showing you exercised reasonable care, and that is the showing a § 1592 negligence case turns on.

The legal reality is stark: Your broker is a conduit to ACE, not an insurance policy against CBP enforcement.

## How the Entry Desk Is Actually Run

To understand why Customs Brokers systematically make errors that expose importers to severe civil liability, one must stop looking at the broker as a boutique consulting firm and start looking at the cold, mechanical economics of modern customs brokerage.

Commercial customs brokerage is a high-volume processing business. A modern brokerage unit runs on transaction velocity, not accuracy.

**The Economics of Entry Processing**

Consider the operational financial model of a standard entry processing department:

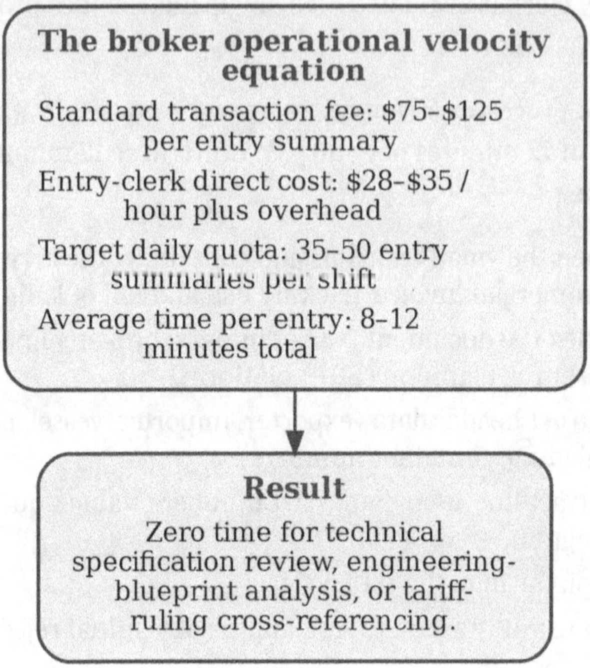


An entry processing unit charges an importer a transactional fee of $75 to $125 per entry summary. The revenue is not the pressure: at volume, that fee comfortably covers clerk salaries, software licensing (CargoWise, Descartes, BluJay), overhead, and margin. The pressure is throughput. A brokerage earns by processing more entries per clerk per day, and it measures its clerks on exactly that, which is what compresses the time available for any one entry. A clerk paid to move volume cannot spend 45 minutes analyzing an engineering schematic, researching General Rules of Interpretation (GRIs), or checking Explanatory Notes, not because the margin forbids it, but because the throughput target does. A note on the numbers in this section: the per-entry fees, the files-per-shift, and the minutes-per-entry figures are representative of what I have seen in the field, not published rates. Treat them as the shape of the economics rather than exact constants. The pressure they describe is the point, and it is real.

An entry clerk is evaluated on a single metric: files processed per day.

If a clerk processes 40 entries in an eight-hour shift, they have an average of 12 minutes per entry. Within those 12 minutes, the clerk must:

1. Open the email transmission containing the arrival notice, commercial invoice, packing list, and bill of lading.
2. Index the document packet into the broker's Enterprise Resource Planning (ERP) platform.
3. Extract header data (exporter, importer, vessel, port of unlading, container numbers).
4. Extract line-item data (part numbers, values, quantities, weights).
5. Input or map the HTS codes.
6. Transmit the data to ACE and resolve initial rejection edits.

**The "Clear First, Correct Never" Mindset**

Under this extreme operational velocity, the entry clerk's primary objective is to get the cargo released from CBP custody so the freight can move off the pier or out of the air cargo terminal, avoiding demurrage and storage fees. Velocity is rewarded; pause and investigation are penalized.

This creates a structural conflict of interest between the broker and the importer:

- The importer's goal: accurate classification, duty minimization through legal tariff engineering, full compliance with partner government agencies, and the creation of a durable 5-year audit trail.
- The broker's operational goal: rapid transmission, immediate system release, zero container dwell time, and maximum daily transaction throughput.

When an entry clerk encounters an ambiguous product description on a foreign vendor's commercial invoice, for example, "Control Box Model X-200", the clerk has two choices:

1. Option A (Stop the Line): Put the entry on hold, email the importer's compliance manager, request a detailed technical data sheet, electrical schematics, and an explanation of the box's function, wait 24 hours for a response, incur potential pier storage fees, and drop below their daily entry quota.
2. Option B (The Path of Least Resistance): Look up what HTS code was used last time, search the broker's system database for "Control Box," or select a generic, catch-all "basket provision" HTS code that carries a safe, high duty rate and instantly clears ACE validation rules.

Under quota pressure, the path of least resistance usually wins, and that default is the birth of the disinterested-agent trap.

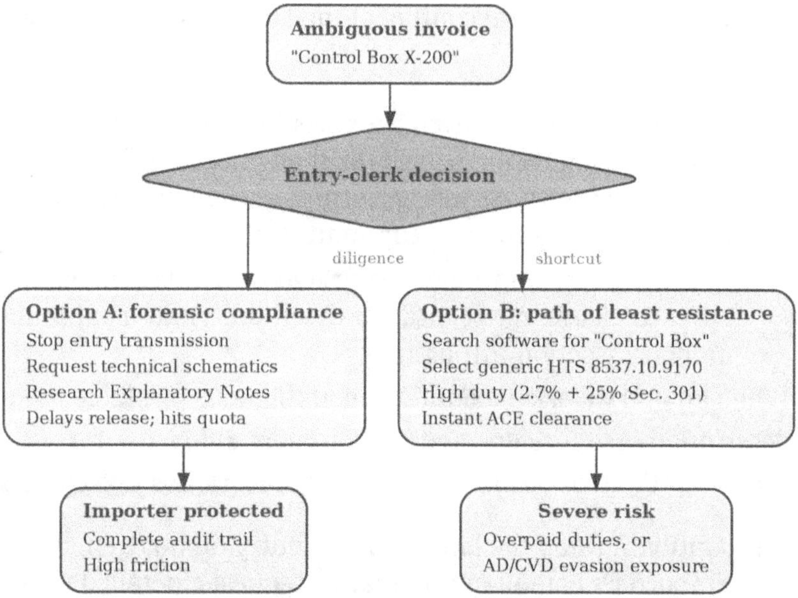


## Fallback Classification: The Generic High-Duty Codes

To avoid system rejections in ACE, entry clerks frequently default to generic "basket provisions": codes that end in `.90` or `.9000` ("Other: Other").

These basket provisions are designed by the World Customs Organization (WCO) and the U.S. International Trade Commission (USITC) as statistical catch-alls for items that do not fit into specific, highly technical tariff subheadings. Because basket provisions rarely trigger specific PGA restrictions or complex conditional duty exemptions, they flow through CBP's automated targeting systems like water through a sieve.

However, defaulting to generic basket codes creates two immense financial and legal liabilities for the Importer of Record:

1. Massive Duty Overpayment: Basket provisions frequently carry higher base column 1 duty rates and are almost universally captured under Section 301 trade remedies (China tariffs). An item that legally belongs in a specific, duty-free technical subheading (e.g., specialized medical

device parts under Chapter 90) gets routinely classified under a generic machinery basket code in Chapter 84 carrying a 3.7% base duty plus a 25% Section 301 surcharge. Over a multi-year period, an importer can quietly bleed millions of dollars in overpaid tariffs. Two clocks govern the recovery. Before liquidation, the Post-Summary Correction window, 300 days from the date of entry, or fifteen days before scheduled liquidation, whichever comes first (longer where liquidation is suspended or extended), lets you fix the entry administratively; on a good-faith overpayment like this one, that carries no penalty. After liquidation, a protest under 19 U.S.C. § 1514 must be filed within 180 days. Miss both and the entry is generally closed. Chapter 10 covers the first; Chapter 6 covers the second.

2. Silent AD/CVD Evasion: Even more dangerous is when a generic fallback code is used for merchandise that is actually subject to Antidumping or Countervailing Duty orders. If an entry clerk misclassifies an imported aluminum extrusion component under a generic "Articles of Aluminum" basket code instead of flagging it under the specific AD/CVD scope order, ACE will issue an automated release. The importer believes everything is compliant because the goods cleared the port.

Two years later, CBP's Trade Regulatory Audit (TRA) directorate executes a data-mining query against the importer's ACE ES-001 reports, cross-references physical bills of lading, and issues a formal Demand for Payment for 200% retroactive AD/CVD duties, accompanied by a Section 1592 civil penalty notice for gross negligence.

When the panicked importer calls their broker, the broker points to the standard boilerplate terms and conditions on the back of their invoice, which limit the broker's financial liability, for a claim arising from customs business, to $100 per entry or the brokerage fee paid for that entry, whichever is less.

## The National Permit Shift and the Loss of Port Intelligence

The structural vulnerability of the importer-broker relationship was dramatically amplified by CBP's sweeping regulatory overhaul of Customs Broker operations under the 19 CFR Part 111 modernization (final rule published October 18, 2022, effective December 19, 2022), which culminated in the final transition to the National Permit Framework.

To understand the profound operational danger this framework introduced, one must contrast it with the historical "District Permit" model that governed U.S. customs entry for nearly a century.

### The Historical Reality: District Permits and Port Expertise

Historically, under the legacy 19 CFR Part 111 regulations, a customs brokerage firm was required to maintain a physical office, a licensed individual Customs Broker, and a "District Permit" in every single customs district where it conducted customs business.

**The historical district-permit model**

Port of Long Beach → local broker office and licensed broker

Port of Chicago → local broker office and licensed broker

Port of New York → local broker office and licensed broker

**Operational characteristics**

Physical proximity to the piers and cargo terminals

Personal relationships with local CBP import specialists

Knowledge of port-specific examination protocols

Real-time inspection of detained merchandise

Under this local framework, if an importer brought a vessel shipment of specialized industrial valves through the Port of Long Beach, the entry was handled by a licensed broker physically located in Long Beach. That local broker knew the specific CBP Import Specialist assigned to the Machinery Center of Excellence.

They understood the local port's specific dockside examination habits, knew how local agriculture inspectors handled dunnage, and could physically drive to the terminal warehouse to inspect a damaged container label or verify a country-of-origin marking before an entry summary was finalized.

There was local intelligence, human accountability, and direct physical proximity to the merchandise.

## The Modern Reality: National Permits and Centralized Processing Factories

Under the modernized Part 111 regulations, CBP eliminated district permits entirely, establishing a single National Permit system. A brokerage firm now needs only one national permit and one designated licensed broker to process entries at ports nationwide.

This regulatory shift allowed large global logistics conglomerates to consolidate their entry processing operations into massive, centralized data-entry hubs located in low-cost labor markets.

> **The modern national-permit model**
>
> Long Beach, Miami, Seattle, and Laredo all feed one centralized entry factory (a remote processing hub) that transmits via ACE from 1,500 miles away.

> **Operational reality**
>
> Zero physical presence at the port of unlading
>
> No personal contact with local CBP personnel
>
> Total reliance on digital PDF invoice indexing
>
> Zero physical visibility of the merchandise

Today, an entry for a complex chemical compound unlading at the Port of Houston is frequently processed by an entry clerk sitting in a cubicle farm in Charlotte, North Carolina, or in a processing center on the other side of the world.

This structural centralization has severed the vital feedback loop between the entry filer and the physical realities of the port:

1. Zero Physical Visibility: The entry filer has never seen, touched, or physically inspected the merchandise. They are entirely dependent on whatever low-resolution, poorly translated PDF commercial invoice is uploaded into their document management platform.
2. Anonymized CBP Interaction: The filer no longer interacts with a known local Import Specialist. Entries flow into CBP's national Centers of Excellence and Expertise (CEEs). When a system hold or CBP Form 28 (Request for Information) is issued, it is generated by an anonymized CEE team located anywhere in the country. The centralized entry clerk has no relationship with the issuing officer and no contextual understanding of the local port conditions that triggered the inquiry.
3. The "Remote Location Filing" (RLF) Blind Spot: Remote Location Filing allows entry summaries to be transmitted electronically across any port. However, when physical anomalies occur on the pier, such as a container being selected for a specialized NII (Non-Intrusive Inspection) gamma ray scan, or an FDA physical sampling hold, the remote entry processing factory is completely blind. They routinely fail to notify the importer until storage and demurrage fees have accumulated into thousands of dollars.

**The Severed Feedback Loop**

This national consolidation has created a profound operational disconnect. Importers assume their broker has "feet on the ground" watching their cargo and protecting their interests at the port. In reality, their entry is being processed by an overworked remote clerk managing a digital queue of 300 entries from 40 different corporate clients across 12 different time zones.

When CBP issues a notice of action, the remote clerk's immediate reaction is not to fight for the importer or defend a technical classification position; it is to pass the notice to the importer with a generic cover email stating: "Please see attached notice from Customs and advise how you wish to proceed."

The broker offers no legal strategy, no technical defense, and no regulatory context. They act as a glorified bulletin board, passing regulatory notices to an importer who rarely understands the severe legal clock that has just started ticking.

The transition from localized port expertise to centralized entry processing factories has permanently stripped the broker of local intelligence. An importer without its own oversight of these remote processing hubs carries the full liability with none of the visibility.

# Chapter 3: The New Enforcement Era: Penalty Floors & Loss of Import Privileges

## Deconstructing the June 2026 Executive Order: The Death of Negotiated Mitigation

On June 3, 2026, the trajectory of U.S. international trade compliance shifted. President Donald Trump signed the landmark Executive Order titled "Strengthening Customs Enforcement" (Executive Order 14411). The underlying duty did not change that day: reasonable care has sat with the importer since 1993. What the order sets out to change is the cost of falling short of it.

While trade publications initially focused on headlines about restrictions on foreign entities: Section 2(b) of the order bars foreign importers of record from filing informal entries. The true enforcement core of the Executive Order lies in its overhaul of civil penalty mitigation and Customs Broker liability. (The suspension of duty-free de minimis treatment came from a separate action: Executive Order 14324, "Suspending Duty-Free De Minimis Treatment for All Countries" (30 July 2025), as continued by Executive Order 14388, not from this order.)

For over thirty years, following the passage of the Mod Act in 1993, the standard operating procedure for trade compliance defense followed a predictable, well-trodden path. When CBP's Office of Fines, Penalties, and Forfeitures (FP&F) issued a massive civil penalty notice under 19 U.S.C. § 1592 for misclassification, undervaluation, or origin misstatements, the importer's trade counsel would file a Supplemental Petition for Relief.

Under the legacy administrative mitigation guidelines (published in 19 CFR Part 171, Appendix B), FP&F officers work within defined ranges rather than at large. For duty-loss cases the guidelines set a statutory maximum and a mitigation floor at each culpability level: negligence mitigates to between 0.5 and 2 times the loss of duty (the floor sits at one-quarter of the 2× maximum); gross negligence to between 2.5 and 4 times (a floor at roughly 62.5% of the 4× maximum); and fraud to between 5 and 8 times (again about a 62.5% floor). Within those ranges, trade counsel moved cases substantially by stacking recognized mitigating factors:

- First-time violation status.
- Demonstrated cooperation with CBP inquiries.
- The existence of a written, corporate compliance policy.
- Remedial measures taken post-violation.

The largest reductions, though, rarely came from mitigating below the floor. They came from contesting the culpability level (negligence rather than gross negligence, which drops the maximum from 4× to 2×) and from disputing the calculated loss of duty itself. Either way, executives came to view customs penalties not as threats to the business but as a manageable "cost of doing business": a negotiable legal expense that trade counsel could quietly smooth over.

Two things follow, and they matter for reading the Executive Order. First, if you take the order's "not less than 50 percent of the assessed penalty" at face value, it actually cuts in different directions: for negligence, where the current guideline floor is one-quarter of the maximum, a 50 percent floor is a sharp tightening; for gross negligence and fraud, where the guideline floor is already about 62.5 percent, a flat 50 percent floor is no tightening at all and could even read as more lenient, which is why the details of how CBP defines "assessed penalty" in the revised guidelines will decide how much actually changes. Second, whatever the floor does, the order's separate command to eliminate mitigation for repeat offenders is the provision with real teeth, because it removes the ranges entirely for anyone who lands in that category.

The June 3, 2026 executive order sets out to dismantle this safety net, directing CBP to rewrite its mitigation rules within 90 days.

A word on timing before we go further. An executive order is a directive to agencies, not a change to the statute. Section 4 tells the Secretary to revise the mitigation standards within 90 days; Section 2 tells CBP to stand up the good-standing registry within 180 days. As of this writing the 90-day mitigation deadline of September 1, 2026 has passed with nothing published: 19 CFR Part 171's mitigation appendices remain unamended, while the 180-day good-standing deadline of November 30, 2026 has not yet arrived. That the first deadline slipped is itself instructive: the direction is unchanged, the order stands, and the Secretary is still directed to act, but agency deadlines in executive orders slip, which is exactly why you build against the direction rather than against a date. (An earlier, 45-day milestone for legislative recommendations fell on July 18, 2026.) Read the sections that follow as the enforcement regime the order builds toward, not as rules already in force. That distinction is the difference between preparing for the shift and betting your continuous bond on a standard that can still be narrowed, delayed, or challenged in court.

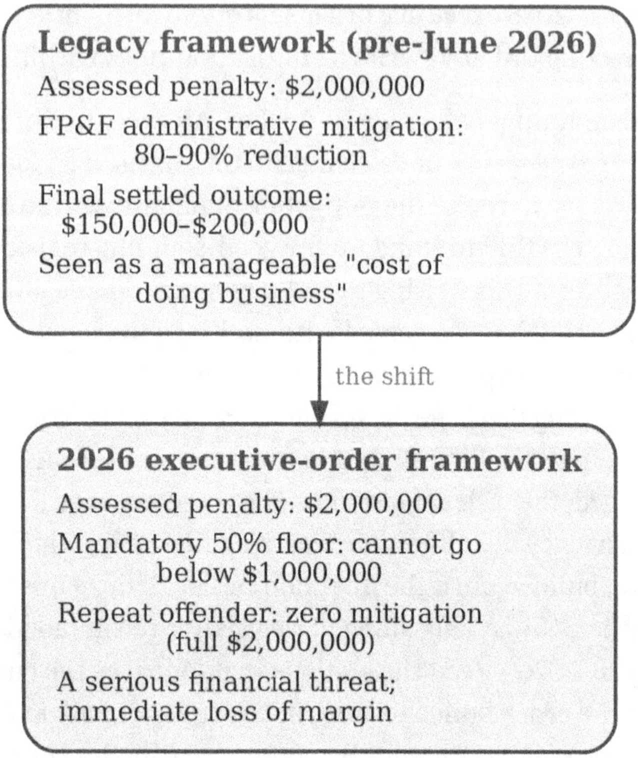


### The 50% Penalty Floor the Order Directs

Section 4(c) of the Executive Order directs the Secretary of Homeland Security to revise the administrative penalty mitigation guidelines within 90 days, and it specifies what those revisions must include:

> *"Within 90 days of the date of this order, the Secretary shall take steps to revise all mitigation standards consistent with the policy of this order. These revisions shall include establishing a minimum penalty floor of not less than 50 percent of the assessed penalty, absent exceptional circumstances that materially impact national security; establishing a minimum liquidated damages floor; and eliminating mitigation for repeat offenders." (§ 4(c))*

Read that carefully, because the distinction matters. The 50 percent floor is written into the order, but as a standard the Secretary is *directed to establish* through revised guidelines, not as a rule already in force. Section 12(b) says the order "shall be implemented consistent with applicable law, including the Administrative Procedure Act," and § 12(c) says it creates no right "enforceable at law or in equity by any party." Until CBP actually amends its mitigation guidelines, the operative text is still the old one: as of this writing, 19 CFR Part 171, Appendix B carries its last amendment credit of T.D. 00-41 (2000), unchanged. So state the effect conditionally. If and when CBP revises the guidelines as directed, and CBP then issues a $5,000,000 penalty for systemic misclassification or duty evasion, the floor would mean FP&F could not settle it below $2,500,000, and the discretion FP&F officers have long used to grant leniency for commercial errors would be sharply curtailed. That is the regime the order builds toward; build for it, but do not treat the floor as a number FP&F is bound by today.

**No Mitigation for Repeat Offenders**

More severe still is the bar on mitigation for "repeat offenders."

The order directs CBP to eliminate mitigation for "repeat offenders," but it leaves the definition of that term to rulemaking. How a repeat offender will be identified, a rolling window, a second enforcement action, violations spanning different product lines, is not yet fixed. It is worth keeping the terminology straight, because these forms recur throughout this book: a CBP Form 28 is a Request for Information and a Form 29 is a Notice of Action. Neither is itself a penalty assessment. The penalty, if it comes, is assessed later under Section 1592.

For a repeat offender, mitigation is meant to fall to zero: under the rule the order directs, CBP would be barred from reducing the assessed penalty by a single dollar. The full statutory penalty, up to the domestic value of the merchandise under gross negligence or fraud, must be paid in full, backed by immediate enforcement against the importer's continuous customs bond.

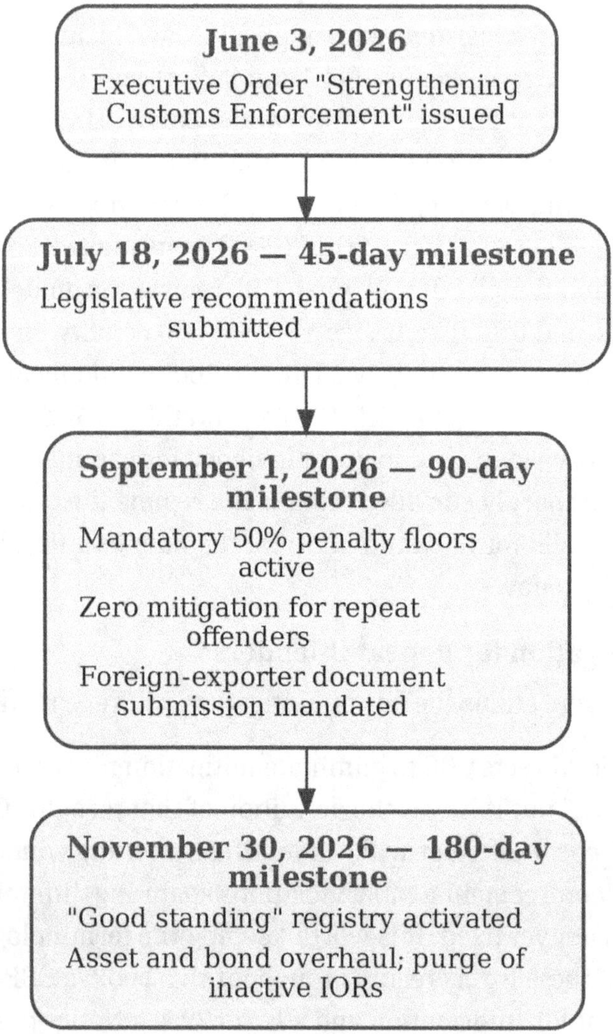


**The End of the "Broker Error" Defense**

To prevent importers from attempting to evade these penalty floors by pointing fingers at their filing brokers, the Executive Order establishes a parallel directive commanding the Secretary of Homeland Security to impose maximum statutory penalties on

Customs Brokers who fail to exercise due diligence, repeatedly represent non-compliant clients, or fail to respond promptly to CBP requests for information.

This sets off a three-move squeeze that ends on the importer's desk:

1. CBP to Importer: "We are assessing a 50% minimum penalty floor against your continuous bond for negligence. You cannot negotiate this down."
2. Importer to Broker: "You filed this wrong entry summary, so you must pay this penalty."
3. Broker to Importer: "Under our standard terms and conditions, the NCBFAA model language on the back of our invoice, our legal liability is limited to $100, or the brokerage fees you paid, whichever is less. And under federal law, you are the Importer of Record who signed the ACE entry summary. Pay CBP directly." (Note what the broker does not say: no regulation caps its liability. Part 111 contains no limitation of broker liability: the cap is purely a contract term, which is exactly why the addendum in Chapter 4 can rewrite it.)

The era of relying on trade counsel to quietly smooth over broker-generated entry errors at FP&F is ending, and while the rulemaking that ends it missed its September 1 deadline, the direction is set and the Secretary is still under order to act. In the post-June 2026 regulatory environment, an un-audited broker relationship is an unpriced risk sitting on your balance sheet.

### Personal Liability: The Officer Behind the Entry

There is a third source of pressure, and it reaches past the company to the people who sign for it. In United States v. Trek Leather, Inc., 767 F.3d 1288 (Fed. Cir. 2014), the Federal Circuit, sitting en banc, held that a company's sole officer was himself a "person" who could be held personally liable under 19 U.S.C. § 1592(a) for introducing merchandise into U.S. commerce by means of material false statements or omissions: here, entries that omitted the value of fabric "assists" (material the importer supplied to the manufacturer at no or reduced cost) and so understated the dutiable value of the imported suits. The court affirmed the Court of International Trade's judgment that Mr. Shadadpuri was grossly negligent; it did not make that finding itself, and expressly said it was "presented no issue about whether Mr. Shadadpuri was grossly negligent." What the en banc court decided was the reach of the statute to the individual: it did not need to pierce the corporate veil to get to him; his own conduct in the entry process was enough. As the opinion put it, "[a]pplying the statute to Mr. Shadadpuri does not require any piercing of the corporate veil."

The reading for a trade director, controller, or procurement lead is direct. If you personally approve or transmit a commercial invoice you know, or should know, misstates transaction value, understates assists, or buries non-dutiable charges to lower the duty owed, you are exposed in your own name, not only your company's. That exposure is greatest under a DDP or DAP arrangement, where the temptation to accept a foreign seller's single-figure, duty-inclusive invoice is strongest, and it runs to gross negligence, which reaches the lesser of the merchandise's domestic value or four times the duty loss (Chapter 2 sets out the full penalty tiers). Trek Leather is the decision that turns a paperwork shortcut into personal risk.

## The "Good Standing" Matrix: Loss of Import Privileges

The penalty floor is a hit to cash. The provision that should worry you more is the one that goes after your ability to import at all.

Historically, a dispute with CBP over duties, penalties, or classification stayed financial. Cargo kept moving under your continuous bond while counsel argued about the entry summaries. Except in cases involving public-safety seizures or criminal indictments, CBP rarely suspended an established company's basic ability to file entries.

Section 2 of the June 3, 2026 executive order sets out to change that. And because this is the provision most likely to be misdescribed in the trade press over the next year, it is worth reading what the order actually says before we get to what it will probably mean.

**What the Order Actually Says**

Here is Section 2(d), in full:

> *"Within 180 days of the date of this order, the Secretary shall require all IORs to maintain 'good standing' with CBP, and CBP shall define 'good standing' based on the IOR's and its affiliates' history of compliance with U.S. customs and trade laws and regulations and payment of required customs liabilities, among other relevant considerations. For example, IORs that have been found by CBP to have illegally imported fentanyl, nitazene, or other illicit substances or contraband, including precursor chemicals for the purposes of manufacturing illicit substances, shall, consistent with applicable law, not be in 'good standing' with CBP. IORs not in 'good standing' with CBP shall not be allowed to import into the United States or otherwise conduct activities directly related to the importation of goods, including designating a customs broker to act as IOR on their behalf."*

That is the entire definition. Read it carefully, because three things about it matter.

First, it is a delegation, not a standard. The order does not define good standing. It tells CBP to define it, and gives two factors to build on: compliance history, yours and your affiliates', and payment of customs liabilities. Everything else is "among other relevant considerations," which is regulatory language for we will tell you later.

Second, the only named disqualifier is illicit substances. Fentanyl, nitazenes, precursor chemicals. That is the example the order chose, and even there the language is hedged: such importers "shall, consistent with applicable law, not be in 'good standing.'" The order does not say forced labor. It does not say UFLPA. Forced labor appears elsewhere in the order: Section 4(b) directs CBP to prioritize enforcement against forced-labor imports, misclassification, undervaluation and illegal transshipment, including EAPA investigations, but none of it is tied to good standing. If you read somewhere that a UFLPA finding costs you your import privileges, that is someone's forecast, not the order.

Third, the last sentence is the sharp one. You cannot route around a block by hiring a broker to serve as importer of record on your behalf. That door is explicitly closed.

Two adjacent provisions belong in the same picture, and they are frequently confused with the good-standing rule because they sit in the same section:

- Section 2(a) directs CBP, within the same 180 days, to revise importer eligibility rules, requiring minimum tangible domestic assets, bonding, or both, and requiring IORs to disclose anticipated import volumes, ownership and beneficial ownership, business affiliations, and domestic assets. These are conditions of being an IOR at all. They are not the good-standing test, though CBP may well fold them together.
- Section 2(e) directs CBP to create "risk-based tiers for IORs based on compliance history, enforcement actions, and audit results, among other things." That is the closest thing in the order to the tiering architecture the trade press has described.

Foreign importers of record get their own treatment under Sections 2(b) and 2(c): barred from filing informal entries, barred from relying on a continuous bond except where CBP finds the revenue fully protected, and required either to be CTPAT-validated themselves or to use a CTPAT-validated licensed broker. If your supplier has been serving as IOR on your behalf, that arrangement is directly in the order's sights, and you should be planning for it now.

Before you conclude this is only your supplier's problem, read Section 10, because it defines "foreign IOR" far more broadly than "a company overseas." An entity is a U.S. IOR only if it is "organized under the laws of the United States, is located in the United States, and has at all times controlling beneficial owner(s) who are United States citizens or lawful permanent residents", or owns "a significant amount of real property in the United States" (§ 10(a)). An entity that fails *any* one of those tests is a foreign IOR (§ 10(b)). Run the two questions that follow from that text against your own company:

1. Are your controlling beneficial owners U.S. citizens or lawful permanent residents? A U.S.-incorporated subsidiary with a U.S. address and a U.S. EIN, but a foreign parent, answers no, and is therefore presumptively a foreign IOR, regardless of how domestic it looks on paper.
2. If not, do you own a significant amount of U.S. real property? If neither is true, the § 2(b) informal-entry bar, the § 2(c) restriction on continuous-bond reliance, and the CTPAT-validation requirement all reach *you*, not just an overseas supplier.

Section 10(c) sharpens the "located in the United States" test further, requiring a genuine U.S. principal place of business, physical presence, and tangible U.S. assets, expressly to catch "shell companies, sham transactions, or artificial corporate or organizational structuring." Outside counsel have called the definition one that casts a wide net over legitimate U.S.

subsidiaries of foreign-owned groups. If that describes your company, treat this section as yours to plan against.

### What CBP Will Probably Require: A Forecast, Clearly Labeled

CBP has not yet defined good standing; the deadline to do so is November 30, 2026. But Section 2 is no longer entirely quiet. On 19 August 2026 CBP published "Accuracy of Importer of Record Data Submitted to CBP," implementing Section 2(e) and effective 18 September 2026: it requires the IOR's physical address on the CBP Form 5106 to be the actual business location, not a registered agent, P.O. box, or third-party address, requires the e-mail and phone on file to belong to the IOR rather than the broker, states that CBP will void IOR numbers containing inaccurate information, and imposes broker due-diligence and direct-POA obligations. A separate ANPRM, "Heightened Import Disclosures for Supply Chain Visibility," was published 2 September 2026 under Section 3, with comments due 1 December. What has not published is Section 2(a) eligibility and bonding, 2(b) informal entry, 2(d) good standing, or 2(f) vetting. If your 5106 currently shows the broker's address or the broker's e-mail, your IOR number is now at risk of being voided: the first concrete consequence of this order to land on importers, and an independent reason to act on the direct-communication argument in Chapter 4.

So what follows is my forecast, not the law. I am setting it out because a forecast you can plan against is more useful than a shrug, but you should hold it loosely, and you should confirm the final rule before you make a decision that depends on it.

I expect CBP to build good standing around four things:

1. Compliance and payment history. Outstanding penalty assessments and unpaid duty demands are the two items the order names directly, so they will almost certainly be

disqualifying at some threshold. I expect an error-rate component drawn from ACE transmission data as well, because CBP already computes it. What the thresholds will be is anyone's guess, and "zero tolerance" is unlikely to survive comment.

2. Financial substance. The Section 2(a) tangible-assets and bonding requirements are eligibility conditions on their face, but CBP has an obvious incentive to make continued satisfaction of them a condition of standing, not just of entry. Expect bond sufficiency to be evaluated against your actual Section 301 and AD/CVD exposure rather than a flat formula.
3. Ownership transparency. Beneficial ownership, corporate parents, business affiliations. The order requires the disclosure; making standing contingent on keeping it current is the natural next step.
4. Affiliate contagion. This is the one I would watch most closely, because it is in the order's actual text and almost nobody is discussing it. Good standing turns on "the IOR's and its affiliates' history of compliance." If you operate multiple IOR numbers, or sit inside a corporate group with other importers, a sister company's penalty file may become your problem. Map your affiliated IORs now.

Notice what is not on that list. I do not expect a UFLPA finding to trigger automatic revocation, because the order does not say so and because the forced-labor program already has its own detention and exclusion machinery. Could CBP fold forced labor into standing? It could. It has not said it will.

The trade bar is pushing back on the breadth of all of this. The National Customs Brokers and Forwarders Association of America has urged CBP that good standing should be revoked only for egregious, direct violations, and through a fair and uniform process. The U.S. Chamber of Commerce filed comments on July 14, 2026 urging CBP to proceed by notice-and-comment rulemaking and flagging the definition of good standing, minimum bond levels, the scope of required disclosures, and the risk-tiering methodology as areas needing care. Neither is binding on CBP. Both tell you the final rule is likely to be narrower than the order's language permits.

### How a Block Would Probably Work

The order says an IOR out of good standing "shall not be allowed to import." It does not say how. It contains no reference to ACE, to sureties, to bonds being canceled, or to general order.

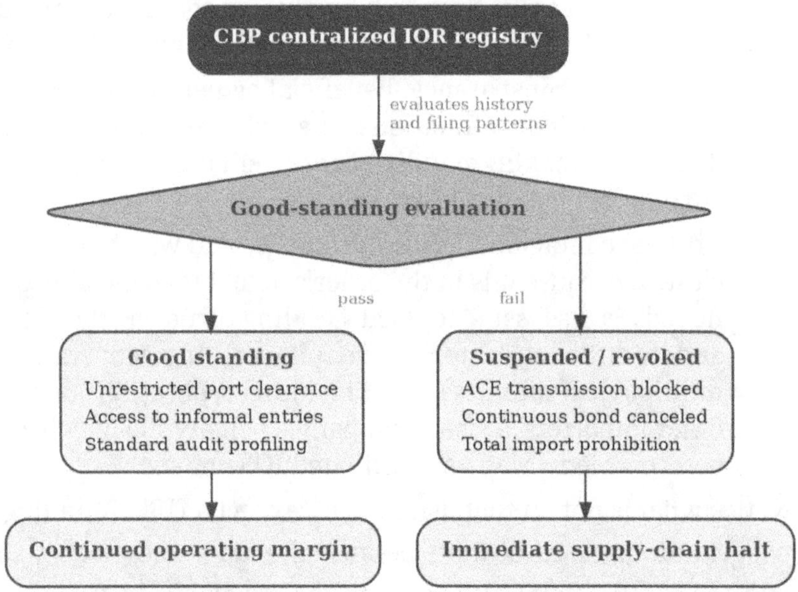


Here is how a block like this would most plausibly operate, based on how ACE already handles bond and IOR validation failures today. Treat it as informed speculation about mechanics, not as a description of published rules:

- An ACE validation block. The most likely implementation is a hard edit against the IOR number at entry summary transmission, rejecting the filing the way ACE already rejects an entry against an insufficient bond. No broker could file under that number, which is consistent with the order's bar on designating a broker as IOR.

- Bond consequences. Whether CBP would notify the surety and move to terminate the continuous bond, or simply stop accepting filings against it, is unknown. Either produces the same operational result.
- Cargo already in transit. This is the part that should keep you up at night, and the order is silent on it. Containers on the water when a status changes arrive with no way to clear. Demurrage and terminal storage run in the hundreds of dollars per container per day, and cargo not entered within fifteen calendar days after arrival becomes general order, and the carrier must arrange its transfer to a general-order warehouse by the twentieth day under existing rules, where costs climb further and the merchandise eventually becomes subject to sale or destruction.

None of that is in the order. All of it follows from how the system already works.

**The Domino Effect of Broker Misfilings**

Now put the pieces together, with the caveat that every link in this chain depends on rules that have not yet published.

A mid-sized manufacturer imports specialized electronic assemblies. Its broker, unbeknownst to the compliance director, repeatedly applies an incorrect low-duty HTS code to move entries faster. Over twelve months, 400 entries go out with the same error.

CBP's targeting system flags the anomaly and issues a Form 28. The broker's entry desk receives it, does not recognize its significance, does not forward it, and answers with a brief unvetted email that CBP reads as evasive.

Under the regime the order builds toward, here is the exposure:

- CBP issues a finding of negligence and assesses a penalty.
- Whether 400 entries carrying one systemic error make the company a "repeat offender" is precisely the question the order leaves to rulemaking. It could be defined by a rolling

window, by a second enforcement action, by violations spanning product lines, or by something else. If the definition reaches this fact pattern, mitigation goes to zero and the assessed penalty is paid in full. If it does not, the 50 percent floor still applies once the mitigation rules are revised: a sharp change for negligence cases in particular, where the guideline floor has long sat at a quarter of the statutory maximum.
- If the company's standing is affected, incoming shipments stop at the pier, and the assembly line stops shortly after that.

I have laid this out as a chain because that is how it would unfold. But be clear about what is load-bearing: the underlying liability is settled law and has been since 1993. The penalty floor depends on a rule that was due September 1 and, as of this writing, has not published. The repeat-offender bar depends on a definition that does not yet exist. The standing consequence depends on a rule due November 30.

The direction is not in doubt. The mechanics are still being written. Plan for the direction, and confirm the mechanics before you rely on any specific one.

What is not speculative is the cause. All of it started because an entry clerk made a series of unaudited data-entry choices, and the importer assumed the broker was its compliance shield.

## The Broker's Divided Loyalty: Deconstructing 19 CFR § 111.39

For decades, importers operated under the assumption that their relationship with their Customs Broker enjoyed a form of quasi-privilege. That a broker was an ally who would help cover up operational errors, quietly fix mistakes in the background, or at least keep compliance disputes internal.

That assumption does not survive a careful reading of 19 CFR § 111.39.

Section 111.39 does not make your broker your ally, and it does not turn the broker into an informant who reports you to Customs. What it does is require the broker, once it knows of a client's non-compliance or error, to advise the client promptly and to keep a record of that advice. The rule also forbids the broker from withholding information from the client, from knowingly conveying false information, and from suggesting a plan to evade the law. It contains no duty to file a report against the client with CBP. The pressure it creates is quieter and, for the importer, just as dangerous: a broker that has advised you of a problem you refuse to fix will protect its own license before it protects your account.

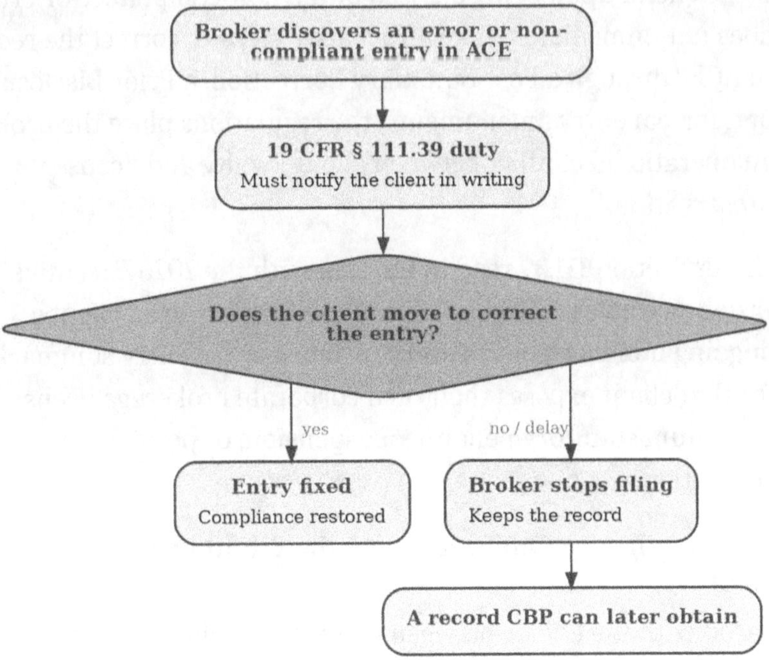


**The Mechanics of 19 CFR § 111.39**

19 CFR § 111.39(c) is direct:

> *"If a broker knows that a client has not complied with the law or has made an error in, or omission from, any document, affidavit, or other record which the law requires the client to execute, he must advise the client promptly of that noncompliance, error, or omission. The broker must advise the client on the proper corrective actions required and retain a record of the broker's communication with the client in accordance with §§ 111.21 and 111.23."*

That second sentence is new since the 2022 Broker Modernization rule, and it is the one your own file may turn on: the duty to advise on corrective action and to retain a record of the communication is exactly why the broker keeps written proof that it advised you.

If the client, upon being advised of the non-compliance or error, does not immediately take affirmative steps to correct the record in ACE (through a Post-Summary Correction, a Prior Disclosure, or a formal entry amendment), the regulations place the broker in an operational conflict between client loyalty and license preservation.

Under Section 111.39 read in tandem with the 2026 Executive Order directives, a Customs Broker who discovers a client's ongoing non-compliance and continues to file entry summaries for that client exposes their own corporate brokerage license to maximum statutory penalties, suspension, or permanent revocation.

### The Regulatory Choice: Protect the Client or Save the License

Faced with the choice between protecting a client who hesitates to pay back-duties and preserving a corporate brokerage license that generates tens of millions of dollars in transaction fees across hundreds of other accounts, the broker's incentives point one way, and you should assume they will follow them.

Better-run brokerages have begun embedding explicit automated compliance triggers into their operating software (CargoWise/Descartes). When an internal audit flag or CEE inquiry identifies an uncorrected classification, valuation, or PGA error:

1. The system automatically generates a formal, written "Notice of Non-Compliance" to the importer's designated point of contact.
2. The notice sets a strict time limit (typically 5 to 10 business days) for the importer to authorize a Post-Summary Correction (PSC) or file a formal Prior Disclosure under 19 U.S.C. § 1592(c).
3. If the importer refuses to correct a known error, the broker faces its own exposure under 19 CFR § 111.39: it may not withhold information, convey false information, suggest any illegal plan for evading duties (§ 111.39(d), the section's fourth command), or keep advancing a filing it knows to be wrong. In practice, the broker stops filing for the account rather than risk its national permit, and it keeps the written record showing that it advised you.

That record, the broker's written notice to you and its internal file notes, is not transmitted to CBP automatically. But it exists, it is a customs business record, and CBP can obtain it later through an audit, a summons, or litigation discovery.

In that moment, your broker's contemporaneous record becomes evidence that you were on notice.

Once CBP has that record, it can build a Section 1592 case on it. A documented notice that you knew and did not act speaks directly to the state of mind the statute turns on, and that is what moves a violation from simple negligence toward gross negligence.

### The Operational Imperative

Importers can no longer view their broker as a confidential confidant or a buffer against federal enforcement. Under 19 CFR § 111.39, the broker's first duty runs to its own license, not to your account. It will advise you, document that it did, and stop filing rather than jeopardize its permit, and none of that shields you.

If your internal compliance architecture is not actively auditing your entry summaries, identifying errors before your broker's automated routines flag them, and executing corrective measures under your own control, you are operating with an unresolved liability inside your supply chain.

The picture is complete. The legal mandate is clear. The enforcement landscape of 2026 demands that importers dismantle the myth of broker protection and build an internal broker-oversight program.

# PART II: CONTRACTUAL DEFENSE & POWER OF ATTORNEY (POA) ARCHITECTURE

# Chapter 4: Rebalancing the POA: Removing Clause-Level Liability Traps

## Deconstructing the Standard Broker POA Package: Identifying One-Sided Liability Traps

In the high-stakes theater of federal customs enforcement, the Customs Power of Attorney (POA) is one of the most consequential documents an Importer of Record (IOR) will ever sign.

To the untrained corporate legal department, a Customs POA appears to be a boilerplate administrative form: a routine authorization granting a licensed Customs Broker permission to file entry summaries, pay duties, and communicate with U.S. Customs and Border Protection (CBP) on behalf of the principal. Corporate signers regularly treat it as a trivial onboarding document, signing standard templates provided by freight forwarders and Customs Brokers without changing a single word.

It is the most consequential document most companies sign without reading.

The POA itself is short. Most brokers use CBP Form 5291 or the sample power of attorney at 19 CFR § 141.32, and neither contains a liability cap, a sub-agency clause, or a data-sharing clause. What makes the package one-sided is what the POA page incorporates by reference: the broker's Terms and Conditions of Service, where the liability cap and the indemnity actually live. (NCBFAA does publish standardized power-of-attorney forms, so this is not a document the association leaves to each broker. But the liability cap and the one-sided indemnity do not live on the POA page. They live in the Terms and Conditions of Service the POA page incorporates by reference. That is the document to read.) So when you sign a standard broker POA, usually on a page that also acknowledges those Terms and Conditions, you are not merely appointing an agent; you are accepting a set of terms that concentrate regulatory risk on you, and most importers never read them.

To rebalance the arrangement in favor of the importer, you must first take the standard broker POA package apart, the POA plus the Terms and Conditions it incorporates, exposing the liability traps embedded in the standard text.

What a Standard Broker POA Package Does: the POA plus its incorporated Terms and Conditions

| POA LIABILITY TRAP | WHAT THE STANDARD TEMPLATE DOES |
|---|---|
| Liability limitations | Caps broker liability at $100 or your brokerage fee, whichever is less; waives consequential damages; waives direct financial loss. |
| One-sided indemnity | Importer holds the broker harmless and pays the broker's legal fees, even for the broker's own errors. |
| Sub-agency & data waiver | Blank-check delegation to un-vetted third-party sub-agents; unlimited cross-sharing of confidential commercial data. |

## 1. The Limitation of Liability Clause, and What It Is Actually Worth

Embedded in every standard broker terms-and-conditions agreement, incorporated by reference into the POA execution page you sign, is the liability cap. Most importers have never read it. Most have never checked which version of it they signed.

Check the number before you argue about it. The figure has moved. Older NCBFAA revisions, and the many house forms derived from them, set the cap at $50 per shipment, and $50 is the number still quoted in most trade-press commentary. The base figure is effectively a fill-in field: live broker forms carrying NCBFAA attribution show $35, $50, and $100, so read the number in your own broker's operative revision rather than assuming any one of them. The current NCBFAA Terms and Conditions of

Service (rev. 9/2023) set it at ¶ 9(c) as follows: one hundred dollars per shipment or transaction for activities other than customs business, and, for claims arising from customs business,

> *"$100.00 per entry or the amount of brokerage fees paid to Company for the entry, whichever is less."*

Read that second prong again, because it is the one that governs everything in this book. It is not $100. It is $100 or your brokerage fee, whichever is less. If your negotiated rate is $75 an entry, your contractual remedy for a broker error on that entry is $75. The harder you squeezed procurement on price, the smaller your recovery.

Now put that against the operational reality. An entry clerk at a centralized processing desk omits an AD/CVD case number on a high-value shipment of industrial machinery, or selects a generic basket code that pulls in a $750,000 Section 301 assessment. CBP issues a demand for duty and assesses a penalty under 19 U.S.C. § 1592. You are out three-quarters of a million dollars because of a data-entry failure you had no visibility into.

You go to the broker. The broker cites ¶ 9(c) and offers you seventy-five dollars.

**Is the cap actually enforceable? The honest answer, which is better than you think.**

Here is where most treatments of this subject stop, with some version of "courts consistently uphold these clauses, so don't bother." That is not accurate, and believing it costs you the leverage you actually have.

What the case law establishes is narrower and more useful. Enforceability turns on two questions: was the clause validly incorporated into your contract, and what degree of fault is being alleged.

On incorporation, the broker usually wins, because of how you have behaved. Courts enforce these caps where the terms were on the invoices you paid without objection, over and over. In Insurance Co. of North America v. NNR Aircargo Service (USA), Inc., 201 F.3d 1111 (9th Cir. 2000), the Ninth Circuit enforced a $50-per-shipment limitation against a loss of roughly $257,285, holding that 47 prior identical invoices over three years had put the shipper on notice. The Seventh Circuit reached the same result on the same course-of-dealing doctrine in Capitol Converting Equipment, Inc. v. LEP Transport, Inc., 965 F.2d 391 (7th Cir. 1992), where the parties' course of dealing supplemented an oral agreement that was silent on liability. And in ABN AMRO Verzekeringen BV v. Geologistics Americas, Inc., 253 F. Supp. 2d 757 (S.D.N.Y. 2003), aff'd, 485 F.3d 85 (2d Cir. 2007), the closest thing to a case about this specific form, the court enforced the cap in terms and identified the clause by name as the NCBFAA-approved Terms and Conditions of Service.

The lesson of that line of cases is not "the cap is untouchable." It is that silence is assent. Every invoice you pay without objection builds the broker's record. Which is precisely why the addendum later in this chapter has to be executed and dated, and why it has to say in terms that it controls over anything the broker sent before or sends after.

On degree of fault, the ground is much softer than brokers like to suggest. The case usually cited for the proposition that a cap survives even gross negligence is Calvin Klein Ltd. v. Trylon Trucking Corp., 892 F.2d 191 (2d Cir. 1989), where the Second Circuit enforced a $50 limitation against a stipulated case of gross negligence and remanded with instructions to enter judgment for fifty dollars.

Calvin Klein is a common carrier case. It rests on the released-rate bargain: the shipper accepted a lower freight rate in exchange for a declared-value cap, and having taken the cheaper rate, was held to the trade. That doctrine has deep roots in carriage law, and it applies with far less force outside carriage, but "no application" would overstate it. Courts in this circuit have extended Calvin Klein to non-carrier intermediaries: in the ABN AMRO case cited above, the court invoked it to enforce a $50 limitation for a freight forwarder, a defendant it described as "little more than a 'travel agent'", not just for a trucker. So the honest statement is that its application to a Customs Broker filing entries is weaker and more contestable, not that it is absent.

New York's own law draws the line at gross negligence, though more narrowly than the cap's opponents suggest. In Sommer v. Federal Signal Corp., 79 N.Y.2d 540 (1992), a case about a central-station fire-alarm company, a defendant the court treated as carrying a public-interest-inflected duty, the Court of Appeals held that limitation-of-liability clauses are enforceable against *ordinary* negligence, and let the case go to trial only because whether the conduct rose to gross negligence was a jury question. On that gross-negligence point the court held that New York's public-policy bar on contracting away such liability

> *"applies equally to contract clauses purporting to exonerate a party from liability and clauses limiting damages to a nominal sum."*

Note what Sommer is and is not: it does not cite or overrule Calvin Klein, and both remain good law. A Customs Broker performing customs business is not a common carrier and did not sell you a released rate, so on a gross-negligence theory, a systemic pattern of ignoring your written classification instructions, say, rather than a single mistyped digit, Sommer keeps the door open in a way Calvin Klein does not. But be candid about the counter-authority, because your broker's counsel will be: in ABN AMRO that same New York standard was applied to a customs intermediary and the gross-negligence attack *failed*: the conduct did not "smack of intentional wrongdoing" or "evince a reckless indifference to the rights of others," and the $50 cap held, affirmed by the Second Circuit. The way through is to distinguish it, and the distinction is real: ABN AMRO's defendant was a forwarder doing cargo handling, the "travel agent", not a broker exercising the classification and filing judgment Part 111 places on a licensed professional, and the conduct there was ordinary negligence at worst. Sommer keeps the gross-negligence door open; it does not walk you through it, and New York sets the threshold high. That is a real argument, and a better hand than the trade press gives you, but it is an argument, not a guarantee.

If your governing law is California, the ground has shifted further in your favor and recently. Civil Code § 1668 voids contracts that exempt a party from responsibility for willful injury or violation of law, and in New England Country Foods, LLC v. VanLaw Food Products, Inc., 17 Cal. 5th 703 (2025) (No. S282968, decided on a certified question from the Ninth Circuit), the California Supreme Court held that § 1668 bars not only full exculpation but damages caps limiting liability for willful injury. The court left room to limit damages for ordinary breach of contract absent an independent duty within § 1668's scope. Gross negligence sits on a separate track, and it is already settled the same way: in City of Santa Barbara v. Superior Court (2007) 41 Cal.4th 747, the court adopted the majority rule that an agreement purporting to release liability for future gross negligence generally is unenforceable as a matter of public policy. Its holding is framed in the recreational-services context, a limit a broker's counsel will be quick to raise, but the public-policy reasoning is not confined to it. A contractual cap on a broker's gross-negligence liability therefore runs into a well-established bar, not an open question, and New England Country Foods, discussing that line of authority, treats it as settled while extending § 1668 to reach willful-injury damages caps as well.

**Two things nobody tells you.**

First: no reported decision squarely resolves this question in the customs-penalty setting. Every case above involves lost or damaged cargo. I could not find a decision holding on whether a broker's cap is enforceable where the broker's error produced a CBP duty assessment or penalty rather than a physical loss. That is an open question, and open questions are negotiating room. When a broker tells you the cap is settled law, ask them for the case. I could not find one.

Second: the cap does not bind CBP, and it never did. Whatever ¶ 9(c) says about what the broker owes you, it has no effect at all on what the government can do to the broker directly. CBP disciplines brokers under 19 U.S.C. § 1641(d), implemented through 19 CFR Part 111, Subpart E (§§ 111.91 through 111.95; § 111.96 sets the fee schedule), and no private contract limits that. Executive Order 14411 § 4(a) directs the Secretary to impose maximum penalties on brokers who fail to conduct due diligence, repeatedly represent noncompliant clients, or fail to respond to CBP requests in a timely manner.

So your broker faces two exposures. One is capped by a clause they wrote. The other, a § 1641(d) discipline proceeding, carries a monetary penalty that § 1641(d)(2)(B) sets "not to exceed $30,000 in total for a violation or violations of this section" (and that $30,000, unlike almost every other federal penalty figure, has never been inflation-adjusted, because Tariff Act of 1930 penalties are expressly carved out of the Federal Civil Penalties Inflation Adjustment Act: a point worth having ready, since practitioners assume every such figure has been indexed upward). But the exposure that actually concentrates a broker's attention is not the money: it is the license and the national permit the discipline reaches, on which the broker's entire book of business depends. That exposure is uncapped in the way that matters, and it is about to get worse. That asymmetry is the most under-used piece of leverage an importer has in this negotiation, and it is the honest basis for the conversation the addendum is designed to start: the government is going to hold you to a standard regardless. Let's write down what that standard is, together, before either of us needs it.

**2. The One-Sided Indemnification Clause**

While the broker limits their own liability to a nominal fee, they demand un-capped indemnification from the importer. Representative indemnity language of the kind found in commercial broker Terms and Conditions runs like this:

> *Customer agrees to indemnify, defend, and hold harmless Company from and against any and all claims, liabilities, losses, damages, fines, penalties, court costs, and attorney's fees arising out of or related to any act, omission, or instruction of Customer, or arising from any entry, filing, or declaration made on behalf of Customer.*

(That is representative language, not a verbatim quotation of any one broker's form; check the actual Terms and Conditions your broker incorporates.)

This clause creates a structural legal asymmetry. Under this text, if CBP opens a § 1641(d) discipline proceeding against the broker, or a third party brings a claim arising out of the broker's filing, the broker can use this clause to push its own legal defense fees and civil fines onto you. (Pick the example with care: late-filing liquidated damages are *not* it. Under 19 CFR § 142.15, the port director demands those against the importer's own continuous bond, on which you are already the principal, so there is nothing for an indemnity to shift. The asymmetry bites where the exposure is genuinely the broker's, such as a § 1641(d) penalty or a third-party claim.)

You are contractually agreeing to fund your agent's legal defense for errors committed while handling your account.

The Structural Legal Asymmetry

| BROKER PROTECTION UNDER STANDARD POA | IMPORTER RISK UNDER STANDARD POA |
|---|---|
| Maximum Financial Liability: Capped at $100.00 (or the brokerage fee, whichever is less) | Financial Liability: 100% of duties & fines |
| Legal Defense Costs: Paid by Importer via Indem | Legal Defense Costs: Paid out-of-pocket |
| Consequential Damages: Completely Excluded | Business Interruption: Uninsured & Uncovered |
| Errors & Omissions Exposure: Shielded | Penalty Floors: Fully Absorbed |

### 3. Blank-Check Sub-Agency Delegation

Standard POAs routinely contain a clause authorizing the appointed broker to delegate their power of attorney to un-vetted sub-agents:

> *"The undersigned grants unto said attorney full power and authority to appoint sub-agents and to execute such power of attorney to such sub-agents as may be necessary to conduct Customs business..."*

By signing this provision, you grant your primary Customs Broker unrestricted authority to transfer your power of attorney to local drayage brokers, third-party logistics (3PL) contractors, or independent filing desks across the country. Without notifying you, without disclosing who holds your power of attorney, and without verifying the sub-agent's internal compliance controls.

When a breach of confidentiality or a gross entry error occurs at the sub-agent level, the primary broker disclaims liability by pointing to the sub-agency authorization clause, leaving the importer to pursue a phantom sub-agent with whom they have no direct contractual relationship.

**4. The Data Share and Commercial Confidentiality Waiver**
Modern freight forwarders operate multifaceted logistics enterprises, running freight brokerage, warehouse management, customs entry, and supply chain advisory services under a single corporate umbrella. Standard POAs routinely incorporate clauses permitting the broker to share the importer's proprietary commercial data across their internal corporate divisions and with third-party software vendors.

This data includes your vendor lists, factory purchase prices, bills of materials, unit margins, and product transport routes.

Allowing your Customs Broker to freely share this data exposes your enterprise to commercial espionage, supplier poaching, and data breaches. Your master customs data is high-value commercial intelligence; handing a broker a blanket waiver to distribute that data is an unacceptable corporate vulnerability.

## Direct Communication and Eliminating Forwarder Shields (19 CFR § 111.36)

One of the riskiest operational arrangements in modern trade compliance occurs when an importer allows an international freight forwarder to act as an intermediary shield between the importer and the licensed Customs Broker actually filing the entries in ACE.

In this common 3PL setup, the importer contracts with a freight forwarder for end-to-end transportation. The forwarder then subcontracts the customs entry work to an independent or affiliated licensed Customs Broker. The forwarder instructs the importer to execute a POA directly to the forwarder or to the forwarder's chosen broker, but all day-to-day communications, entry approvals, and billing flow strictly through the forwarder's operational account managers.

This operational structure runs against the policy behind 19 CFR § 111.36 and creates an informational vacuum that routinely leads to severe compliance failures. Be precise about what the rule is, though: § 111.36 is a Part 111 duty the broker owes to CBP, which CBP enforces under 19 U.S.C. § 1641(d) and 19 CFR §§ 111.91 through 111.95. An importer has no private right to enforce it, and the arrangement does not automatically "violate" it, as the close reading below shows, § 111.36(c)'s conditions attach only where the broker compensates the forwarder for referrals. The leverage here is therefore contractual: hold the broker to these conditions in your own agreement, as the addendum does.

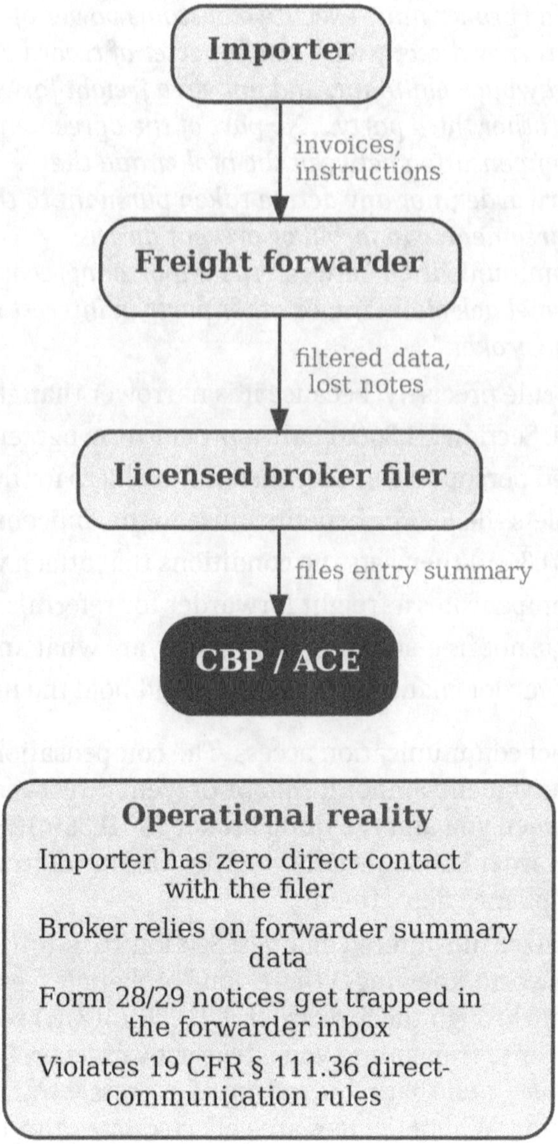


## Deconstructing 19 CFR § 111.36

Recognizing the potential for fraud, misrepresentation, and operational interference when third parties insert themselves between importers and Customs Brokers, 19 CFR § 111.36 governs a broker's relationships with unlicensed intermediaries. Its strongest sentence, at § 111.36(c)(3), is the one you actually want:

> *"The broker must execute a customs power of attorney directly with the importer of record or drawback claimant, and not via a freight forwarder or other third party.... No part of the agreement of compensation between the broker and the forwarder, nor any action taken pursuant to the agreement, can forbid or prevent direct communication between the importer of record, drawback claimant, or other party in interest and the broker."*

Read the rule precisely, because it is narrower than it is often described. Section 111.36(b) bars a broker from agreeing with an unlicensed person to transact customs business for others in a way that lets the fees or benefits inure to the unlicensed person. Section 111.36(c) then sets the conditions that attach when a broker compensates a freight forwarder for referrals. Those conditions, not free-standing commands, are what an importer using forwarder-managed logistics should hold the broker to:

1. Direct communication access. The compensation arrangement cannot forbid or prevent direct communication between you and the filing broker (§ 111.36(c)(3)). The forwarder cannot legally wall the broker off from your compliance department.
2. Itemized, un-filtered charges. Section 111.36(c)(2) draws a line worth knowing. Where your brokerage fees are collected by or through the forwarder, § 111.36(c)(2)(i) requires the broker to transmit to you a true copy of its brokerage charges, and that requirement is expressly waivable in writing. Where the fees are collected by or through the broker itself, § 111.36(c)(2)(ii) requires the broker to give you an itemized account of its charges, and that one is not waivable. So part of what you might assume you have to secure by contract is already guaranteed by regulation. Know which of the two regimes your arrangement falls under before you negotiate for it.

3. A POA executed directly with you. Section 111.36(c)(3) requires the POA to run directly between the importer of record and the broker, not through the forwarder.

Separately, § 111.36(a) requires a broker employed by a non-importer unlicensed person to transmit a copy of the bill or the entry to the actual importer, unless the goods were bought on DDP terms or the importer waived that in writing.

**The Informational Shield Hazard**

When an unlicensed freight forwarder acts as an operational shield, they prioritize transportation speed and freight margin over regulatory precision. When CBP issues a CBP Form 28 (Request for Information) or CBP Form 29 (Notice of Action) electronically in ACE, the notification lands in the filing broker's queue.

If the filing broker does not maintain direct communication with the importer, the regulatory escalation sequence breaks down:

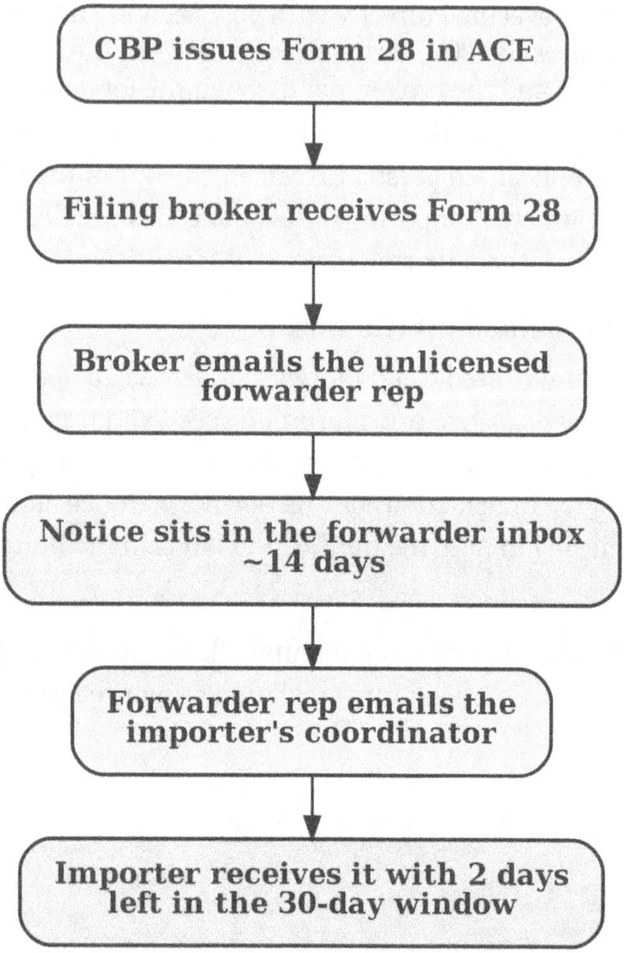


By the time the importer's legal or compliance team sees the Form 28, the thirty-day response window printed on the form has virtually expired. The importer is forced to rush out an un-vetted, incomplete response, or face an automated CBP Form 29 Notice of Action reclassifying the merchandise at the highest available duty rate, accompanied by an immediate rate advance and bond lock.

### Enforcing Direct Communication

To harden your POA architecture against this vulnerability, every importer using forwarder-managed logistics should enforce direct communication:

- Tri-party POA registration: execute POAs directly with the underlying licensed Customs Broker, incorporating a clause that references 19 CFR § 111.36 and obligates the broker to copy the importer's internal compliance email address (`compliance@importer.com`) on 100% of regulatory transmissions, ACE notifications, and entry summary confirmations.
- Elimination of Forwarder Data Filtering: Contractually prohibit freight forwarders from altering, summarizing, or re-keying invoice data. The filing broker must receive original, un-edited commercial invoice datasets generated directly from the importer's ERP platform.
- Direct Duty Remittance via ACH: Never pay customs duties through a freight forwarder's general invoice. Establish an Automated Clearing House (ACH) Payer Account directly with CBP. Under ACH Payer status, duty payments are pulled directly from the importer's bank account by CBP, eliminating forwarder markups, preventing forwarder duty-float schemes, and ensuring immediate, traceable proof of duty payment directly on CBP statement records.

## The Customized POA Addendum: Clause-by-Clause Drafting Strategies

To transform the POA from a tool of broker protection into an instrument of importer control, you must never sign a standard broker POA as presented. Instead, you must attach a controlling, overriding Customized Power of Attorney Addendum.

A caution before the clauses, because it determines whether any of them bind. A customs power of attorney is a *unilateral* grant of agency authority from the principal to the broker (19 CFR § 141.31(a); the standard form is at § 141.32). It is signed by the principal alone and is typically unsupported by consideration. An addendum that only reshapes the *scope* of the authority you are granting works as part of that unilateral grant. But every clause below that imposes an affirmative obligation on the *broker*, indemnity, joint-and-several liability for sub-agents, confidentiality and data duties, 24-hour escalation, is a contract offer, and an offer binds no one until it is accepted. Because CBP never receives the POA (19 CFR § 141.46), nothing external will ever surface the defect; you discover it the first time you try to enforce a clause the broker never signed. So put these obligations where they will hold: in a broker services agreement, or in an addendum that is *countersigned by an authorized officer of the broker*, with recited consideration. Treat an addendum returned unsigned as having no effect, and note that Chapter 6 assumes exactly this, walking through what to do when "your broker has declined to sign it."

This Addendum must contain explicit legal language establishing that in the event of any conflict between the broker's standard terms and conditions and the Addendum, the Addendum shall strictly govern and control.

Below are the five essential, clause-by-clause drafting strategies required to construct a strong POA Addendum.

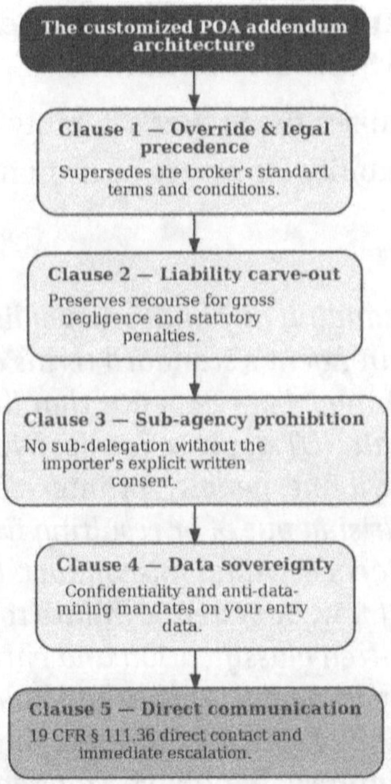


## Clause 1: Override and Legal Precedence

This clause destroys the broker's boilerplate terms and conditions, establishing legal priority for the importer's controls.

Model Draft Text:

> *"This Addendum amends, controls, and legally supersedes any power of attorney form, credit application, service agreement, or standard terms and conditions executed between Importer of Record ('Principal') and Customs Broker ('Agent'). In the event of any inconsistency, ambiguity, or conflict between the terms of this Addendum and any standard agreement or terms and conditions provided by Agent, the terms of this Addendum shall strictly govern and control, regardless of whether Agent's standard agreement was executed prior to or subsequent to this Addendum."*

### Clause 2: Carve-Out for Gross Negligence, Willful Misconduct, and Statutory Penalties

This clause neutralizes the broker's liability cap and forces financial accountability for severe operational failures.

Model Draft Text:

> *"Notwithstanding any limitation of liability clause contained in Agent's standard terms and conditions or NCBFAA model agreements, that limitation of liability shall NOT apply to any loss, fee, liquidated damage, civil fine, penalty, or interest incurred by Principal arising out of or resulting from Agent's gross negligence, willful misconduct, intentional violation of law, or systemic failure to follow explicit written classification and entry instructions provided by Principal. Agent shall hold harmless and indemnify Principal for direct financial losses, including interest, liquidated damages, statutory penalties under 19 U.S.C. § 1592 or 19 U.S.C. § 1641, and the reasonable professional and administrative costs of correction, caused directly by Agent's gross negligence or failure to exercise due diligence under 19 CFR Part 111. This indemnity does not extend to the underlying duties, taxes, and fees themselves, which Principal owes to CBP by statute regardless of fault."*

A drafting note on that last sentence, because it is a deliberate narrowing. The rest of this book proves that the duties are yours under 19 U.S.C. § 1484 no matter who made the error, so asking the broker to indemnify "assessed CBP duties" asks it to pay a liability that is yours by statute: the one demand a broker's counsel can refuse on principle without seeming unreasonable, and a clause that invites a fight over the whole indemnity. Narrowing the indemnity to the *incremental* harm the broker's fault actually caused, interest, penalties, liquidated damages, and the cost of cleanup, is what makes the clause both fair and signable.

A second, easily missed gap: neutralizing the liability *cap* does nothing about the broker's *time bar*. The NCBFAA model terms and most house forms carry a Limitation of Actions provision that runs two separate clocks, and you have to disarm both. The first is a written notice-of-claim requirement: ninety days under the rev. 9/2023 terms (§ 3(a)), where "the failure to give the Company timely notice shall be a complete defense" to the claim. The second is a suit-limitation period: § 3(b)(iv) requires any suit on an import-entry claim to be brought within seventy-five days from the date of liquidation. Confirm both periods in your broker's operative revision. A carve-out from the cap that leaves these provisions standing is close to worthless, because your own operating model guarantees both bars fire: a quarterly audit finds the error more than ninety days after the event, so the notice bar closes, and a § 1592 demand or rate advance usually lands well after liquidation, so the seventy-five-day suit bar closes too. Whichever revision your broker uses, the addendum must expressly extend or disapply it, for example: "Any contractual notice-of-claim or limitation-of-actions period in Agent's terms is extended such that Principal must give written notice of a claim within 30 days of Principal's discovery of the underlying error, and may bring suit within two years of that discovery." Without that, the silence in the case law that Chapter 6 reads as leverage is at least partly a time bar quietly disposing of these claims before they ever generate an opinion.

**Clause 3: Sub-Agency Restriction and Explicit Consent Controls**

This clause revokes the broker's blank-check authority to delegate your power of attorney to un-vetted third parties.

Model Draft Text:

> *"Agent's authority to appoint sub-agents under this Power of Attorney is strictly restricted. Agent shall not delegate, assign, or transfer customs business authority to any third-party Customs Broker, sub-agent, or independent contractor without securing the prior written consent of Principal's Corporate Compliance Officer. Any sub-agent approved by Principal must execute a written agreement agreeing to be bound by all terms, restrictions, and confidentiality mandates contained within this Addendum. Agent remains fully, jointly, and severally liable for all acts, omissions, and entries filed by any approved sub-agent acting under this Power of Attorney."*

Know what this clause does and does not add. If you are a **U.S.-resident** importer: most of this book's audience, 19 CFR § 141.43(a) already bars the holder of your POA from appointing a subagent at all (except to file Electronic Export Information), and provides that any such subagent "cannot delegate his power." For you, the free-standing sub-POA authority in a broker's form is largely unenforceable to begin with, so treat this clause as belt-and-suspenders rather than a top-tier fight. The joint-and-several liability sentence is the part still doing real work. Where the clause genuinely matters is for **nonresident** principals: § 141.43(b), read with § 141.36, does allow a subagent for a nonresident, subject to residency and service-of-process conditions. If your structure is nonresident, this is a first-order clause; if it is resident, spend your negotiating capital on the time bar and the indemnity above.

**Clause 4: Data, Confidentiality, and Anti-Mining**

This clause locks down your master customs data, treating commercial information as protected intellectual property.

Model Draft Text:

> *"All commercial data, technical specifications, product descriptions, HTS classification databases, vendor identities, unit pricing, purchase orders, and entry summary data provided by Principal or generated by Agent under this Power of Attorney shall remain the exclusive intellectual property and confidential information of Principal. Agent is strictly prohibited from selling, sharing, mining, aggregating, or disclosing Principal's data to any third party, affiliate, freight forwarding division, or commercial entity for any commercial purpose. This prohibition does not restrict disclosures the law requires or expressly permits, namely: transmission to CBP and partner government agencies to execute entries; production of records under 19 CFR § 111.23 and 19 CFR Part 163; disclosure to the surety on a particular entry as permitted by 19 CFR § 111.24; response to a subpoena, court order, or other compelled legal process; and transmission to Agent's own ABI software and ACE service providers who are bound by equivalent confidentiality obligations. Agent shall maintain modern cybersecurity controls consistent with SOC 2 Type II or ISO 27001 standards to protect Principal's data from unauthorized access or exfiltration."*

Draft the carve-outs, and draft them generously, because a clause that bars the broker from doing what § 111.23, Part 163, or a court order require is a clause no competent broker's counsel will sign, and if one does, you have manufactured breaches you never wanted. Track § 111.24's own exception set rather than inventing a narrower one.

### Clause 5: 19 CFR § 111.36 Direct Communication and Immediate Escalation

This clause codifies direct communication pathways and forces immediate escalation of CBP inquiries.

Model Draft Text:

> *"Agent acknowledges its regulatory obligations under 19 CFR § 111.36 and agrees to maintain direct, un-impeded communication with Principal's dedicated compliance team. Agent shall transmit copies of all ACE entry summary data (CBP Form 7501), commercial invoices, and duty payment confirmations directly to Principal's designated email portal (`compliance@importer.com`). Agent shall immediately, and in no event later than twenty-four (24) hours from receipt, forward to Principal's designated email portal any CBP Form 28 (Request for Information), CBP Form 29 (Notice of Action), CBP Form 4647 (Notice to Mark and/or Redeliver), or any formal inquiry, detention notice, or communication received from U.S. Customs and Border Protection or any Partner Government Agency (PGA). Agent shall not take a substantive position, or submit substantive responsive content, to CBP or any PGA in Principal's name without securing prior written authorization and approved response content from Principal; this does not bar Agent from acknowledging receipt, confirming factual matters within Agent's own knowledge, or requesting an extension of time."*

# Chapter 5: Building an Enforceable Service Level Agreement (SLA)

## Defining "Customs Business" SLA Metrics: Establishing Quantifiable Benchmarks

A Power of Attorney grants legal authority; a Service Level Agreement (SLA) enforces operational performance.

Without a binding, metrics-driven SLA attached directly to your broker contract, your account is managed according to the broker's operational convenience. Entry clerks will process your work when time permits, default to high-duty fallback codes during volume surges, delay filing Post-Summary Corrections (PSCs) until statutory deadlines loom, and ignore partner government agency (PGA) data elements until ACE issues an entry rejection.

To construct a rigorous SLA, you must translate the legal concept of "due diligence" under 19 CFR § 111.29(a) into quantifiable, trackable, and enforceable Key Performance Indicators (KPIs) that govern every aspect of "customs business."

The Customs Business SLA KPI Metric Matrix

| OPERATIONAL DOMAIN | TARGET PERFORMANCE METRIC | MEASUREMENT WINDOW & FORMULA |
|---|---|---|
| Entry Summary Timeliness | 100% filed within 5 days of release | Daily ACE ES-001 Audit Report |
| Classification Accuracy | >= 99.5% match to Master HTS Table | Monthly Random Line-Item Audit |
| CBP Form 28/29 Escalation | 100% forwarded within 24 Hours | Timestamp Log Verification |
| PGA Transmission Accuracy | 100% zero-reject rate on PGA flags | ACE Automated Edit Log |
| PSC Execution Turnaround | Completed within 10 Business Days | Request-to-Filing Timestamp |

**Metric 1: Entry Summary Timeliness and Duty Remittance**

Under 19 CFR § 142.12(b), the entry summary documentation must be filed with estimated duties attached within 10 working days after the time of entry (19 CFR § 141.68), which usually, but not always, coincides with release. Relying on this 10-working-day regulatory maximum as your operational baseline is a critical error; it leaves zero margin if data discrepancies emerge. Your SLA in the next chapter sets a tighter five-business-day standard measured from release; that is a deliberate tightening, and it works precisely because you know the regulatory clock and the contract clock are different instruments.

- SLA Standard: 100% of standard consumption entry summaries (Entry Type 01) and Section 301/AD/CVD entries (Entry Type 03) must be fully transmitted, validated, and duty-scheduled in ACE within five (5) business days of cargo release.
- Measurement Formula: Entry Timeliness % = (Entries Filed within 5 Days / Total Entries Released) × 100
- Threshold: Any monthly score below 98.0% triggers an immediate operational review and fee credit. The gap between the 100% standard and the 98% trigger is deliberate: the 100% figure is what you hold the broker to, and the two-point band absorbs the occasional benign release-timing edge case, a Friday-afternoon release, a carrier data lag, without firing a remedy. That is why this metric's standard and trigger differ, while the classification metric below sets both at the same 99.5% line: an unauthorized code change, unlike a late filing, has no benign explanation to absorb.

**Metric 2: Line-Item Classification Match Rate**

Brokers must be strictly evaluated on their adherence to the importer's pre-vetted Master HTS Database. Entry clerks are prohibited from modifying 10-digit HTS codes, applying secondary tariffs, or changing PGA flag declarations without system authorization.

- SLA Standard: The HTS codes, unit value declarations, and country of origin entries transmitted in ACE must achieve a 99.5% exact match rate against the importer's authorized master item database.
- Measurement Formula: Classification Match % = (1 – Unauthorized HTS Modifications / Total Transmitted Line Items) × 100
- Threshold: A match rate below 99.5% in any calendar month requires the broker to audit 100% of all entry lines filed during that month at the broker's expense.

**Metric 3: CBP Form 28 / 29 / 4647 Notification Velocity**

When CBP issues an inquiry or notice of action, time is the ultimate asset. The SLA must set a firm metric for escalation speed.

- SLA Standard: 100% of all official notices, informal emails from CEE Import Specialists, and system-generated ACE forms (CBP Forms 28, 29, 4647, 6043) received by the broker must be logged, scanned, and transmitted to the importer's compliance team within twenty-four (24) hours of receipt by the broker.
- Measurement Formula: Timestamps recorded on the ACE notification log versus the electronic delivery timestamp to the importer's compliance portal.
- Threshold: A failure to notify the importer of a CBP Form 28 or 29 within 48 hours constitutes a material breach of the SLA, resulting in an automatic contract audit and financial penalty.

A note on the escalation clocks, because four different numbers appear across this book and a careful reader will ask which one goes in the contract. They measure different things. Twenty-four hours is the contractual standard: the window in which the broker must forward a CBP notice to you. Forty-eight hours is the breach threshold, because you want a defined cure gap rather than a hair trigger: miss twenty-four and you are late, miss forty-eight and it is a material breach. Four hours is the internal routing target once a notice reaches your own compliance inbox: a different clock, inside your own organization, not a duty on the broker. And two business days is the counter you should be willing to accept from a mid-market broker (Chapter 6). Set the twenty-four-hour standard in the contract, hold the forty-eight-hour breach line, run the four-hour clock internally, and know that two business days is a fair landing point.

### Metric 4: Post-Summary Correction (PSC) Execution Speed

When the importer's internal audit identifies a broker entry error (e.g., incorrect value declaration, missing SPI claim, or misapplied HTS code), the error must be corrected via ACE Post-Summary Correction before liquidation occurs: within 300 days of the date of entry, or fifteen days before the scheduled liquidation date, whichever is earlier.

- SLA Standard: Upon receiving a written request for a Post-Summary Correction from the importer's compliance team, the broker must execute, validate, and transmit the PSC in ACE within ten (10) business days.
- Measurement Formula: PSC Turnaround Time = Date PSC Transmitted in ACE – Date PSC Requested by Importer
- Threshold: Any PSC request taking longer than 15 business days to execute without written justification incurs an automatic SLA financial offset.

## Gating Rules for High-Liability Entries

The most powerful mechanism in a modern SLA is a set of automated entry gates.

An entry gate is a system-enforced stoppage point in the entry filing workflow. It prevents a Customs Broker's entry clerk from transmitting an entry summary into ACE unless explicit, pre-defined compliance conditions are met and verified in writing.

Without gating protocols, entry clerks routinely bypass complex regulatory requirements to maintain processing speed. By embedding binding gating protocols directly into your SLA contract, you forcibly align the broker's software workflow with your corporate risk tolerance.

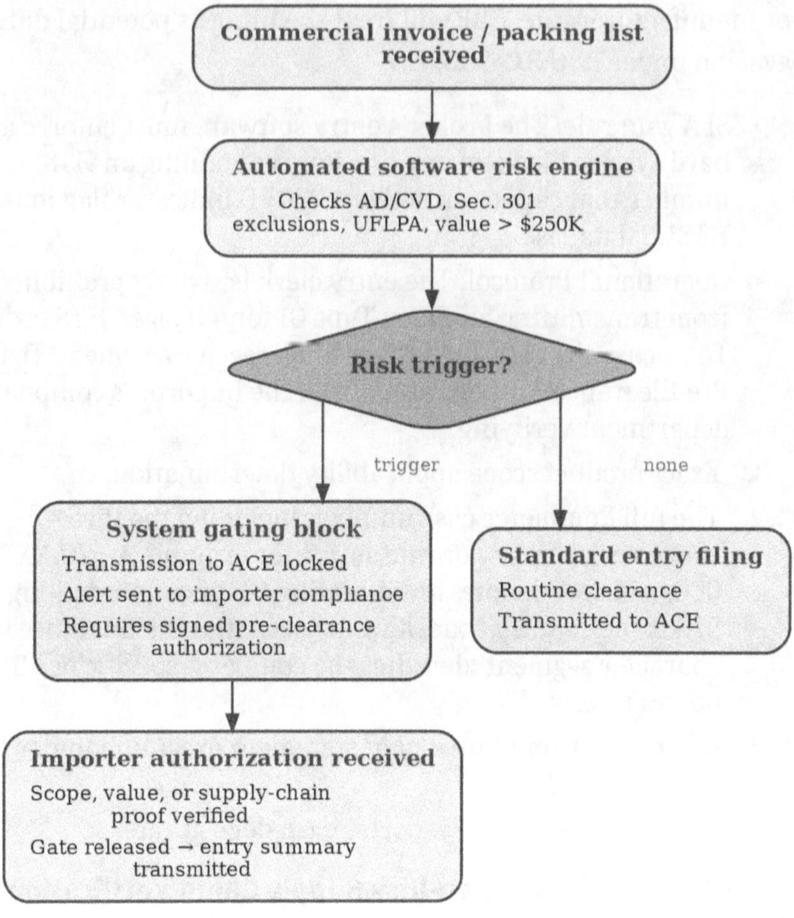


Below are the three gating rules to codify in your SLA.

### Gate 1: The Antidumping / Countervailing Duty (AD/CVD) Hard Lock

Antidumping and Countervailing Duty entries (Entry Type 03) represent the highest potential civil penalty exposure in international trade. AD/CVD cash deposit rates routinely exceed 100% to 300% of the entered value. If an entry clerk files a line item under Entry Type 01 (Consumption) when it is legally subject to an AD/CVD order, or enters an incorrect case number or manufacturer rate, CBP will treat the filing as potential duty evasion under 19 U.S.C. § 1592.

- SLA gate rule: The broker's entry software must enforce a hard system block on any line item containing an HTS number that carries an active AD/CVD indicator flag in the HTSUS database.
- Operational Protocol: The entry clerk is strictly prohibited from transmitting an Entry Type 01 for a flagged HTS code. To release the gate, the broker must receive a signed AD/CVD Pre-Clearance Authorization from the importer's compliance department verifying:

1. Exact product scope applicability determination.
2. The full Commerce case number, including the three-character company or rate suffix, for example A-570-XXX-000, where A denotes antidumping (C for countervailing), 570 is the country code, XXX the case, and the final three-character segment identifies the company-specific or all-others rate.
3. Correct non-reimbursement statement execution under 19 CFR § 351.402(f).
4. Exact manufacturer/exporter cash deposit rate.

### Gate 2: The UFLPA / High-Risk Supply Chain Verification Gate

Under the Uyghur Forced Labor Prevention Act (UFLPA), merchandise mined, produced, or manufactured in whole or in part in the Xinjiang Uyghur Autonomous Region (XUAR), or produced by entities listed on the UFLPA Entity List, is subject to the UFLPA's rebuttable presumption of forced labor (Pub. L. 117-78, § 3), which bars the goods from entry under 19 U.S.C. § 1307 and triggers detention at the port.

- SLA gate rule: The broker's entry platform must enforce a hard system lock on any entry originating from specific geographic regions, high-risk HTS chapters (e.g., Chapter 52 cotton and Chapters 61–62 apparel, Chapters 7 and 20 tomatoes and tomato products, Chapter 85 electronics, Chapter 76 aluminum), or involving foreign vendors flagged on the importer's internal UFLPA watch list.
- Operational Protocol: The entry clerk cannot transmit the entry summary until the broker receives a verified UFLPA Clearance Certificate from the importer's supply chain compliance team, confirming that the tier-1 through tier-4 supply chain mapping records, raw material bills of lading, and mill test certificates have been audited and archived in the importer's compliance repository.

**Gate 3: High-Value and Section 301 Exclusion Expiration Gate**

- SLA gate rule: The broker's system must enforce an automated hold on:

1. Any individual entry summary where the entered declared value exceeds $250,000.00.
2. Any entry line applying a specific Section 301 tariff exclusion under HTS heading 9903.

- Operational Protocol: For high-value entries, the broker must verify transaction value calculations, valuation assists, international freight/insurance deductions, and currency conversion rates against the importer's pre-entry clearance sheet. For Section 301 exclusions, the broker must verify that the specific exclusion Chapter 99 heading remains legally active in ACE and matches the precise physical and technical description of the imported product.

## Financial Remedies & Audit Escalation: Structuring SLA Offsets and Penalties

An SLA without financial teeth is merely a set of non-binding recommendations. To make the standard bind, build a contractual framework of financial offsets, audits, and escalation paths.

When a broker breaches an SLA metric, the financial consequences must be immediate, direct, and automatically applied as fee credits against outstanding service invoices.

SLA Financial Remedy & Escalation Matrix

| SLA Breach Event | Contractual Financial Remedy | Escalation Action |
|---|---|---|
| Entry summary filed after the 5-business-day SLA standard but within the 10-working-day regulatory window | Service credit you set (e.g., a fixed per-entry credit or a step credit on the month's fees), price it, or the 5-day standard is aspirational | Account manager review |
| Late entry summary filing (>10 days in ACE) | 100% fee credit plus the importer's internal administrative cost fee | Broker account manager; formal review meeting |
| Discrepancy match rate drops below 99.5% | 25% reduction in monthly entry-processing fees across the account, rising to 50% if the rate drops below 98.0% | 100% line audit at the broker's expense |
| Failure to notify of CBP Form 28/29 within 48 hours | Broker reimburses 100% of assessed liquidated damages and penalties | Executive VP escalation; right to instantly terminate |
| Systemic un-authorized HTS substitution by entry clerk | Fee credit of $250.00 per misclassified line item | Formal notice to broker's corporate officer / licensed broker under 19 CFR § 111.28 |

### 1. Contractual Fee Offsets for Performance Failure

The SLA contract must incorporate an explicit Fee Offset Schedule, but drop the word "non-contestable," because self-help set-off is never non-contestable. If you unilaterally withhold or deduct fees, the broker can dispute it, and doing so can trip the broker's general lien over your documents and goods (the lien Chapter 6 warns about, connect the two, because this remedy is what triggers it). Structure the offsets as agreed service-credit price adjustments applied on the next invoice, not as a self-help withholding you declare unanswerable:

- Late Filing Offsets: If the broker fails to transmit an entry summary within the regulatory 10-working-day window, resulting in CBP issuing a Notice of Liquidated Damages (CBP Form 5955A), the broker shall:

1. Immediately pay 100% of the liquidated damages claim assessed by CBP.
2. Issue a 100% fee credit for the transactional brokerage fee associated with that entry.
3. Pay the importer a flat administrative fee of $500.00 per incident to cover internal legal and compliance review costs.

- Accuracy Threshold Offsets: The two accuracy remedies in this SLA are complementary, not alternatives, and both trigger at the same 99.5% line. The 100% line audit at the broker's expense (Metric 2) is the corrective remedy: it forces the broker to find and fix the errors, while the fee discount below is the financial offset that compensates the importer for the month the standard was missed. When the broker's monthly HTS match rate drops below the 99.5% threshold, the broker shall run the 100% audit at its own expense and automatically apply a 25% discount across all entry-processing invoice fees billed to the importer for that operating month. If the match rate drops below 98.0%, the discount increases to 50% while the audit obligation remains. None of these figures is a regulatory or industry-mandated benchmark; there is no published CBP or trade standard fixing a broker match rate, so treat 99.5% as a negotiated commercial target you set with your broker, not a number the law supplies.

**2. The Audit Escalation Path**

When performance metrics deteriorate, the SLA must trigger a structured, multi-stage Audit Escalation Protocol that moves quickly up the broker's corporate hierarchy:

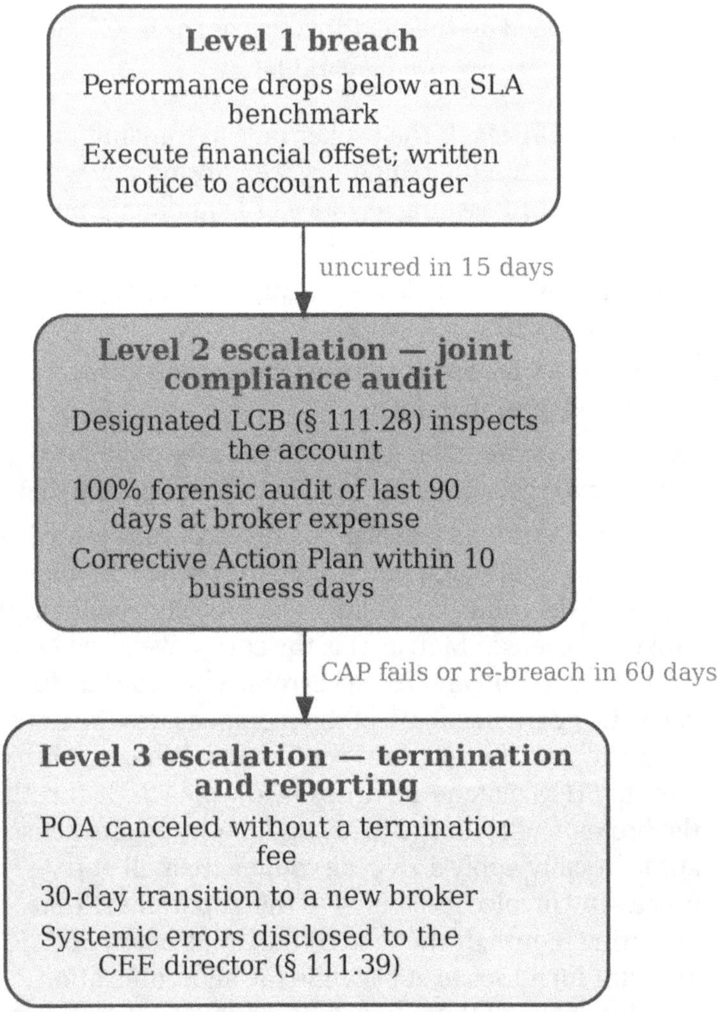


**3. Carve-Out for Direct Third-Party Financial Recovery**

The SLA must contain an explicit legal clause establishing that the financial remedies provided under the SLA are in addition to, and do not replace or limit, the importer's right to seek full financial recovery for direct losses caused by the broker's gross negligence, fraud, or intentional misconduct.

Model SLA Clause Text:

> *"The financial offsets, fee credits, and administrative remedies set forth in this Service Level Agreement represent agreed operational price adjustments for deficient service performance and shall NOT operate as a ceiling on damages or limit Principal's right to seek full legal indemnification for interest, liquidated damages, statutory penalties, or court costs resulting from Agent's gross negligence, willful misconduct, or failure to exercise responsible supervision and control under 19 CFR § 111.28."*

Two enforceability cautions your counsel should weigh before this goes in a contract. First, fixed per-line and per-incident sums ($250 per misclassified line, $500 per incident) are enforceable as liquidated damages only if actual damages were genuinely hard to estimate at signing and the sum is a reasonable pre-estimate of the loss. A flat figure that is identical for a $12 line and a $400,000 line has the classic profile of an unenforceable *penalty*: a court may strike it. Second, and this is why the carve-out above is drafted as it now reads, a schedule that hands the importer both the fixed sums *and* full actual damages for the same breach invites a court to characterize the fixed sums as punitive and take down the whole schedule. The safer structures are elective: the importer elects the service credit *or* actual damages, not both, or an explicit service-credit price adjustment that is deducted from any damages later awarded. (Note that the indemnity here is drawn, deliberately, to interest, liquidated damages, penalties, and costs, not the underlying duties, which are the importer's by statute regardless of fault, for the reason given in Chapter 4.)

A power of attorney sets who is liable. A service level agreement sets what "acceptable" means. Most importers have signed the first and never written the second, which is how a relationship ends up governed entirely by the party with the most to lose from writing it down.

# Chapter 6: When the Broker Says No

You have taken the addendum from Chapter 4 to your broker. Your broker has declined to sign it.

This chapter is about what happens next, and it starts with the least satisfying fact in it: your broker's refusal is usually not bad faith, and treating it as bad faith is the fastest way to lose the negotiation.

**Why they actually say no**

Four reasons, in rough order of how often you will meet them.

**The person you asked cannot say yes.** Account executives at national brokerages have no authority to modify terms. The addendum has to go to legal, legal is in another city, and the path of least resistance for everyone in between is a polite no. This is the most common refusal and the least meaningful one. Ask who *can* say yes, and ask in writing.

**Their errors-and-omissions insurance is written against the standard terms.** A broker who accepts uncapped liability for gross negligence may be accepting exposure their carrier does not cover. That is a real constraint, not an excuse, and it points at the productive version of the conversation: not "remove the cap" but "what will your carrier support, and what is the number?"

**The margin genuinely does not support it.** If you competed the account down to forty-five dollars an entry, you bought a service priced for volume processing, and you are now asking for a liability profile priced for professional judgment. You cannot have both at that number. This refusal is the honest one, and the answer is usually not legal.

**They believe they do not have to.** Some brokers refuse because the standard terms have always held and no client has pushed.

This is the only category where the refusal is really a test, and Chapter 4's case law is your answer.

### Ask for the right things

The addendum has five clauses. They are not equally important, and going to the table treating all five as non-negotiable is how you end up with none of them.

**The three that matter:**

**1. Escalation of CBP communications.** Every CBP Form 28, 29, or 4647, and every informal inquiry from a Center, forwarded to your compliance address within one business day, with the broker barred from responding substantively without your written authorization.

This is the clause to fight for and it is the one you are most likely to win. It costs the broker essentially nothing: it is a workflow rule, not a liability transfer, and it protects them too, because it stops an entry clerk from making an unvetted statement to CBP in your name. A broker who refuses *this* is telling you something important about how they operate.

**2. The gross-negligence carve-out.** The liability cap does not apply to loss caused by the broker's gross negligence, willful misconduct, or systemic failure to follow your written instructions.

Chapter 4 explains why this is a smaller ask than it sounds: outside the common-carrier context, a damages cap purporting to shield gross negligence is on shaky ground in New York and, since 2025, on ground that is at least contested in California, and increasingly so. You are asking them to write down a rule that probably already applies. Say so, without gloating.

One tension worth naming before your broker's counsel does. The escalation clause bars the broker from taking a position with CBP in your name without your authorization, and the June 2026 order separately penalizes brokers who fail to respond promptly to CBP. A careful broker will point out that a flat "do not respond" clause could put it crosswise with Executive Order 14411 § 4(a), which penalizes brokers who fail to respond promptly to CBP, and with its own due-diligence duty under § 111.29. Resolve it the way it actually gets resolved: the clause bars substantive positions taken in your name, not the broker's acknowledging receipt, confirming facts within its own knowledge, or requesting an extension. Draft it that way, as the addendum in this book now does, and the objection narrows sharply. It does not vanish, and you should not pretend to your broker that it does: a broker cannot contract out of § 111.32 (it must not file a document it knows to be false) or § 111.39(c) (it must promptly advise a client of a known error and the corrective action required), and EO 14411 § 4(a) now points squarely at brokers who fail to cooperate with CBP in time. So give the clause a deemed-authorization backstop: if you do not respond within a stated period before the CBP deadline, the broker may respond, with contemporaneous notice to you and a copy of whatever it files. That keeps the broker onside with its own non-waivable duties without handing it free rein to speak in your name. It is one more instance of knowing what the broker is going to say before it says it.

**3. Sub-agency consent.** The broker does not transfer your power of attorney to another filer without your written consent, and remains liable for any sub-agent it does use.

Cheap to grant, and it closes the gap where you have no contractual relationship with the party that actually made the error.

**The two you can trade:** the data-sovereignty clause and the override-and-precedence language matter, but they are where you have room to concede structure in exchange for the first three.

### Scale the ask to your size

**Under 500 entries a year.** Ask for escalation and sub-agency consent. Skip the liability carve-out. You do not have the volume to win it, and pressing it costs you the two you could have had. Get the escalation clause in an email confirmation if you cannot get a signed addendum; a documented written commitment is worth considerably more than nothing.

**500 to 5,000.** All three core clauses are realistic. Bring them into the annual rate conversation rather than raising them cold, and be prepared to pay for them.

**Over 5,000.** You are a national account and the terms are negotiable. Put the addendum in the RFP, per Chapter 13, so it is priced in from the start rather than renegotiated after award.

### What you can actually trade

You have more to offer than you think, and none of it is money alone.

- **Term and volume.** A two-year commitment is worth real concessions.
- **Rate.** The single most effective sentence available to you is: *"I am not asking you to do this at forty-five dollars. What is the number where you can?"* It reframes the conversation from a liability fight to a pricing conversation, which is one brokers know how to have.
- **Cleaner data on your side.** Every hour their clerk spends chasing your vague invoice is margin. Committing to structured product data, complete origin detail, and itemized values is a genuine gift, and it also happens to be the master-data work in Chapters 8 and 9. *Horizon Products*, in Chapter 2, is the case that shows what happens when the importer sends bad instructions. You are asking your broker to accept accountability, and you should accept your half of it in the same document.

- **The scorecard as protection.** A broker performing well has every reason to want a documented record of it. Frame the scorecard as evidence they can use, because it is.

### The counter you should take

A reasonable broker's counter usually looks like this: escalation accepted with a two-business-day window instead of one; the gross-negligence carve-out accepted but capped at a stated dollar figure or at annual fees paid; sub-agency consent accepted with a carve-out for emergency port coverage.

**Take it.** A capped carve-out at a real number is enormously better than a hundred-dollar cap, and a two-day escalation window still gets you inside the clocks that matter. Perfect terms you cannot get are worth less than good terms you can.

### When "no" is the answer

Some refusals are information. Walk if you see these:

- They will not commit to forwarding CBP inquiries in **any** timeframe.
- They will not tell you who actually files your entries, or where.
- They will not confirm whether sub-agents touch your account.
- They refuse to give you a copy of the terms currently governing your relationship.
- They tell you the liability cap is settled law and decline to discuss it. Ask for the case. In my own search I could not find a reported decision holding that a broker's cap is enforceable where the error produced a CBP penalty rather than cargo loss, which is not proof that none exists, and is the stronger line for it: I looked and could not find one, so show me yours.
- Your quarterly check keeps finding the same error after you have raised it in writing.

That last one is the real signal. Everything else is negotiation.

## Changing brokers without a filing gap

If you do leave, the mechanics are more forgiving than most importers fear, with two traps.

**Your bond travels with you.** The continuous bond is *yours*. You are the principal, the surety is the co-obligor, CBP is the obligee, and **your broker is not a party to it.** Changing filers requires no bond action at all. There is no rider for changing brokers: 19 CFR § 113.24 accepts all authorized rider types, and none of them addresses the filer, because the broker is not on the instrument. (Section 113.27(a) requires a termination request to reach the Revenue Division; where no effective date is requested, termination takes effect on the tenth business day after receipt, which is the default that traps people.)

If you do decide to move the bond to a new surety agent, know that there is no CBP procedure for changing an "agent of record". That is surety-industry language, not a customs term. The route is to terminate the existing bond under § 113.27 and file a new one, and **the sequencing is the trap**: only one continuous bond per activity per principal is authorized (§ 113.12(b)), and termination takes effect no earlier than ten business days after the Revenue Division receives the request. Get the dates wrong and you are either double-bonded and rejected, or unbonded and stopped. Most importers changing brokers should simply leave the bond alone.

**You can run two brokers at once.** Nothing in the regulations limits how many valid powers of attorney you may have outstanding. Overlap deliberately: appoint the new broker, run both for a period, then revoke. Do not create a gap to prove a point.

**Revocation is simpler than you expect.** Under 19 CFR § 141.35, a power of attorney "shall be subject to revocation at any time by written notice given to and received by CBP, either at the port of entry or electronically." No form, no notice period, no waiting. One practical oddity: § 141.46 provides that the broker retains the POA and is *not* required to file it with CBP, so CBP is not actually holding the document you are revoking. In practice, revoke by written notice to the broker, and copy CBP as a belt-and-suspenders step.

**Your old broker's errors can still be fixed: by your new broker.** This is the trap most importers assume and get backwards, so it is worth stating plainly.

**A different filer may file a Post-Summary Correction on an entry summary originally filed by another filer, with the importer of record's authorization.** CBP does not check powers of attorney at the transaction level; it assumes the authorization exists. So firing your broker does not strand the entries they filed, as long as those entries are still inside the correction window from Chapter 10.

Two qualifications.

The entry number itself permanently carries the *original* broker's three-character filer code: the entry does not become yours in that sense, and never will.

And there is a confidentiality consequence you need to think about before you file. Under CBP's current PSC rules, when a new filer submits a correction, **the original filer retains full access to it.** CBP's own notice says an importer "should not file a PSC... if the importer does not want the original entry summary filer or any PSC filer for the same entry to have full access to all information contained within a subsequent PSC that was filed by a different filer." Correcting a sensitive valuation error or an AD/CVD scope position through a new broker means showing that correction to the broker you just fired. Sometimes that is fine. Sometimes it is a reason to talk to counsel first.

**If the window has closed**, you are not without options, but they narrow sharply. You may file a **protest** under 19 U.S.C. § 1514 within 180 days of liquidation, and importantly, **you can file it yourself.** 19 CFR § 174.12(a) permits protests by the importer or consignee shown on the entry papers; you do not need any broker's cooperation. Where the error involves an underpayment, the prior disclosure route in Chapter 10 is available.

What is *not* available is the old escape hatch. For merchandise entered, or withdrawn from warehouse for consumption, on or after December 18, 2004, CBP has no authority to reliquidate to correct a clerical error, mistake of fact, or inadvertence where no valid protest was filed. The provision that used to allow it, former 19 U.S.C. § 1520(c), was repealed by the Miscellaneous Trade and Technical Corrections Act of 2004 (Pub. L. 108-429, § 2105). Miss the PSC window and miss the protest window, and the entry is closed.

**Records are the one place the law does not help you.** No customs regulation requires a departing broker to hand over your file. 19 CFR § 111.23 requires the broker to retain **originals** for five years, which means even a cooperative broker gives you copies. Be precise about § 111.24, because it is easy to over-read: it is a confidentiality duty the broker owes *to CBP*, and it lists the client among the persons to whom the broker's records may be disclosed without breaching that duty. It confers no delivery entitlement on you at all. The provision that actually runs your way is § 111.39(a): "A broker must not withhold information from a client relative to any customs business it conducts on behalf of a client who is entitled to the information." That is the sentence to put in front of a broker sitting on your file, enforceable only by CBP, not by you directly, but a real referral threat. Whether a broker may withhold records over unpaid fees is contract and state law, and many brokerage terms contain a general lien clause.

Meanwhile your own five-year recordkeeping duty under 19 CFR Part 163 is **independent and parallel** to the broker's. Using a broker does not discharge it. If CBP demands records under § 163.6 and the only copy sits with a broker you parted from badly, the penalty is **yours**, and read its structure carefully, because it is the lesser of two figures, not the greater. For negligent failure to produce, 19 U.S.C. § 1509(g) and 19 CFR § 163.6(b) set it at the lesser of $10,000 or 40% of the appraised value of the merchandise, *per release of merchandise*; for willful failure, the lesser of $100,000 or 75%. The "per release" unit is what makes the number frightening: on a demand spanning many entries, it multiplies.

Two conclusions follow, and they are the most practical sentences in this chapter. Negotiate a records-turnover clause *before* you engage a broker, not while you are leaving one. And maintain your own ACE Portal account from day one, so your independent copy of the entry record never depended on the relationship in the first place.

**The order of operations**

1. Stand up your own ACE Portal account, if you have not (Chapter 1).
2. Appoint the new broker; do not revoke the old one yet.
3. Pull your full entry history from your own portal account.
4. Request records from the outgoing broker in writing, citing your services agreement.
5. Identify every unliquidated entry still inside the PSC window and decide what needs correcting.
6. Run both brokers in parallel through at least one full cycle.
7. Revoke the old POA in writing; copy CBP.
8. Leave the bond alone unless you have a specific reason not to.

## When There Is No Other Broker

Everything above assumes you can walk. Sometimes you cannot. The most common version is the captive affiliate: your freight forwarder owns, or is owned by, the licensed broker that files your entries, and in your lane there appears to be no one else. The negotiation loses its teeth when "we will take our business elsewhere" has no elsewhere behind it.

Be precise about how much of that is real. The broker files under a power of attorney you granted, and that authority is yours to pull. 19 CFR § 141.35 makes a customs POA "subject to revocation at any time by written notice given to and received by" CBP. No cause, no notice period. And § 111.36(c)(3) requires the broker to execute that POA "directly with the importer of record" and not by way of a freight forwarder or other third party. The captive broker is your agent, holding your revocable authority. The forwarder is not a party to that grant.

The "no one else in the lane" premise is largely a commercial illusion, not a rule. Since the Part 111 modernization took effect on December 19, 2022, a single national permit lets any licensed broker conduct customs business throughout the customs territory of the United States, and district permits were eliminated. Any broker holding an active national permit can file your entries, nationwide, whatever port your cargo moves through. The lane does not choose your filer. The forwarder's routing preference does.

Even inside the captive arrangement, § 111.36 preserves your access. Under § 111.36(c)(1) a broker may not take a forwarder's referral fee unless you were notified in advance of the name of the broker the forwarder selected: leverage you hold in practice, even though, as Chapter 4 notes, § 111.36 gives an importer no private right to enforce it directly. Under § 111.36(c) no agreement between the forwarder and the broker can forbid or prevent direct communication between the importer of record and the broker. A forwarder that walls you off from your own filer is not exercising a right. It is breaking the rule that governs the arrangement.

The rest of the leverage you already hold. You can keep your own ACE portal account and see everything filed under your number without the broker's cooperation (Chapter 1). You can file your own protests, 19 CFR § 174.12(a) extends that right to the importer shown on the entry, no broker required, and your own Post-Summary Corrections. You can pay duty directly to CBP by ACH rather than through the broker or forwarder (§ 141.1(b)(2), which routes to the payment means in § 24.1(a); ACH mechanics are at §§ 24.25–24.26). And you can move the problem upstream, to the purchase order: buying on FCA or EXW terms, rather than a delivered price where the seller arranges U.S. clearance, puts the customs leg and the choice of filer in your hands. That last one is a contracting decision under Incoterms, not a customs rule, and it shifts more of the freight and risk onto you earlier in the move. But it is the cleanest way to take the filer decision back.

None of this makes a captive broker a bad broker. Plenty are competent, and if yours does careful work and will accept the addendum, keep it. But the relationship persists on inertia and bundled pricing, not on any rule that locks you to the forwarder's affiliate. You have more room to move than the bundle is built to let you see.

# PART III: FORENSIC DATA MINING & ACE PORTAL EXPLOITATION

# Chapter 7: Mining the ACE Portal: Extraction & Data Schema Mapping

## Beyond the Dashboard: Setting Up, Scheduling, and Automating Customized ACE Reports

In the trade compliance ecosystem, the Automated Commercial Environment (ACE) Portal is marketed by U.S. Customs and Border Protection (CBP) as a modern, user-friendly digital interface designed to give Importers of Record (IOR) seamless visibility into their trade activity. Most trade managers use the portal this way: high-level summary dashboards, ad-hoc liquidations, an annual duty tally when accounting asks, and it is not their fault. Nothing in CBP's interface suggests there is a deeper layer. There is. To the forensic customs auditor, the standard ACE web dashboard is a summary layer that was never built for forensic work. It is not hiding anything. It simply is not the view CBP's own auditors use. CBP's Office of Trade, Trade Regulatory Audit (TRA) directorate does not evaluate your trade compliance by looking at dashboard summary widgets. It works from line-level transaction data: the same line-level facts that sit in the Entry Summary reports available to you in ACE Reports. CBP does not publish its targeting schemas, and no importer can query the exact environment its enforcement teams use; you do not need to. What matters is the level you work at: if you are not extracting, structuring, and programmatically auditing your own raw ACE line-item data, you are reading the summary view while CBP is reading the lines, and that gap is where the findings come from.

CBP Office of Trade, Trade Regulatory Audit (TRA), Raw ACE Reports (automated recurring extracts)

| ES-001 / ES-002 / ES-003 (ENTRY SUMMARY) | CR-004 / CR-005 (CARGO RELEASE) | MNFST-001 (MANIFEST / IN-BOND) |
|---|---|---|
| Header, line and tariff-line detail | Cargo release and bill-of-lading fields | In-bond movement and manifest |
| Liquidation, duties, HTS, values, MID | Ports, carrier, release status | In-bond entry tracking |

All of these feed the internal broker-management engine, which runs the SQL automated discrepancy audits detailed below.

To take control of your broker oversight, you must bypass the standard ACE UI and establish an automated, scheduled data pipeline utilizing the Entry Summary reports in ACE Reports: ES-001 (Entry Summary Header Details), ES-002 (Entry Summary Line Details), and ES-003 (Entry Summary Line Tariff Details), supplemented by the Cargo Release and Manifest universes for bill-of-lading and in-bond data.

> *A note on report identifiers and fields, because this is the layer where books go stale. ACE Reports is reorganized by CBP periodically, and both report IDs and column names change between refreshes. The identifiers below are current as of the August 2022 ACE Reports Catalog for Trade; CBP has added reports since (for example ES-022 in 2025-26 refund guidance). Before you build a pipeline, pull the current ACE Reports Catalog for Trade and confirm both the report IDs and the exact column names in your own account. The field lists below are a working guide, not a substitute for the live catalog.*

### 1. The Core ACE Report Set

The ACE Forensic Report Specification

| REPORT ID | REPORT NAME | FORENSIC UTILITY & DATA FIELDS EXPOSED |
|---|---|---|
| ES-001 | Entry Summary Header | Header-level audit: Filer code, |

| REPORT ID | REPORT NAME | FORENSIC UTILITY & DATA FIELDS EXPOSED |
|---|---|---|
| | Details | Entry #, Summary/Import Date, Liquidation Status, Duty Paid, ACH Total Entered Value, Bond ID, Surety Code. |
| ES-002 | Entry Summary Line Details | Line-level audit: Line #, MID Code, Line Entered Value, SPI Indicators, Country of Origin, Net Quantity. |
| ES-003 | Entry Summary Line Tariff Details | Tariff-line audit, the report for classification and duty work: 10-digit HTS, Primary Rate of Duty, AD/CVD Case Number, Section 301 heading, duty amounts at the tariff line. |
| CR-004 / CR-005 | Cargo Release Line / Entry Details | Cargo-release reconciliation: entry and line release data. Bill-of-lading fields sit in the Cargo Release ("Cargo Release New") data universe; CR-009 lists entries without a follow-up summary. |
| MNFST-001 | In-Bond Details | In-bond and manifest movement: in-bond entry tracking, ports, carrier. |
| ES-013 | CBP Form 28/29/4647 Status Report | Historically tracked the status of CBP Forms 28, 29 and 4647 against your entries, but it has been offline since May 2022 (CSMS #51852023) pending re-pointing to the modernized Forms data universe. Do not rely on it. Track Form 28/29/4647 status instead through the ACE Portal CBP Forms application in Portal mode (see Chapter 12). |

### ES-001: The Financial & Macro-Compliance Anchor

The ES-001 report operates at the Entry Summary (CBP Form 7501) header level. While it does not expose product-level line items, it is the primary tool for auditing financial timelines, broker filing speed, duty payment reconciliations, and liquidation status. Fields to look for: Filer Code, Entry Number, Entry Type,

Importer of Record Number, Entry Date, Import Date, Summary Date, Payment Due Date, Liquidation Date, Liquidation Code, Estimated Duty Amount, Interest Amount, Total Entered Value, Broker Reference Number, Surety Code, Continuous Bond Account Number. (Confirm the exact column names against the current catalog.)

### ES-002 and ES-003: The Line-Item and Tariff Audit

Line-level and tariff-line data is the single most critical dataset in trade compliance. ES-002 breaks each entry summary into its individual commercial lines: MID, value allocation, country of origin, quantity and SPI claims, and ES-003 carries the tariff-line detail you audit classifications and duties against: the 10-digit HTS, the primary rate of duty, the AD/CVD case number, and the Section 301 heading. You join the two on entry and line number. Fields to look for: Line Item Number, 10-Digit HTSUS Code, Special Program Indicator (SPI) Code, Manufacturer Identification (MID) Code, Country of Origin, Entered Value (USD), Net Quantity (HTS Units), AD/CVD Case Number, AD/CVD Duty Paid, Section 301 heading, Primary Rate of Duty, and PGA disposition. (As above, verify the field split between ES-002 and ES-003 in the current catalog before you build against it.)

### Cargo Release and Manifest: The Physical Reality Check

Brokers frequently enter data based strictly on commercial invoices provided electronically, detached from the cargo-release and manifest record. The Cargo Release universe (CR-004 Cargo Release Line Details, CR-005 Cargo Release Entry Details, and CR-009 Entries Without a Follow-Up Summary) and the Manifest / In-Bond universe (MNFST-001 In-Bond Details) let you reconcile what was actually released and moved against what the broker declared. Fields to look for: Master and House Bill of Lading, Carrier Code (SCAC), Vessel Name / Flight Number, Foreign Port of Loading, U.S. Port of Unlading, Piece Count, Container Numbers, and In-Bond Entry Numbers.

**2. Automating the Extraction Pipeline**

Relying on manual monthly downloads executed by a compliance analyst clicking through the ACE Portal guarantees gaps in your audit log. Analysts miss weeks, files get misplaced, or download date parameters overlap, creating duplicate or missing records. Configure the ACE Reporting engine to run automated weekly data extracts:

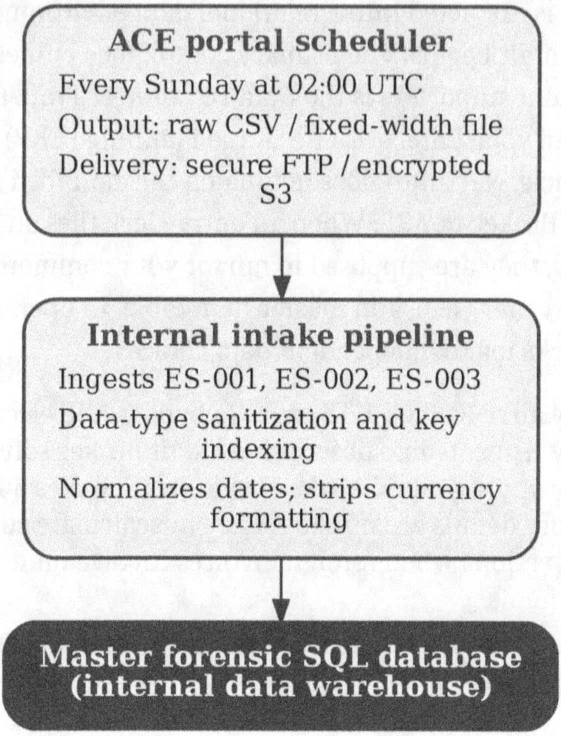


Scheduling raw CSV exports during off-peak hours does two things. It pipes clean transactional records into your data environment on a cadence a human will not forget, and it gets you out of the portal's interactive display limits, which are built for reading on screen rather than for bulk analysis. CBP's own reporting documentation warns that large standard reports become unwieldy well before you reach the volume a year of entries produces, and directs high-volume users toward scheduled extracts and the authorized data-extract path for exactly this reason. If you are pulling a year of line-item detail through the browser a page at a time, you are fighting the tool.

## The Line-Item Audit: Cross-Referencing ACE Data Against Your Systems

Once raw ACE data (ES-001, ES-002/ES-003, and the Cargo Release extracts) is extracted into a relational data environment, the forensic audit begins. The primary compliance vulnerability for high-volume importers is the Data Disconnect Trap: the data residing in your Enterprise Resource Planning (ERP) platform (SAP, Oracle, NetSuite) does not match the data filed by your Customs Broker in ACE. When an entry clerk files an entry summary, they are supposed to mirror your commercial invoice, purchase order (PO), and master item table. In operational reality, entry clerks make independent data choices:

- They alter 10-digit HTS codes to bypass ACE electronic edits. They truncate line descriptions to fit broker software fields. They apply generic MID codes to clear entries quickly when factory details are missing. They miscalculate currency conversions when foreign invoices involve multi-currency line items.

To expose these discrepancies, you match three independent data streams for every import transaction.

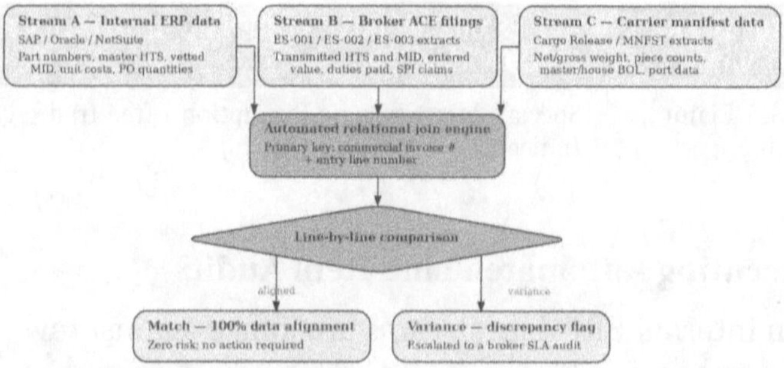


## 1. Establishing Relational Data Mapping Schemas

To execute programmatic cross-referencing, you must build a database schema that maps fields from internal ERP tables directly to corresponding ES-002/ES-003 fields using explicit join parameters.

Relational Data Mapping Schema Table

| INTERNAL ERP FIELD NAME | ACE ES-002/ES-003 FIELD NAME | FORENSIC AUDIT JOIN RULE |
|---|---|---|
| ERP_Invoice_Number | Commercial_Invoice_Number | Reconciliation reference only, the commercial invoice number is not a reliable ACE entry-summary key; join on entry number + entry-summary line via a broker crosswalk (see the join caution below). |
| ERP_Line_Item_Seq | ACE_Line_Item_Number | Resolved through the broker crosswalk, not a direct join, one consolidated ACE line can map to several ERP sequences. |
| ERP_Master_HTS | HTS_10_Digit_Transmitted | Hard comparison / classification match. Store and compare both sides as 10 digits with no dots (8542310000); dots are for human-readable display only. |
| ERP_Vendor_MID | Transmitted_MID_Code | String match / origin verification |
| ERP_Line_Extended_Val_USD | Entered_Value_USD | Numeric range match (± tolerance) |
| ERP_Net_Quantity | Declared_HTS_Quantity | Unit of measure conversion check |

| INTERNAL ERP FIELD NAME | ACE ES-002/ES-003 FIELD NAME | FORENSIC AUDIT JOIN RULE |
|---|---|---|
| ERP_SPI_Claim_ Eligible | Special_Program_ Indicator | Exemption / free-trade agreement match |

## 2. Executing Automated Line-Item Audits

When internal ERP data streams are joined against raw ACE ES-002/ES-003 records, automated scripts run four critical reconciliation passes across every line item:

### Audit Pass 1: Classification Deviation Analysis

The system compares ERP_Master_HTS against HTS_10_Digit_Transmitted . If the broker transmitted an HTS code that differs by even a single digit from your vetted master catalog, the record is flagged. Forensic Significance: Exposes instances where entry clerks overrode internal engineering-approved codes to force entry acceptance, or defaulted to high-duty fallback provisions.

### Audit Pass 2: Valuation Variance Audit

The system compares ERP_Line_Extended_Val_USD against Entered_Value_USD . Forensic Significance: Identifies entry clerk mathematical errors, misapplied currency exchange rates (e.g., failing to convert EUR or JPY to USD), un-reported Assists (tooling/mold costs), or omitted international freight and insurance deductions.

### Audit Pass 3: Manufacturer Identification (MID) Divergence

The system cross-references ERP_Vendor_MID against Transmitted_MID_Code . Forensic Significance: Catches brokers using generic, high-risk, or inaccurate MIDs. In an era of heightened enforcement under the Uyghur Forced Labor Prevention Act (UFLPA) and Section 301 anti-circumvention rules, transmitting a wrong MID code can incorrectly tie your goods to an entity on a sanction list or subject to Antidumping duties.

**Audit Pass 4: Free Trade Agreement & SPI Exclusion Verification**

The system compares ERP_SPI_Claim_Eligible (e.g., USMCA, GSP, Israel FTA) against Special_Program_Indicator fields in ACE.

Forensic Significance: Exposes "missed money" opportunities where the broker failed to claim preferential tariff treatment despite clear internal master data instructions, or conversely, claims an SPI when supporting origin documentation is missing, exposing the firm to duty recovery penalties.

## Spotting Broker Typing Errors: Building Automated SQL & Excel Audit Engines

The single greatest source of compliance noise and regulatory risk in daily entry operations is not intentional fraud by the importer; it is systemic fat-fingering by entry clerks. Under extreme transaction velocity quotas, entry clerks type hundreds of characters per minute across clunky data entry screens. They make predictable, repeated data entry errors that pass basic ACE system validation checks but inject severe errors into your regulatory record. Below are the four most common broker fat-finger errors, complete with production-ready SQL Query Scripts and Excel Formula Architectures to catch them within 24 hours of filing.

The Four Broker Fat-Finger Error Archetypes

| Error Archetype | Operational Manifestation & Compliance Risk |
|---|---|
| 1. MID Code Transposition ("CN" vs. "TW" or generic MID) | Entry clerk transposes country or producer codes, incorrectly tying shipments to restricted or unverified manufacturers and defeating AD/CVD and UFLPA screening. |

| Error Archetype | Operational Manifestation & Compliance Risk |
|---|---|
| 2. Valuation Decimal Slippage (over- or under-valuation) | Decimal point placed incorrectly ($10,000.00 entered as $1,000,000.00), triggering massively overpaid duties or, in reverse, an undervaluation penalty. |
| 3. Unit of Measure Conversion Failure | Transmitting gross weight (KG) in place of net pieces or square meters, altering unit values by orders of magnitude and distorting the duty calculation. |
| 4. HTS Digit Transposition / Truncation | Transposing internal digits (e.g., 8471.60 vs. 8741.60), shifting items into high-tariff or AD/CVD categories. |

## 1. The SQL Audit: Detecting Fat-Finger Errors

Below is a SQL script template that queries raw ES-002/ES-003 and ES-001 tables joined with an internal ERP master item table ( tbl_ERP_Master_Items ). It targets valuation slippage, MID transpositions, and HTS classification overrides. Treat `tbl_ACE_ES002_LineItems` as a flattened line-level view that already joins the ES-002 line report to the ES-003 tariff-line report on filer, entry, and line number, so the 10-digit HTS and AD/CVD fields resolve at the line.

One caution before you run anything, because getting the join wrong will make an honest broker look guilty. Two problems sit in the obvious approach. First, the commercial invoice number is **not** a field CBP exposes in the ACE entry-summary universe. Invoice-level data reaches ACE only through the optional electronic invoice (AII), and CBP's ACE entry-summary instructions do not allow AII for entry type 03 (AD/CVD): the very entries you most want to audit. Second, ACE entry-summary line numbers are filer-assigned, and brokers routinely consolidate several ERP or invoice lines that share HTS, country of origin, and MID into a single entry-summary line. So joining `es002.Line_Item_Number` to your ERP's invoice-line sequence is not a key: on any consolidated entry it pairs the wrong rows and manufactures false HTS, value, MID, and quantity "mismatches" across the whole entry, which the remediation protocol later in this chapter would then fire at a broker that did nothing wrong. The only dependable join is **entry number + entry-summary line**, matched to a **broker-supplied line-to-invoice-line crosswalk** that you obtain contractually through the SLA (Chapter 5), not from ACE. Value and quantity reconcile reliably only in aggregate per entry summary unless the broker commits in writing to 1:1 line mapping. Read the queries below as templates to run against that crosswalk, and confirm every column name against the current ACE Reports catalog before you rely on a single flag.

```
-- ==========================================================
-- FORENSIC AUDIT SCRIPT: BROKER ERROR EXTRACTION ENGINE
-- Target: Identifies Valuation Slippage, HTS Mismatches,
   and Invalid MID Filings
-- ==========================================================

SELECT
    es001.Filer_Code,
    es001.Entry_Number,
    es001.Entry_Date,
    es002.Line_Item_Number,
    xwalk.Commercial_Invoice_Number,

    -- HTS Audit Logic
    es002.HTS_10_Digit AS ACE_Transmitted_HTS,
    erp.Master_HTS     AS ERP_Approved_HTS,
    CASE
        WHEN erp.Master_HTS IS NULL
            THEN 'NO ERP MATCH - VERIFY'
        WHEN es002.HTS_10_Digit <> erp.Master_HTS
            THEN 'FLAG: UNAUTHORIZED HTS OVERRIDE'
        ELSE 'MATCH'
    END AS HTS_Audit_Status,

    -- Valuation Slippage Audit Logic (detects > 5%
       deviation)
    es002.Entered_Value_USD AS ACE_Entered_Value,
    erp.Expected_Value_USD  AS ERP_Expected_Value,
    ABS(es002.Entered_Value_USD - erp.Expected_Value_USD)
        AS Valuation_Variance,
    CASE
        WHEN erp.Expected_Value_USD > 0
             AND ABS(es002.Entered_Value_USD -
                 erp.Expected_Value_USD)
                 / erp.Expected_Value_USD > 0.05
            THEN 'FLAG: SEVERE VALUATION SLIPPAGE'
        ELSE 'MATCH'
    END AS Valuation_Audit_Status,
```

```
-- MID Code Transposition Logic
es002.Transmitted_MID_Code AS ACE_Transmitted_MID,
erp.Approved_MID_Code      AS ERP_Approved_MID,
CASE
    WHEN es002.Transmitted_MID_Code <>
        erp.Approved_MID_Code
        THEN 'FLAG: MID CODE MISMATCH'
    WHEN es002.Transmitted_MID_Code LIKE '%XX%'
         OR es002.Transmitted_MID_Code LIKE
            '%GENERIC%'
        THEN 'FLAG: GENERIC MID USED'
    ELSE 'MATCH'
END AS MID_Audit_Status,

-- Unit of Measure Conversion Verification
es002.Declared_Quantity AS ACE_Transmitted_Qty,
erp.Expected_Quantity   AS ERP_Expected_Qty,
CASE
    WHEN es002.Declared_Quantity <>
        erp.Expected_Quantity
        THEN 'FLAG: QUANTITY / UOM MISMATCH'
    ELSE 'MATCH'
END AS UOM_Audit_Status
```

```sql
-- (continued) FROM / JOIN / WHERE / ORDER BY
FROM tbl_ACE_ES002_LineItems es002

INNER JOIN tbl_ACE_ES001_Headers es001
    ON  es002.Filer_Code   = es001.Filer_Code
    AND es002.Entry_Number = es001.Entry_Number

-- Join via the broker-supplied crosswalk (SLA, Ch. 5):
-- entry number + entry-summary line, the only safe key.
-- ACE exposes no invoice-to-line linkage; unmatched
-- lines fall to NULL and read as VERIFY, never as a flag.
LEFT JOIN tbl_Broker_Line_Crosswalk xwalk
    ON  es002.Entry_Number     = xwalk.Entry_Number
    AND es002.Line_Item_Number = xwalk.Entry_Summary_Line
LEFT JOIN tbl_ERP_Master_Items erp
    ON  xwalk.ERP_Item_Key = erp.ERP_Item_Key

WHERE
    es001.Entry_Date >= DATEADD(day, -30, GETDATE())    --
        last 30 days
    AND (
            (es002.HTS_10_Digit <> erp.Master_HTS OR
                erp.Master_HTS IS NULL)
         OR (erp.Expected_Value_USD > 0
             AND ABS(es002.Entered_Value_USD -
                 erp.Expected_Value_USD)
                 / erp.Expected_Value_USD > 0.05)
         OR es002.Transmitted_MID_Code <>
             erp.Approved_MID_Code
         OR es002.Declared_Quantity <>
             erp.Expected_Quantity
    )
ORDER BY es001.Entry_Date DESC, es001.Entry_Number ASC;
```

## 2. The Excel Audit: Quick Desktop Scanning

For trade analysts working outside a SQL database environment, you can build an automated Excel forensic audit sheet using dynamic array formulas.

### The Excel Layout Structure

- Sheet 1: ACE_Raw_Import (Paste raw CSV extract from ACE ES-002/ES-003).
- Sheet 2: ERP_Master_Catalog (Export of internal item master with Part Numbers, Approved HTS, Approved MIDs, and Standard Costs).
- Sheet 3: Forensic_Audit_Dashboard (Calculates automated flags).

### Excel Formulas for Key Discrepancies

Three dynamic-array formulas drive the audit dashboard. Each compares a transmitted ACE value against the ERP master catalog, keyed on the Part Number in column B.

```
' Valuation Slippage Flag (cell G2)
=IF(ISBLANK(A2),"",LET(v,XLOOKUP(B2,
    ERP_Master_Catalog!$A:$A,ERP_Master_Catalog!$C:$C,""),
    IF(v="","NO ERP MATCH - VERIFY",IF(ABS(C2-v)/v>0.05,
    "CRITICAL: VALUATION VARIANCE > 5%","OK"))))

' HTS Substitution Flag (cell H2)
=IF(ISBLANK(A2),"",LET(h,XLOOKUP(B2,
    ERP_Master_Catalog!$A:$A,ERP_Master_Catalog!$B:$B,""),
    IF(h="","NO ERP MATCH - VERIFY",IF(TEXT(D2,
    "0000000000")<>TEXT(h,"0000000000"),
    "FLAG: HTS OVERRIDE","MATCH"))))

' MID Code Validation Flag (cell I2)
=IF(ISBLANK(A2),"",LET(m,XLOOKUP(B2,
    ERP_Master_Catalog!$A:$A,ERP_Master_Catalog!$D:$D,""),
    IF(m="","NO ERP MATCH - VERIFY",IF(E2<>m,
    "WARNING: MID MISMATCH","MATCH"))))
```

Valuation slippage compares the entered line value (column C) against the ERP standard value and flags variances over 5%. The HTS check forces 10-digit string formatting to preserve leading zeros before comparing the transmitted ACE HTS (column D) against the approved HTS. The MID check compares the transmitted MID (column E) against the approved vendor MID.

A note on the valuation tolerances, because two different numbers appear across the program and a sharp reader will ask why. The operational checks, the SQL sweep and its companion Excel engine in this chapter, and the Tool C master query in the appendix, all flag valuation variance over 5%. The annual scorecard in Chapter 13 holds a stricter 1% tolerance. This is by design, not an inconsistency: the monthly operational pass at 5% is tuned to surface real errors at speed across thousands of lines without drowning you in rounding noise, while the annual forensic audit is where you hold the line to the penny. Set the tolerance that matches the job the check is doing, and keep the strict one for the backstop.

### 3. The Post-Audit Workflow

Finding typing errors in your ACE data is only half the battle. Once an error is exposed through your SQL or Excel audit engine, you must execute a strict 3-Step Remediation Workflow:

```
[AUDIT ENGINE FLAGS ERROR]
          |
          v
[STEP 1: Log Discrepancy in Centralized Broker Scorecard
    Engine]
* Record Filer Code, Entry #, Error Type, Financial Impact
   ($).
* Automatically assign error points against Monthly SLA
   Scorecard.
          |
          v
[STEP 2: Issue Automated Corrective Action Demand to
    Filing Broker]
* Send standardized PDF "Notice of Discrepancy" to Broker
   Compliance Manager.
* Attach SQL audit extract proof showing original ERP data
   vs. ACE entry.
* Require Broker to confirm filing of Post-Summary
   Correction (PSC) within 5 business days.
          |
          v
[STEP 3: Verify Transmission in Subsequent Weekly ACE
    ES-002/ES-003 Extract]
* Re-run SQL script to verify PSC transmission indicator
   in ACE.
* Close audit ticket only when corrected data is confirmed
   directly in ACE database
```

The point of all of this is not the queries. It is that you stop asking your broker whether the entries are right and start knowing. Those are different relationships, and only one of them is oversight.

# Chapter 8: Master Data Synchronization: Eliminating Entry Clerk "Guesswork"

## The Master Data Disconnect: Why PDF Commercial Invoices Drive Rogue Classifications and Default PGA Filings

For decades, the standard operating model of international trade has relied on a fundamental operational flaw: the PDF commercial invoice transfer. In the typical supply chain workflow, an overseas vendor generates a commercial invoice and packing list as flat PDF documents, attaches them to an email, and sends them to a logistics coordinator or freight forwarder. The forwarder or importer then forwards those PDFs to an entry processing desk at a customs brokerage firm. At that precise moment, the integrity of the Importer of Record's (IOR) compliance program breaks down completely.

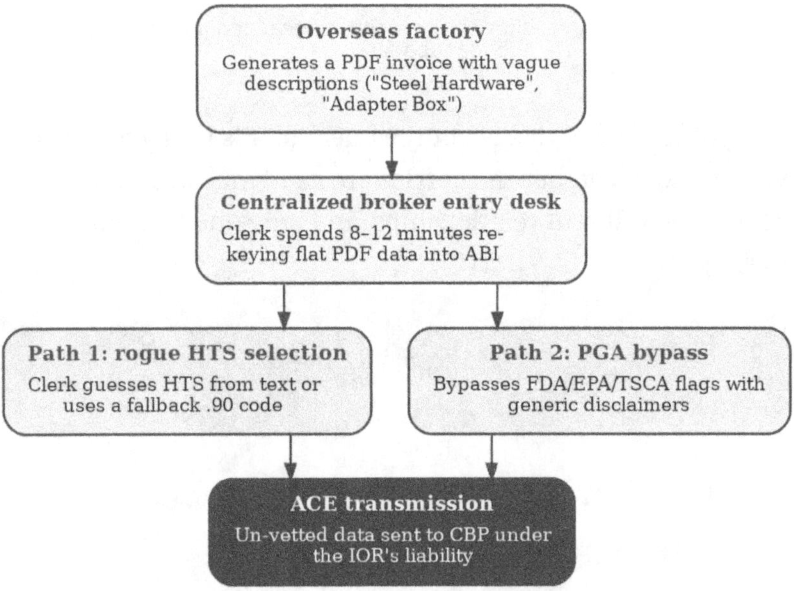


When an entry clerk receives a static PDF, they are not looking at your enterprise item master, your engineering drawings, or your

Customs and Border Protection (CBP) binding rulings. They are looking at alphanumeric text printed on a digital sheet of paper, often written by an overseas vendor whose primary language is not English and whose knowledge of the U.S. Harmonized Tariff Schedule (HTSUS) is non-existent. Descriptions like "Metal Parts," "Power Adapter," "Industrial Controller," or "Plastic Fittings" create an immediate dilemma for an entry clerk working under a quota of 40 entries per shift:

1. Optical Character Recognition (OCR) Limitations: Even when brokers deploy AI-driven document extraction tools or OCR parsing engines to ingest PDF invoices, OCR engines only digitize the text printed on the page. If the vendor wrote "Steel Adapter," the OCR tool extracts "Steel Adapter." It cannot infer carbon content, alloy composition, manufacturing method (cold-drawn vs. hot-rolled), or structural dimensions required to determine a 10-digit HTSUS classification.
2. The Keyboard Interpretation Engine: Because the clerk lacks technical product specifications, they perform keyword searches inside their brokerage software (such as CargoWise or Descartes). They type "Adapter" into an internal search bar and select the first code that pops up, often a generic "Other" catch-all subheading ( .9000 ) carrying high Column 1 duty rates and Section 301 tariffs, or worse, an HTS code that bypasses applicable Antidumping/Countervailing Duty (AD/CVD) flags.
3. Default Partner Government Agency (PGA) Disclaimers: When a transmitted HTS code triggers an automated PGA indicator in the Automated Commercial Environment (ACE), such as an Environmental Protection Agency (EPA) TSCA flag, a Food and Drug Administration (FDA) device code, or an APHIS Lacey Act plant declaration, the clerk lacks the specific registration numbers, 510(k) clearances, or chemical CAS numbers. To prevent the entry from rejecting in ACE, clerks routinely apply default disclaimer codes (e.g., transmitting PGA Disclaimer Code A - Not Regulated). (A note for electronics importers: the FCC is *not* a PGA in the

ACE message set. The FCC eliminated its Form 740 import declaration effective November 2, 2017, so radio-frequency equipment authorization is an internal pre-shipment control you verify under 47 CFR § 2.1204. There is nothing FCC-related to transmit at entry. Do not build an ACE gate on it.)

This manual re-keying of PDF data is where rogue classifications and illegal PGA disclaimers enter your public customs record. You may possess an internal compliance team that spent six months classifying your product catalog with specialized trade counsel, but if that compliance data sits inside an isolated internal PDF or ERP spreadsheet while your broker manually re-keys entries from vendor PDFs, your internal work is completely useless. CBP enforces 19 U.S.C. § 1484 based on what is transmitted electronically into ACE via the Automated Broker Interface (ABI), not what sits in a folder on your internal network.

## System-to-System Integration: Pushing Pre-Vetted Compliance Databases into Broker Platforms

To eliminate entry clerk guesswork, you must replace flat PDF transmissions with automated, system-to-system master data synchronization. Modern logistics enterprise software platforms, primarily CargoWise (WiseTech Global), Descartes Customs & Compliance Suite, and BluJay Solutions (E2open), do not operate as isolated data silos. They feature robust, real-time application programming interfaces (APIs), asynchronous XML message queues (e.g., CargoWise eAdapter / eHub), and electronic data interchange (EDI) data pipelines specifically architected to ingest external product master tables directly from shipper ERP systems (SAP GTS, Oracle Global Trade Management, NetSuite, or custom enterprise data lakes).

The technical architecture of this pipeline, the middleware validation engine, the mTLS transport, and the platform-specific ingestion paths into CargoWise and Descartes, is diagrammed and specified in Chapter 9.

### 1. How System Integration Works

When an importer establishes a direct API or XML data pipeline into a broker's entry platform, the operational workflow changes completely:

1. Product Master Push: Whenever a new SKU, part number, or raw material item is added or modified inside the importer's ERP system, an automated payload (JSON or XML) is generated and transmitted to the broker's system.
2. Part Number Auto-Matching: When the foreign vendor generates an electronic commercial invoice (via EDI 850/810 or structured XML payload), the shipment invoice lines contain exact, unique Part Numbers / SKUs.
3. Automated Field Injection: As the broker's software ingests the shipment data, it queries its internal Product File (populated by your API push). The platform automatically injects the pre-vetted 10-digit HTSUS code, the verified Manufacturer Identification (MID) code, the exact Special Program Indicator (SPI) claim, and all mandatory PGA data elements directly into the CBP entry summary record.

The entry clerk is transformed from a data-guessing typist into an operational supervisor whose sole job is to review system-matched records for structural completeness before hitting transmit.

The field-level mechanics of this pipeline, the exact map from each ERP field to its CargoWise eAdapter XML tag and Descartes API element, a sample product-master payload, and the error-handling loop that catches a failed sync, are collected in Chapter 9, which serves as the technical appendix to this chapter. What follows here is the policy that governs the pipeline: the "No-Default" ruleset that decides what an entry clerk may and may not touch, and the exception path for the parts the system has not yet vetted. Turn to Chapter 9 when your IT team is ready to build the connection itself.

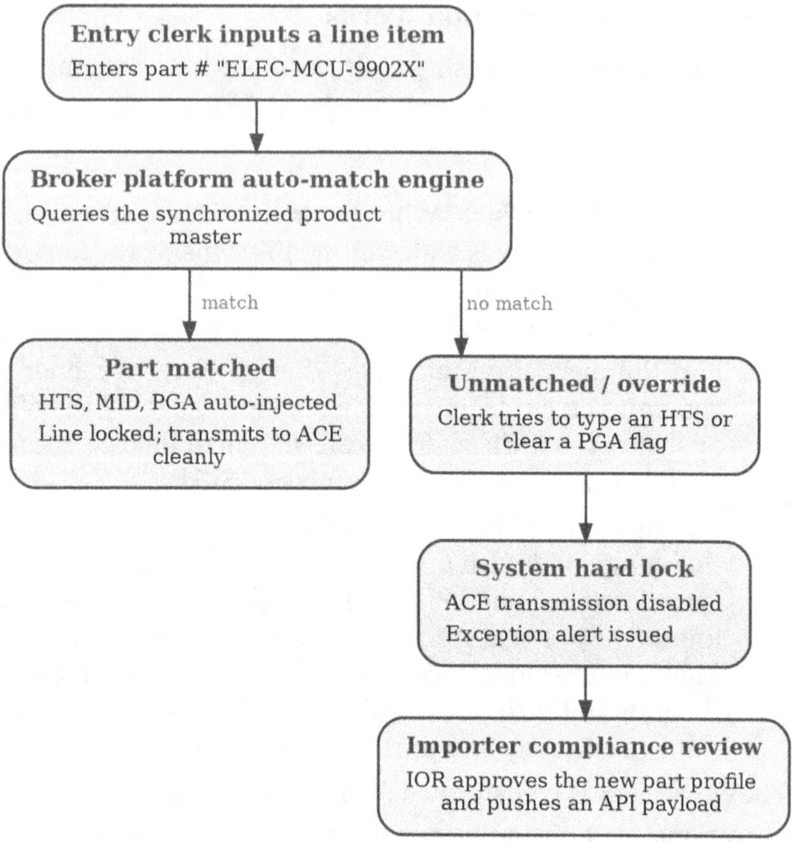


## 1. Defining the "No-Default" Ruleset

A "No-Default" policy is an automated software gate that disables specific entry clerk capabilities within platforms like CargoWise, Descartes, or BluJay. When configured, the software enforces four strict rules:

### Rule 1: Prohibition of Manual Tariff Alterations

If an imported line item contains an established Part Number/SKU present in the synchronized product file, the TariffCode field is permanently locked. The entry clerk cannot delete, edit, or modify the 10-digit HTS code. If the clerk attempts to type over the HTS code, the system generates a hard error:

SECURITY VIOLATION: HTS OVERRIDE RESTRICTED BY IMPORTER COMPLIANCE MANDATE .

**Rule 2: No Fallback HTS Codes**

The broker's software configuration is updated to block entry transmission if specific generic "fallback" HTS codes are selected without an accompanying written authorization key issued by the importer's trade compliance director. Restricted Fallback List: Any tariff line ending in .90.00, .90.90, .00.90, or generic Chapter 84/85 "Other Parts" basket headings.

**Rule 3: Zero PGA Disclaimer Bypass**

If a synchronized part profile flags a required PGA filing (e.g., TSCA statement, FDA product code, Lacey Act plant declaration), the software disables the clerk's ability to select generic disclaimer codes (Disclaimer A, Disclaimer B). The system will not allow the entry to be submitted to ACE until every mandatory PGA field contains a valid, alphanumeric value derived directly from the master API dataset.

**Rule 4: Systemic Manufacturer Identification (MID) Locking**

The software locks the MID_Code field to the specific foreign manufacturer facility assigned to that SKU in the master data database. Entry clerks are barred from using "Corporate Headquarters" MIDs or generic "City-Center" MIDs to clear shipments when factory-floor addresses are omitted from foreign shipping documents.

**2. The Exception Workflow**

When an entry clerk processes a shipment containing a brand-new part number that does not yet exist in the synchronized product master database, the software triggers an Automated Exception Workflow:

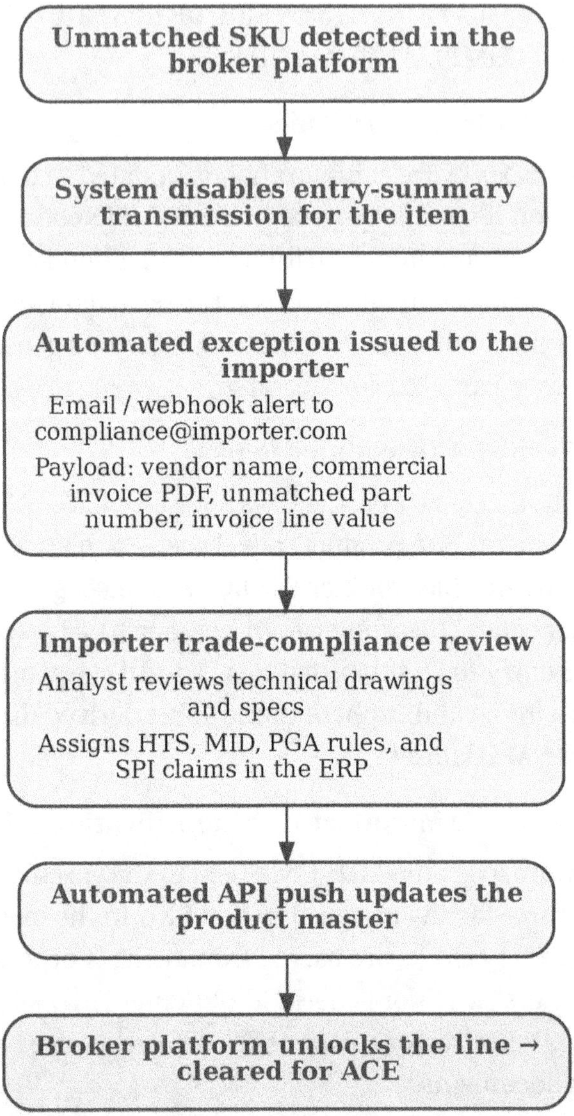


This exception workflow ensures that no entry summary containing an un-vetted part number can ever be transmitted to U.S. Customs and Border Protection. While this creates brief operational friction when new products are introduced, it prevents systemic classification errors from entering your public ACE database. It forces your internal procurement and compliance teams to classify products before they leave the foreign port, rather than allowing a remote entry clerk to guess classifications on the pier while container demurrage clocks are ticking.

## The Audit Trail: Verifying Master Data Integrity

To ensure that your system-to-system integration and "No-Default" rulesets remain effective over time, you must run automated monthly queries against your raw ACE ES-002/ES-003 line-item extracts to measure your Master Data Synchronization Integrity Rate (MDSIR).

```
MDSIR % = ( N_Matched / N_Total ) x 100
  N_Matched = count of transmitted ACE lines matching ERP
      master data 100%
  N_Total   = total count of transmitted ACE lines in the
      ES-002/ES-003 extract
TARGET BENCHMARK: >= 99.8% data match rate across all
    ports nationwide
```

A word on how this 99.8% target relates to the other benchmarks in the book. The 99.5% SLA match rate (Chapter 5) holds the broker to its classification and declaration performance; the audit engine's valuation tolerances are explained where they are set, in Chapter 7. This 99.8% Master Data Sync Integrity Rate (MDSIR) measures something narrower and more mechanical: whether the automated pipeline transmitted your locked master data into ACE without drift. It is held tighter because a system-to-system feed that is working at all should almost never miss; a sub-99.8% MDSIR signals a broken pipe, not a judgment call. If your monthly MDSIR calculation drops below 99.8%, your system pipeline has suffered an operational breakdown: either an entry clerk found a manual software workaround, a third-party sub-agent broker was assigned without receiving your master data feed, or a system API endpoint disconnected. An entry clerk who cannot override your tariff code will never override your tariff code. That is the whole idea. Everything above is plumbing.

# Chapter 9: Software Integration Blueprints: Technical Appendix to Chapter 8

A warning before you turn the page. This is the technical chapter. It has XML schemas, JSON payloads, and an error-handling loop, and it is written for the kind of person who reads those for fun. If that person is you, welcome home, put your feet up. If it is not, if your eyes glazed somewhere around "JSON payload", you are not failing, and you are not the wrong reader for this book. You do not have to build a line of this yourself. Your job as the importer is to know this machine exists, know what it buys you, and know enough to point at it and tell your systems people "we need this one." So read the section openings for the shape of it, then hand the rest to your IT or EDI partner the way you would hand a mechanic the weird noise your car makes at 60 miles an hour. They will be delighted. It is their language. Then meet me back in Chapter 10, where we return to yours: liability, penalties, and how to keep both off your desk.

This chapter is the build-level companion to Chapter 8. Chapter 8 made the case for replacing PDF re-keying with a system-to-system feed and set the policy that governs it: the "No-Default" ruleset and the exception path. This chapter hands your IT and trade-compliance teams the exact schemas to build that feed: the CargoWise eAdapter XML, the Descartes REST JSON, the field-level maps between your ERP and each platform, and the error-handling loop that catches a sync that fails in transit. Read the opening of each section to get the shape of it, then return to the payloads when you are ready to write code. If you are a Tier A or B importer without the IT resources to stand this up, you do not need this chapter yet: adopt the manual ACE spot-audit in Chapter 7 first, and come back here when volume justifies the integration.

## Connecting Your ERP to CargoWise and Descartes

The pipeline connects internal enterprise systems, such as SAP Global Trade Services (GTS), Oracle Global Trade Management (GTM), or NetSuite, directly with the dominant customs brokerage execution platforms: WiseTech CargoWise and Descartes CustomsInfo / Customs Suite. The architecture below is the technical realization of the master-data-synchronization concept introduced in Chapter 8.

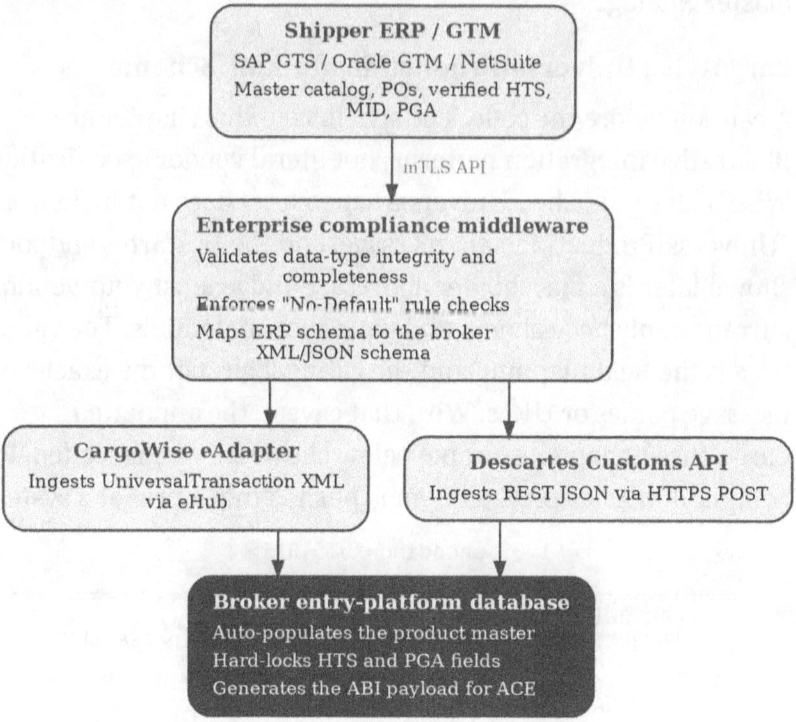


## CargoWise eAdapter Integration Blueprint (UniversalTransaction XML)

WiseTech CargoWise is the dominant software platform used by international freight forwarders and customs brokerage firms worldwide.

To push master product tables, commercial invoice line items, and compliance rules directly into CargoWise, external systems interface with the CargoWise eAdapter Engine using the UniversalTransaction (UT) or UniversalShipment (US) XML schema specification.

The eAdapter engine ingests XML payloads transmitted via secure HTTPS POST requests to the broker's eHub endpoint, automatically creating or updating the broker's internal product master catalog.

### CargoWise UniversalProductMaster XML Schema

A caution before the code. The schemas in this chapter are illustrative integration patterns, not literal vendor specifications. WiseTech's published Universal schema set does not include a "UniversalProductMaster" message, and the Descartes endpoint shown later is a placeholder address. Build against your vendor's current published schema and your own credentials. The value here is the field mapping and the gating logic, not the exact message names or URLs. With that caveat, the annotated CargoWise eAdapter example below shows how a pre-vetted, PGA-compliant master product item is pushed into a broker's system.

```
<?xml version="1.0" encoding="UTF-8"?>
<!--
============================================================
     CARGOWISE eADAPTER INTEGRATION SCHEMA (ILLUSTRATIVE)
     Target: UniversalProductMaster / Enterprise SKU
         Synchronization
     Description: Ingests pre-vetted HTS, MID, SPI, and
         PGA rules into CargoWise
     ==========================================================
         -->
<UniversalProductMaster
xmlns="http://www.wisetechglobal.com/schemas/Universal/
    2011/11"
    version="1.1">
    <Header>
        <SenderID>SAP_GTS_PROD_01</SenderID>
        <RecipientID>BROKER_CARGOWISE_MAIN</RecipientID>
        <MessageNumber>UPM-20260722-99021</MessageNumber>
        <SendTime>2026-07-22T14:30:00.000Z</SendTime>
    </Header>
    <Data>
        <Product>
```

```xml
<!-- Core Product Identification -->
<PartNumber>ELEC-MCU-9902X</PartNumber>
<Description>Microcontroller Unit 32-Bit ARM
    Cortex-M4 Silicon Integrated
    Circuit</Description>
<ShortDescription>Microcontroller
    IC</ShortDescription>
<ProductGroup>SEMICONDUCTORS</ProductGroup>

<!-- Importer of Record Identification -->
<OrganizationCode>IMP123456</OrganizationCode>
<ClientEmployerIdentificationNumber>
    12-3456789</
    ClientEmployerIdentificationNumber>

<!-- Customs & Classification Parameters -->
<CustomsSpecifications>
    <CountryOfOrigin>TW</CountryOfOrigin>
    <HarmonizedTariffCode>8542310000</
        HarmonizedTariffCode>
    <PrimaryUnitOfMeasure>PCS</
        PrimaryUnitOfMeasure>
    <SecondaryUnitOfMeasure/>

    <!-- Manufacturer Identification (MID)
        Hard-Lock -->
    <ApprovedManufacturerCode>TWTMC9932HSIN</
        ApprovedManufacturerCode>
    <ManufacturerName>Taiwan Semiconductor
        Manufacturing Co
        Ltd</ManufacturerName>
    <ManufacturerAddress>No 8 Li Hsin Rd 6
        Hsinchu Science Park Hsinchu
        TW</ManufacturerAddress>

    <!-- Tariff Preference & Special Program
        Indicators (SPI) -->
    <SpecialProgramIndicator>NONE</
        SpecialProgramIndicator>
    <PreferenceCriterion/>
    <Section301Applicable>false</
        Section301Applicable>
    <Section301ExclusionHeading/>
    <ADCVDFlag>false</ADCVDFlag>
    <ADCVDCaseNumber/>

    <!-- Partner Government Agency (PGA)
        Rulesets -->
    <PGASpecifications>
        <!-- Environmental Protection Agency
            (EPA) TSCA -->
        <TSCA>
            <Required>true</Required>
            <CertType>CERT_EXEMPT_ARTICLES</
                CertType>
            <DisclaimerCode>NONE</
                DisclaimerCode>
        </TSCA>
    </PGASpecifications>
</CustomsSpecifications>

<!-- Operational Gating & Security Lock
    Controls -->
<SystemGatingControls>
    <IsHTSLocked>true</IsHTSLocked>
```

```
                <IsMIDLocked>true</IsMIDLocked>
                <AllowManualOverride>false</
                    AllowManualOverride>
                <RequireComplianceHoldOnMismatch>true</
                    RequireComplianceHoldOnMismatch>
            </SystemGatingControls>
        </Product>
    </Data>
</UniversalProductMaster>
```

### Technical Explanation of Key CargoWise eAdapter XML Nodes

CargoWise eAdapter XML Field Function Matrix

| XML NODE TAG | TECHNICAL SYSTEM FUNCTION & COMPLIANCE ENFORCEMENT |
|---|---|
| <PartNumber> | Unique SKU / Item Code. Primary key used by CargoWise to match commercial invoice lines to master catalog records. |
| <HarmonizedTariffCode> | Pre-vetted 10-digit HTSUS code. Auto-injected into line 1 of the ACE entry summary interface. |
| <ApprovedManufacturerCode> | Validated MID code (up to 15 characters). Replaces typist input, preventing MID transpositions and origin errors. |
| <IsHTSLocked> | Boolean flag (true). Forces the CargoWise UI to lock the Tariff Code field, disabling entry clerk manual overrides. |
| <AllowManualOverride> | Boolean flag (false). Disables administrative workarounds for entry clerks attempting to clear software rejection edits. |

## Descartes CustomsInfo API Integration Blueprint

Descartes Systems Group provides enterprise trade management suites widely deployed across global brokerage operations. External ERP platforms integrate with Descartes using RESTful HTTPS APIs transmitting JSON payloads.

Descartes CustomsInfo endpoints process inbound product master updates, execute automated classification validation, and populate the broker's entry execution module.

### Descartes RESTful API Integration Spec

API endpoint specifications:

- Method: POST
- Endpoint URL: https://api.customsinfo.descartes.com/v2/importer/productmaster/sync
- Headers: Content-Type: application/json; Authorization: Bearer <OAuth2_JSON_Web_Token>; X-Descartes-Account-ID: IMP-123456-PROD

### Descartes Inbound Product Sync JSON Schema Payload


```
{
  "requestHeader": {
    "senderSystem": "ORACLE_GTM_PROD",
    "transactionId": "TXN-20260722 88102",
    "timestamp": "2026-07-22T14:35:00Z",
    "apiVersion": "2.1"
  },
  "importerIdentity": {
    "iorNumber": "12-3456789-00",
    "companyName": "Global Tech Industries LLC",
    "primaryCeeSector": "ELECTRONICS"
  },
  "productMasterPayload": {
    "sku": "ELEC-MCU-9902X",
    "productDescription":
    "Microcontroller Unit 32-Bit ARM Cortex-M4 Silicon
        Integrated Circuit",
    "commercialCategory": "INTEGRATED_CIRCUITS",
    "classificationDetails": {
      "htsCode10": "8542310000",
      "countryOfOriginIso2": "TW",
      "primaryUom": "PCS",
      "unitValueUsd": 12.50,
      "baseDutyRatePercent": 0.00
    },
    "tradeProgramEligibility": {
      "specialProgramIndicator": "NONE",
      "section301Applicable": false,
      "section301ExclusionCode": null,
      "adCvdSubjectFlag": false,
      "adCvdCaseNumber": null,
      "nonReimbursementStatementOnFile": true
    },
    "manufacturerDetails": {
      "midCode": "TWTMC9932HSIN",
      "manufacturerName":
          "Taiwan Semiconductor Manufacturing Co Ltd",
```

```
        "addressLine1": "No 8 Li Hsin Rd 6",
        "city": "Hsinchu Science Park",
        "stateProvince": "Hsinchu",
        "postalCode": "300",
        "countryIso2": "TW"
      },
      "partnerGovernmentAgencies": [
        {
          "pgaAgencyCode": "EPA",
          "programCode": "TSCA",
          "certIndicator": "CERT_EXEMPT_ARTICLES",
          "disclaimerCode": "NONE"
        }
      ],
      "systemEnforcementRules": {
        "lockClassification": true,
        "lockManufacturerMid": true,
        "blockManualClerkOverride": true,
        "exceptionAlertEmail": "compliance@importer.com"
      }
    }
  }
```

### Descartes API Field Mapping Guidelines

Descartes REST API Field Mapping Specification

| DESCARTES JSON PROPERTY | DATA TYPE | API VALIDATION & ENFORCEMENT RULE |
|---|---|---|
| sku | String (Max 35) | Primary lookup key. Matches PO lines. |
| htsCode10 | String (Exact 10) | Validates against current HTSUS table. Rejects if expired or inactive. |
| midCode | String (up to 15) | Validates MID structure (ISO country + name + address + city; up to 15 chars). |
| lockClassification | Boolean (true) | Sets read-only flag on HTS code in Descartes Entry Filing Module. |
| blockManualClerkOverride | Boolean (true) | Restricts entry clerk from clearing ABI errors without a compliance key. |

## Technical Error Handling & Asynchronous Exception Loops

In enterprise software integration, API payloads and XML message streams will occasionally fail to ingest due to network timeouts, schema validation errors, or inactive HTS codes.

To prevent system-to-system failures from stalling port clearances, the integration middleware must execute an Asynchronous Exception & Remediation Loop.

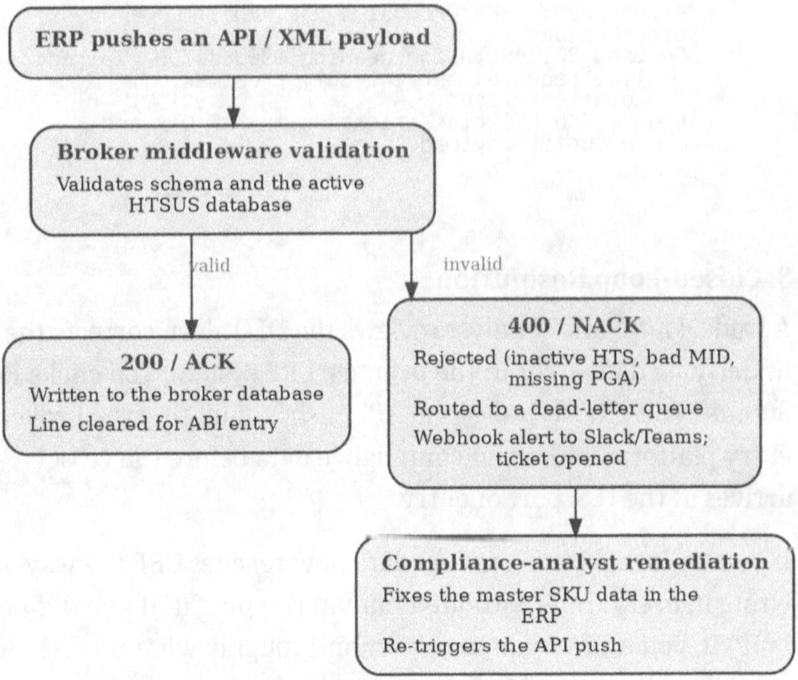


## Error Handling and Remediation

### 1. Dead Letter Queue (DLQ) Isolation

Any XML or JSON payload that returns an HTTP Status 400 (Bad Request) or 422 (Unprocessable Entity) from CargoWise or Descartes is isolated in a secure Dead Letter Queue (DLQ). The broker software is prevented from defaulting to manual entry processing for that SKU.

### 2. Automated Webhook Alerts

The middleware triggers a real-time HTTP webhook payload to the importer's compliance management platform (e.g., Jira, ServiceNow, or internal Slack/Teams compliance channels):

```
{
  "event": "PRODUCT_SYNC_FAILURE",
  "severity": "HIGH",
  "timestamp": "2026-07-22T14:36:12Z",
  "details": {
    "sku": "ELEC-MCU-9902X",
    "brokerSystem": "CARGOWISE_eADAPTER",
    "errorCode": "ERR_EXCLUSION_EXPIRED",
    "errorMessage":
    "Section 301 exclusion heading 9903886700 expired;
        line requires current duty treatment.",
    "remediationAction":
    "Update SKU HTS classification in SAP GTS and
        re-submit payload."
  }
}
```


### 3. Closed-Loop Resolution

A trade compliance analyst reviews the DLQ alert, corrects the underlying data error in the primary ERP system, and clicks Re-Submit. The ERP re-issues the API push, populating the broker's entry platform with valid compliance data before the vessel arrives at the U.S. port of entry.

If you built this, your product data now reaches CBP the way you wrote it, every time, without a human retyping it. If you did not build it, you know what to ask for and roughly what it costs. Both are wins. Chapter 10 is where we get back to law.

# PART IV: HIGH-RISK OPERATIONS & CBP INQUIRY DEFENSE

# Chapter 10: The Post-Summary Correction (PSC) Playbook & Prior Disclosures

## The 300-Day Window: Structuring Internal Pre-Liquidation Audit Routines

In the high-friction environment of international trade compliance, time is the ultimate currency. The moment a customs entry summary (CBP Form 7501) is transmitted to U.S. Customs and Border Protection (CBP) via the Automated Commercial Environment (ACE), a regulatory countdown begins. Too many corporate legal departments and supply chain executives operate under the dangerous assumption that once cargo physically clears the ocean pier or air cargo gateway, the transaction is closed. In operational reality, entry clearance is merely a preliminary permission to enter the stream of U.S. commerce. The legal evaluation of that transaction, the determination of valuation, Harmonized Tariff Schedule (HTS) classification, partner government agency (PGA) flags, and duty liability, remains wide open until liquidation.

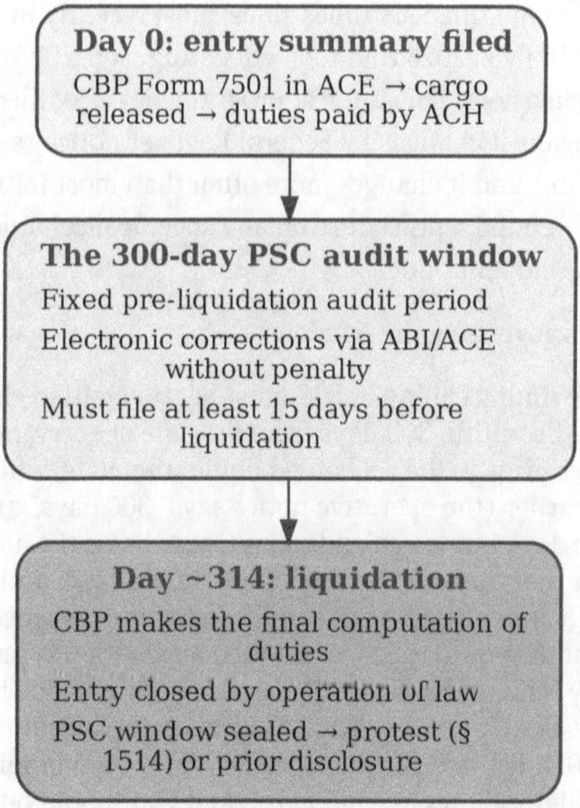


Liquidation is the formal, administrative finalization by CBP of the rate and amount of duties, taxes, and fees owed on an entry. Under 19 U.S.C. § 1504, CBP generally has one year from the date of entry to liquidate a standard entry summary, though liquidation typically occurs on a weekly cycle around Day 314 (approximately 10.3 months post-entry). Between the date of entry summary acceptance and the date of liquidation lies the most critical compliance operational tool available to an Importer of Record (IOR): The 300-Day Post-Summary Correction (PSC) Window.

### Deconstructing the 300-Day PSC Framework

A Post-Summary Correction is authorized under 19 CFR § 101.9(b) as a National Customs Automation Program test, first announced in 2011 and modified six times since, most recently in a notice published July 6, 2026 that took effect August 5, 2026. That currency matters. This is a test program, not a codified regulation, which means it changes by Federal Register notice rather than by rulemaking, and it changes more often than most importers track. Before you build a procedure on any specific mechanic below, check the current notice.

The rules governing the window:

1. The timing ceiling. A PSC must be transmitted electronically in ACE within 300 days from the date of entry, or up to 15 days prior to the scheduled liquidation date, whichever date is earlier (the operative notice says "300 days" and "15 days"; the day-count is calendar days, but that is the author's gloss, not the words of the rule). Both halves bind, and the second is the one that catches people. If an entry is scheduled to liquidate on Day 314, a PSC filed on Day 300 is inside the 300-day limit and still rejects, because it falls inside the 15-day pre-liquidation blackout. Your operating deadline is not Day 300. It is fifteen days before whatever liquidation date ACE actually shows for that entry, and you should be pulling that date, not assuming it.
2. State of the entry summary. To accept a PSC, the entry summary must be in accepted status, fully paid or cleared through Periodic Monthly Statement, and under CBP control. It cannot be under active team review at a Center of Excellence and Expertise, and it cannot have liquidated.
3. Suspended liquidation, and this is where the August 2026 change matters. Where liquidation is suspended beyond 300 days from the date of entry, a PSC may be filed outside the standard window. CBP has now identified qualifying suspension bases, including CVD Suspend, ADD Suspend, AD/CVD Suspend, Subject to EAPA, and Subject to Court Injunction; CBP writes "such as," so treat the list as open and maintain the current one from cbp.gov. Worth noting on the same point: where liquidation is extended rather than suspended, a PSC may still be filed up to fifteen days before

the scheduled liquidation date, which can fall well beyond 300 days, a second recovery route your AD/CVD readers will use.

That third rule deserves more attention than it usually gets, because it inverts the ordinary assumption for a whole category of importers. If you bring in merchandise under an antidumping or countervailing duty order, your entries routinely sit suspended for years pending administrative review. Under the ordinary rule you would have lost the ability to correct them on Day 300. Under this one you have not: the correction window tracks the suspension. If you have AD/CVD entries older than 300 days that you have been treating as closed, they may not be. Pull them and look.

The Pre-Liquidation Audit Cadence

| Audit Cycle | Timing Window | Operational Action & Focus |
|---|---|---|
| Tier 1: Weekly Discrepancy Sweep | Days 1–14 post-release | ACE ES-002/ES-003 extraction; catch typing errors, MID swaps, and gross unit-of-measure mistakes. |
| Tier 2: Monthly Reconciliations | Days 30–45 post-release | Reconcile purchase orders and commercial invoices against PMS payments; audit SPI claims and freight/insurance deductions. |
| Tier 3: Quarterly Transfer Audit | Days 90–120 post-release | Deep forensic review: transfer-pricing adjustments, tooling, and assist values. |
| Tier 4: Pre-Close Liquidation Sweep | Days 240–270 post-release (final safety net) | Final sweep before the 300-day window closes; execute batch PSC filings for any outstanding corrections. |

### Structuring the Pre-Liquidation Audit

Waiting until Day 290 to review broker entry summary filings is a guarantee of failure. High-volume importers must deploy an internal, multi-tiered audit engine that continuously sweeps ACE data extracts (ES-001, ES-002 and ES-003) to flag errors, calculate financial impact, and file PSCs on a rolling cadence.

#### Tier 1: The Weekly Fat-Finger Sweep (Days 1–14)

Every Monday, the compliance engine ingests the prior week's raw ACE ES-002/ES-003 line-item extract. Automated SQL queries cross-reference the transmitted lines against the enterprise item master. The objective at this tier is to catch mechanical entry clerk errors: transposed HTS digits, incorrect Manufacturer Identification (MID) codes, and unit of measure conversion bugs, before the entry summary transitions out of its initial processing phase.

#### Tier 2: The Monthly Valuation & PGA Reconciliation (Days 30–45)

Once Periodic Monthly Statements (PMS) have cleared and duty ACH payments have settled, the compliance team joins the ES-002/ES-003 file with accounts payable ledgers. This sweep verifies that international freight and insurance deductions were properly taken, confirms that SPI claims (e.g., USMCA, GSP) are backed by valid origin certificates, and checks that no PGA disclaimers were illegally inserted by the broker.

#### Tier 3: The Quarterly Forensic & Assist Review (Days 90–120)

At quarterly intervals, compliance coordinates with finance and engineering to review structural valuation adjustments. This includes identifying unreported "assists" (e.g., foreign tooling, molds, or engineering designs provided free or at reduced cost to the foreign manufacturer) and corporate transfer pricing adjustments. If an assist was omitted from the original entry, a batch PSC is designed to adjust the transaction value before liquidation.

**Tier 4: The Pre-Liquidation Final Sweep (Days 240–270)**

This is the hard operational boundary. The compliance engine queries all open entry summaries between 240 and 270 days old. Any un-resolved discrepancy, open CBP Form 28 inquiry flag, or un-corrected broker filing error is immediately escalated to executive compliance for batch PSC execution before the 300-day window permanently seals. Measure the day-count from the date of entry, not release: the 300-day PSC clock runs from entry, and while release and entry usually fall within a day of each other, where they diverge it is the entry date that sets the deadline, which is the whole reason this chapter tells you to pull the actual liquidation date rather than assume it.

## Executing PSCs at Scale: Mechanics, Reason Codes, and Form 28 Avoidance

A Post-Summary Correction is not merely a request to change a data point; in the eyes of CBP, a PSC is a completely new entry summary filing. When a PSC is transmitted via ABI, it completely replaces the original CBP Form 7501 (and any previously filed PSC for that entry). It does not alter the original date of entry or the date of entry summary acceptance, but it replaces every single line-item header, value, duty calculation, HTS code, and PGA declaration.

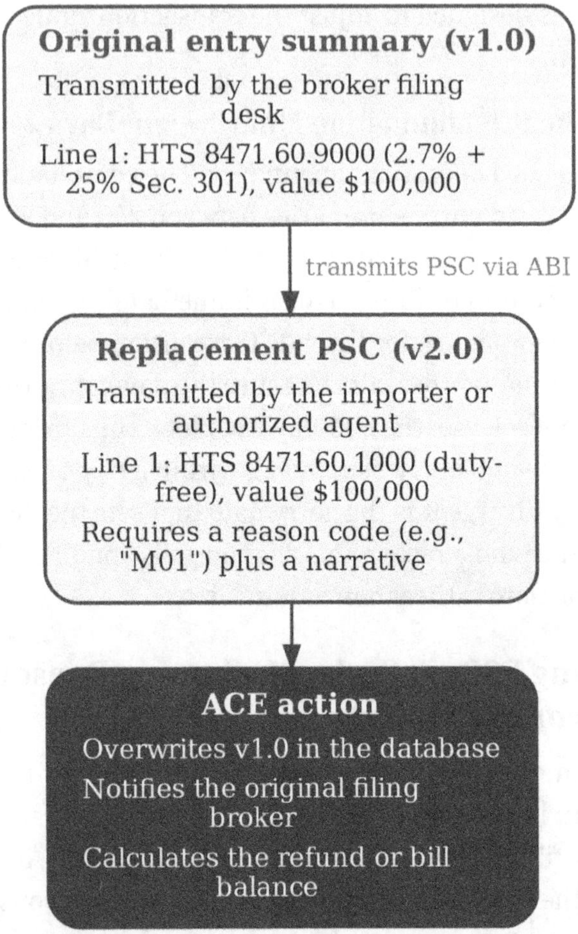


### The Data a PSC Transmission Must Carry

To execute a PSC in ACE, the filing payload must contain specific structural data elements required by CBP's National Customs Automation Program (NCAP) test specifications:

1. Complete Replacement Data Set: The transmission must contain all header and line-item data for the entry, including unchanged data. You cannot transmit only the corrected line item; omitting an unchanged line item permanently deletes that line from the public entry record.
2. Reason Codes (Up to 5 per PSC): The filer must assign at least one CBP PSC reason code identifying the justification

for the amendment. The current valid reason codes are published in the ACE CATAIR entry-summary chapter; the categories in the table below are illustrative and should be confirmed against that source.

3. The Narrative Explanation String: ACE mandates an alphanumeric text description field explaining the precise factual basis for the correction.

CBP publishes the valid PSC reason codes only in the ACE CATAIR Entry Summary Create/Update chapter, transmitted on the 35 record at header level and the 63 record at line level. At least one reason code and a text explanation are required, and up to five reason codes may be identified on a single PSC. Because CBP revises the CATAIR several times a year, pull the current chapter rather than working from any published list, including this one. The categories below are the reasons corrections actually get filed; the codes are whatever the current CATAIR says they are.

| Category | Operational Application |
| --- | --- |
| HTS Classification Change | Correcting a wrong 10-digit tariff classification. |
| Valuation Change | Adjusting declared value, assists, or other additions to price. |
| Quantity Change | Fixing net quantity or a unit-of-measure conversion error. |
| Country of Origin Change | Correcting the declared foreign country of origin or manufacture. |
| SPI / Trade Agreement Change | Adding or removing a USMCA or other free-trade-agreement claim. |
| AD/CVD Case Number Change | Adding, deleting, or altering an AD/CVD case number. |
| PGA Data Elements Change | Correcting EPA/TSCA, FDA, APHIS, or other partner-agency data. |
| Manufacturer ID (MID) Change | Updating the foreign manufacturer address or MID code. |
| Post-Importation Tariff Exclusions | Applying a Section 301 exclusion retroactively. |
| Other Miscellaneous Amendments | Header-level reference or administrative corrections. |

### Executing Duty-Increase vs. Duty-Decrease PSCs

The operational mechanics of a PSC differ radically depending on whether the correction results in additional duties owed to the government or a duty refund owed to the importer.

### 1. Duty-Increase PSCs (Underpayment Correction)

When a PSC identifies a broker error that resulted in an underpayment of duties (e.g., changing a misclassified duty-free code to a 3.7% duty code, or adding an omitted Section 301 tariff):

- Payment Window: The July 6, 2026 notice (91 FR 41053, effective August 5, 2026) changed this. For an ordinary duty increase you no longer have to pay before the PSC will process: a test participant "may choose to pay the full amount of the increase in estimated duties, taxes, and fees resulting from a PSC prior to liquidation or wait to be billed at liquidation." When you do pay a PSC increase, it must be by ACH. Check and cash are no longer accepted. The three-business-day tender window is narrower and still applies to additional antidumping or countervailing duties specifically: for AD/CVD increases, CBP directs the importer to deliver the extra deposit via ACH within three (3) business days of submitting the PSC.
- One-PSC-at-a-time constraint: the same notice provides that you cannot file a subsequent PSC on an entry until the increase from the previously filed PSC "is paid in full and processed by CBP." A partial payment blocks the next PSC. This matters directly to the batch and iterative-correction cadences below: a stuck payment on one entry silently jams the next correction on that same entry.
- Interest Computation: Interest on duty underpayments submitted via PSC before liquidation is NOT calculated automatically at the time of PSC submission. Once the entry liquidates, CBP's Finance Division issues an automated bill for interest computed from the original duty due date under 19 CFR § 24.3a.

**2. Duty-Decrease PSCs (Overpayment Recovery)**

When a PSC corrects a broker error that caused an overpayment of duties (e.g., removing an erroneously applied Section 301 tariff or applying an eligible USMCA free trade preference):

- Refund Processing: CBP does not issue an immediate refund check upon PSC acceptance. The calculated refund is held in suspense until the entry formally liquidates. Upon liquidation, CBP issues an automated refund check (or direct ACH deposit) along with applicable statutory interest.
- Accelerated Liquidation Requests: To expedite the recovery of overpaid funds, the filer can set the Accelerated Liquidation Request Indicator on the PSC, a flag, not a reason code. CBP states on its Post-Summary Correction web page that it will strive to process such requests within 60 calendar days of receipt, and separately (in CSMS #44890398) asks the trade to allow 90 days before making a status inquiry. Treat 60 days as an aspiration, not a cash-flow assumption.

The CBP Form 28 Avoidance Matrix for PSC Filings

| High-Risk PSC Trigger (invites a Form 28 inquiry) | Audit-Proof PSC Preparation |
|---|---|
| Vague narrative: "Correcting HTS per audit" | Detailed narrative: "Correcting 8471.60.90 to 8471.60.10 based on CBP ruling H301992; technical specifications attached." |
| Sudden 90% duty drop without documentation | Upload supporting documentation to the ACE Document Image System (DIS) at the same moment the electronic PSC is transmitted. |
| Switching entry type from 01 to 03 without a non-reimbursement statement | Attach the non-reimbursement statement and the official Commerce AD/CVD case reference. |

## Reducing the Odds of a Form 28

When an importer files a PSC that substantially reduces duty liability or alters sensitive tariff lines, the automated targeting rules at the CEE can flag the PSC for Team Review. If an Import

Specialist sees a sudden $200,000 duty refund claim accompanied by a brief, generic text explanation like "Updating tariff code per internal review," their immediate reaction is to issue a CBP Form 28 (Request for Information), demanding complete accounting ledgers, purchase orders, laboratory analyses, and engineering schematics within 30 days. To execute PSCs at scale without triggering a wave of CBP Form 28 inquiries, you must enforce the Audit-Proof PSC Protocol:

1. Simultaneous Document Image System (DIS) Uploading: Never file a high-value or technical PSC electronically without simultaneously uploading supporting evidentiary documentation into the ACE Document Image System (DIS) tied to the entry summary number. Upload the commercial invoice, packing list, technical specification sheet, and legal justification memo at the exact moment the PSC is transmitted via ABI.
2. Surgical Narrative Writing: Draft the narrative with precision. Reference specific CBP Binding Rulings (e.g., "Reclassifying line 1 pursuant to CBP Headquarters Ruling HQ H312948"), General Rules of Interpretation (GRIs), or explicit Commerce Department AD/CVD scope determination letters.
3. Pre-Emptive CEE Coordination: For large-scale batch PSC filings involving hundreds of entries and millions of dollars in duty adjustments, contact the Chief of the assigned Center of Excellence and Expertise prior to transmission. Providing the CEE with an advance briefing memo and executive summary turns a potential enforcement red flag into a routine, approved administrative adjustment.

## Navigating Prior Disclosures: Managing Systemic Violations Under 19 U.S.C. § 1592

Before going further, be precise about what a PSC does and does not do, because this is the most expensive misconception in the subject. A PSC corrects the entry and the revenue. It is **not** a safe harbor against a civil penalty under 19 U.S.C. § 1592. Section 1592 penalizes material false statements or omissions made with at least negligence; the only thing that caps or eliminates that penalty exposure is a **prior disclosure** meeting § 1592(c)(4) and 19 CFR § 162.74. For a genuine, good-faith error that your own controls caught, a transposed digit, an honest classification miss, filing a PSC typically draws no penalty, because there is nothing culpable to penalize, and CBP's PSC test notice itself asks filers *not* to use a PSC as a prior disclosure and points them to § 162.74 instead. But where the underlying error is a material misstatement made with negligence or worse, a PSC leaves § 1592 exposure fully intact and can hand CBP a documented record that you knew. The rule that follows is simple and it governs everything below: **when the error could be material, the disclosure decision comes first, before you file the PSC.**

With that settled: a Post-Summary Correction is the right mechanism for routine, pre-liquidation corrections, and it has hard limits. A PSC cannot be filed if the entry summary has liquidated, if the window has expired, or where the underlying error is part of a systemic pattern of gross negligence or intentional duty evasion spanning years and hundreds of entries. When an internal audit uncovers a massive, multi-year broker error, such as an entry desk systematically omitting Section 301 tariffs on $50,000,000 worth of imports over a 3-year period, quietly fixing future entries, or filing PSCs without addressing the disclosure question, is legally insufficient. If CBP discovers the un-corrected historical entries independently, it will issue a Penalty Notice under 19 U.S.C. § 1592 assessing civil penalties of two times the lost duties for negligence, four times for gross negligence, or up to the domestic value of the merchandise for fraud. Under the June 3, 2026 Executive Order ("Strengthening Customs Enforcement"), which directs CBP to establish, through revised guidelines not yet in force, a minimum penalty floor of not less than 50 percent and to eliminate mitigation for repeat offenders, an un-disclosed Section 1592 violation can put a corporation's balance sheet at serious risk. The mechanism that insulates the enterprise is the Prior Disclosure (19 U.S.C. § 1592(c)(4) & 19 CFR § 162.74).

### What a Prior Disclosure Buys, Exactly

A prior disclosure under 19 U.S.C. § 1592(c)(4) is a statutory safe harbor. Disclose the circumstances of a violation before, or without knowledge of, the commencement of a formal CBP investigation, and the monetary penalty collapses to a statutory floor.

**Statutory penalty with and without a valid prior disclosure**

| Culpability | Exposure without disclosure | Capped exposure with a valid prior disclosure |
| --- | --- | --- |
| Negligence, § 1592(c)(3) | Lesser of domestic value or 2× lost duties, taxes and fees; or up to 20% of dutiable value where no duty was lost, and subject to the 50% mitigation floor the 2026 order directs | No penalty on unliquidated entries; on liquidated entries, interest only on unpaid duties from liquidation at the § 6621 rate (§ 1592(c)(4)(B)) |
| Gross negligence, § 1592(c)(2) | Lesser of domestic value or 4× lost duties; or up to 40% of dutiable value where no duty was lost | No penalty on unliquidated entries; interest only on liquidated entries (§ 1592(c)(4)(B)) |
| Fraud, with revenue loss, § 1592(c)(1) | Up to the domestic value of the merchandise | 100% of the lost duties (§ 1592(c)(4)(A)(i)); interest under (c)(4)(B) attaches only to negligence and gross-negligence disclosures, not fraud |
| Fraud, no revenue loss, § 1592(c)(1) | Up to the domestic value of the merchandise | 10% of the dutiable value (§ 1592(c)(4)(A)(ii)) |

Three things that table conceals and you should know.

The liquidated/unliquidated split is the one that changes behavior. On a non-fraud disclosure, § 1592(c)(4)(B) measures the "penalty" as interest "computed from the date of liquidation." Before an entry liquidates there is no liquidation date for interest to run from, so on **unliquidated** entries a non-fraud prior disclosure carries **zero**: no penalty and no interest. CBP's own Informed Compliance Publication on prior disclosure says it plainly ("The penalty amount is zero if the importations involve unliquidated (i.e., open) customs entries and no fraud is involved"). Only once entries have **liquidated** does the cost become interest from liquidation to the date you tender. This is decisive for a reader following the audit cadence in this book, because the entries your quarterly sweep is holding are the still-open ones, which is exactly when disclosing is cheapest.

The cap is conditional, not automatic. Under § 1592(c)(4), the reduced penalty applies only if the disclosing party tenders the actual loss of duties, taxes and fees at the time of disclosure, or within 30 days after CBP notifies the discloser of its own calculation. A perfected disclosure with no tender is not a prior disclosure. It is a confession. This is the single most common way a disclosure fails, and it fails after you have already handed CBP the evidence.

Where there is no revenue loss, a negligence disclosure costs essentially nothing. There is no duty base for interest to run against. That is worth knowing before you agonize over disclosing a marking error or a misstatement on a duty-free line. The downside of disclosing is small. The downside of CBP finding it is up to 20% of dutiable value.

### The Structure of 19 CFR § 162.74

The regulation is worth knowing by paragraph, because practitioners cite it constantly and cite it wrong:

- § 162.74(a), the disclosure itself, and the oral option. A disclosure may be made orally, but it must be confirmed in writing within 10 days (absent a good-cause waiver). This is the emergency lever when the clock is the whole game: you can make the disclosure orally to fix the date and confirm in writing days later.
- § 162.74(b), what the disclosure must contain: the class or kind of merchandise; the importations identified by entry number, port, and approximate dates; the material false statements, omissions or acts, with an explanation of how and when they occurred; and the true and accurate information, with a commitment to supply anything still unknown within 30 days.
- § 162.74(c), the tender requirement and Headquarters review. Tender the actual loss at disclosure, or defer until 30 days after CBP notifies you of its calculation; where the claimed loss exceeds $100,000, the deposited-and-reviewed HQ route is available.
- § 162.74(d), the effective time and date of the disclosure. If sent by registered or certified mail, the disclosure is deemed made at the time of mailing, the paragraph that actually decides "legally prior," and the one to build your timestamp around.
- § 162.74(e), the formality that CBP looks for: the words "prior disclosure" conspicuously printed on the face of the envelope containing the disclosure.
- § 162.74(g), when a formal investigation is deemed to have commenced (the date recorded in writing by the Customs Service).
- § 162.74(i). Your knowledge of a commenced investigation, and the rebuttable presumption of that knowledge. Distinct from (g), and it is (i) that CBP will argue.
- § 162.74(j), disclosure using statistical sampling, which is how a five-year, thousand-entry disclosure becomes affordable.

One more benefit the penalty table does not credit: § 1592(c)(4) also provides that on a valid prior disclosure "merchandise shall not be seized." That protection is real and separate from the monetary cap.

**The Race Against the Clock**

The whole contest in prior disclosure practice is establishing that the disclosure was legally prior.

A formal investigation commences on the date recorded in writing by the Customs Service (§ 162.74(g)). But commencement alone does not close the safe harbor. Section 1592(c)(4) protects a disclosure made "before, or without knowledge of" the commencement, so what actually defeats it is CBP establishing that you knew, or are presumed under § 162.74(i) to have known, that the investigation had begun before your disclosure reached the appropriate FP&F officer. That is a burden CBP carries, not an automatic bar: a disclosure filed after an investigation has quietly commenced still qualifies if you filed it without knowledge of that fact. A formal notice of investigation, a search warrant, or a summons served on you is exactly the kind of thing that gives you that knowledge, which is why they matter, but it is the knowledge, not the mere existence of the investigation, that the statute turns on.

Receipt of a routine Form 28 does not by itself mean an investigation has commenced as to the issue you intend to disclose. But if that Form 28 targets the exact product line, HTS code, or valuation issue you were about to disclose, CBP will argue you had knowledge under § 162.74(i), and you will be litigating the presumption rather than relying on the safe harbor.

Hence the operational rule: the moment a systemic error surfaces, file an initial disclosure to fix the date. You do not need the numbers yet. You need the timestamp. Then request an extension, 30 to 60 days is routinely granted on written request, to perfect.

How far back does it reach? Under 19 U.S.C. § 1621, the government has five years, but the trigger differs by culpability, and that difference decides the scope of your disclosure. For negligence and gross negligence, the five years runs from the date of the violation, meaning the entries themselves age out. For fraud, it runs from the date of discovery of the fraud, which may be decades after the entry. Scope your five-year lookback from the violation date, unless you are dealing with facts that could be characterized as fraud, in which case there is no comfortable horizon and you need counsel before you file anything.

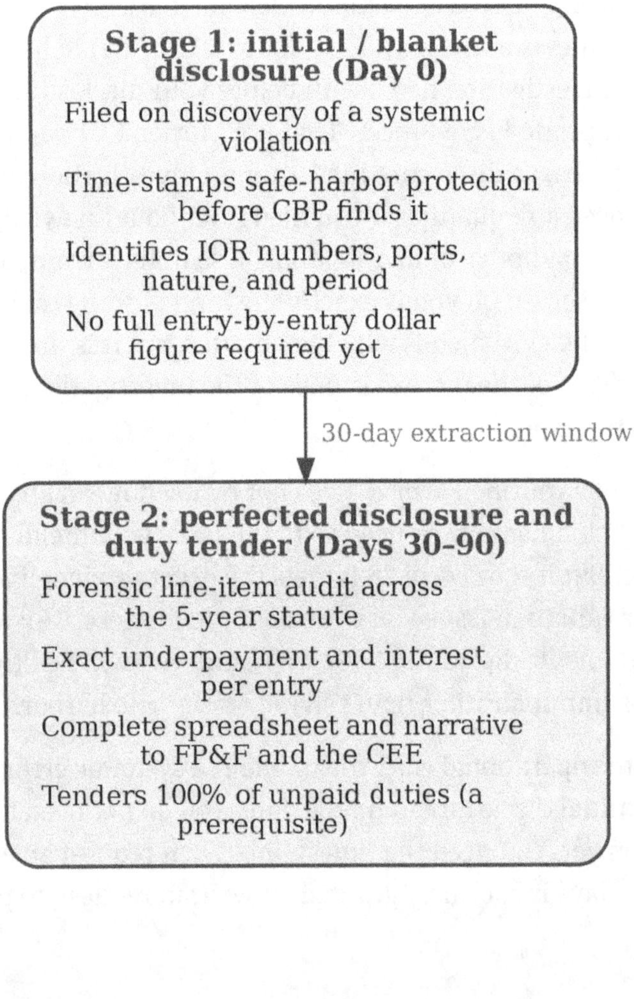

## Step-by-Step Execution of the Two-Stage Prior Disclosure

### Stage 1: Drafting and Submitting the Initial Disclosure

The Initial Disclosure letter is a surgical legal document filed simultaneously with the FP&F Officer at the primary ports of entry and the Center Director of the assigned CEE. The Initial Disclosure must contain four mandatory legal elements under 19 CFR § 162.74(b):

1. Identity of Disclosing Party: Full legal corporate name, IRS Employer Identification Number (EIN), IOR numbers, and corporate address.
2. Class or Type of Merchandise: Precise description of the imported goods affected by the violation.
3. Specified Imports Involved: The ports of entry involved and the approximate time period covering the violations (typically stretching back 5 years under the 19 U.S.C. § 1621 statute of limitations, which for negligence and gross negligence runs from the date of the violation, and for fraud from the date CBP discovered it).
4. Factual Circumstances of the Violation: A concise statement explaining how and why the material false statement, omission, or act occurred (e.g., "An internal compliance audit revealed that between January 2023 and May 2026, entry summaries processed by Customs Broker X inadvertently applied an incorrect HTS code, resulting in an underpayment of Section 301 tariffs").

Critical Practice Rule: State explicitly that the disclosure is being submitted pursuant to 19 U.S.C. § 1592(c)(4) and 19 CFR § 162.74, and formally request a 30-day extension of time to gather full accounting records, calculate exact duty underpayments, and submit the Perfected Disclosure. (CBP routinely grants 30- to 60-day extensions upon written request).

### Stage 2: Data Extraction, Duty Calculation, and Perfection

Once the Initial Disclosure freezes the investigation clock, the forensic audit team executes a complete data extraction:

1. 5-Year ACE ES-002/ES-003 Extraction: Pull every entry summary line filed under the affected IOR numbers for the preceding 60 months.
2. Line-Item Reconciliation: Reconcile transmitted data against purchase orders, commercial invoices, and proof of payment to identify every single entry summary containing the error.
3. Duty and Interest Computation Matrix: Construct an entry-by-entry spreadsheet calculating: 1. Original Entered Value and Original Duty Paid. 2. Corrected Dutiable Value and Corrected Duty Owed. 3. Net Duty Underpayment per Entry Summary.
4. Statutory Interest calculated per 26 U.S.C. § 6621 from liquidation date to tender date.

### Stage 3: Tendering the Duties

Under 19 U.S.C. § 1592(c)(4) and 19 CFR § 162.74(c), a Prior Disclosure is NOT legally valid unless the disclosing party tenders the full amount of unpaid duties, taxes, and fees at the time of disclosure perfection, or within 30 days of receiving a formal duty calculation letter from CBP. Filing a Perfected Prior Disclosure without tendering the underlying unpaid duties strips away your statutory penalty cap. The duty tender must be executed via ACH transfer or cashier's check made payable to U.S. Customs and Border Protection, accompanied by a complete entry-by-entry duty allocation schedule.

### Navigating Broker Liability in Prior Disclosures

When a Prior Disclosure is triggered by systemic broker errors, such as a broker repeatedly using an unauthorized HTS code despite receiving explicit master data instructions, the importer faces a delicate tactical choice. While the Prior Disclosure protects the importer from Section 1592 civil penalties, CBP FP&F Officers will review the disclosure records to determine whether the broker committed actionable violations under 19 U.S.C. § 1641 or 19 CFR § 111.28 (Responsible Supervision and Control). To preserve legal rights and prevent the broker from attempting to disclaim liability:

1. Formally Notify Broker Counsel: Serve the filing broker with a formal Notice of Discrepancy and Indemnification Demand at the exact moment the Initial Disclosure is filed.
2. Expose the Paper Trail: Attach to the Perfected Disclosure all written emails, master data API logs, and SLA contracts proving that the importer provided accurate data and that the error resulted entirely from the broker's failure to follow instructions.
3. Demand Broker Contribution: Use the perfected duty and interest calculation schedule to demand immediate financial reimbursement from the broker for all statutory interest payments and administrative legal costs incurred as a direct result of the broker's gross negligence.

These are counsel decisions, and the sequencing matters more than the substance. Serving an indemnification demand before the disclosure is perfected can turn your filer adverse while it still holds records you need and is still filing your entries, and it can complicate your own culpability position, because if the instructions were that clear and the errors that visible, CBP will ask why your own controls did not catch them sooner. Preserve the evidence immediately; decide with counsel when to deploy it, and whether it goes to CBP at all or only to the broker.

Neither of these tools erases a mistake, and they are not interchangeable. A PSC fixes the entry and the money; a prior disclosure is what limits the § 1592 penalty. What the disclosure decides is who found the error first: an error you disclose before CBP knows of it is an administrative matter; the same error found by CBP two years later is a penalty case. The facts are identical. The difference is a clock, who was watching it, and, where the error is material, whether you reached for the disclosure and not just the PSC.

## Reconciliation: The Pre-Declared True-Up

There is a fourth post-entry tool, and it is the right one for a problem the other three handle badly: the element you cannot finalize at the time you file. Transfer-price adjustments that settle after year-end, assists whose value is not yet allocated, royalties that depend on downstream sales. These are not errors, and they are not corrections. They are numbers that were genuinely open when the entry summary was due. Forcing them into a Post-Summary Correction misdescribes them, and holding the entry until they close is not an option.

Reconciliation, authorized by 19 U.S.C. § 1484(b), is built for exactly this. You flag the entry when you file it, telling CBP that a specified element is undeterminable and will be trued up later, and you enter with your best available figure. Then, within the reconciliation window, you file a single Reconciliation entry that supplies the final numbers across every entry you flagged, and pay or recover the difference. Because CBP was put on notice at entry, the later adjustment is expected. It is not a misstatement, and it does not carry the § 1592 exposure that a late correction of a known error would.

Four kinds of issue are reconcilable. Value is the main one: post-importation price adjustments, assists, royalties, and proceeds. The others are HTSUS heading 9802 (the U.S. content in goods assembled abroad), classification but only where it is pending a ruling, protest, or court decision, and post-importation free-trade-agreement claims under 19 U.S.C. § 1520(d). You cannot use reconciliation to fix a classification you simply got wrong. That is a PSC, or a protest. Three exclusions catch readers arriving from Chapter 11: entry type 02 cannot be flagged for the classification issue, the value issue does not reach latent-manufacturing-defect claims, and AD/CVD merchandise is excluded from reconciliation altogether, so the transfer-price and non-reimbursement adjustments on your AD/CVD entries are not a reconciliation matter, however naturally Chapter 11 leads you to expect they would be.

The clocks are strict, and there are no extensions. For value, 9802, and classification, the Reconciliation entry is due within 21 months of the date of the entry summary of the oldest flagged entry. For free-trade-agreement claims it is 12 months from the date of importation, tracking the one-year post-importation claim period in § 1520(d). The flag is normally set when the entry summary is filed. It is your notice of intent. CBP does allow retroactive flagging, but treat it as a narrow exception, not a fallback: you must request it in writing (to CBP's national reconciliation mailbox), it is granted sparingly, and only if you ask at least 60 days before the entry's scheduled liquidation date. Plan to flag at entry, and keep retroactive flagging in reserve for the entry that slipped through.

Reconciliation runs in ACE. The filer either flags each entry or configures blanket flagging in its own software. CBP no longer applies blanket flags for you. It requires a continuous bond with a reconciliation rider and is limited to entry types 01, 02, and 06. One caution on authority: reconciliation is administered as a National Customs Automation Program test under 19 CFR § 101.9(b), governed by § 1484(b) and the operative Federal Register notices rather than a standalone regulation, so confirm the current mechanics against CBP's reconciliation guidance and the latest CSMS before you build a program on it.

One clock now interacts with another, and it is worth flagging. Under CBP's CAPE refund process (CSMS #69035485, 29 June 2026), a reconciliation-flagged entry is drawn into CAPE only where no Reconciliation entry has yet been filed against it, and

CBP tells filers whose reconciliation deadline falls within 30 days to prioritise the reconciliation filing. If the same entries carry both a CAPE-eligible refund and an open reconciliation flag, the two deadlines can collide. Watch them together, and file the reconciliation entry first where its clock is the shorter one.

The connection to the rest of this book is direct. The quarterly value review in Chapter 1, and the deeper audits in Chapters 7 and 10, are what surface these adjustments: the transfer-price true-up, the assist nobody added, the royalty that belonged in the entered value. Reconciliation is the instrument that lets you correct them prospectively, in one filing, with CBP already on notice, instead of finding them late and reaching for a disclosure.

# Chapter 11: High-Risk Target Lines: AD/CVD, Section 301, and UFLPA Tracing

In the modern federal customs enforcement matrix, standard consumption entries involving routine Column 1 ad valorem duty rates are no longer where corporate existences are won or lost. U.S. Customs and Border Protection (CBP) targeting algorithms, backed by the Department of Commerce's International Trade Administration (ITA) and the interagency Forced Labor Enforcement Task Force (FLETF), have automated the detection of generic commodity import errors. The primary vectors for severe civil financial liabilities, supply chain halts, and corporate blacklisting sit inside three specific high-risk enforcement arenas:

1. Antidumping and Countervailing Duty (AD/CVD) hazards: Where cash deposit rates reaching several hundred percent, coupled with strict statutory rules on duty reimbursement, convert minor clerical filing errors into sharply higher retroactive assessments.
2. Section 301 Trade Remedy Audits: Where aggressive country-of-origin transformation scrutinies and complex exclusion rules turn transshipment strategies into criminal and civil fraud targets.
3. Uyghur Forced Labor Prevention Act (UFLPA) & Forced Labor Gating: Where statutory presumptions of illicit labor require granular, raw-material-level supply chain tracing before cargo can ever clear a U.S. port of entry.

When a high-volume Customs Broker processes high-risk target lines without automated, pre-entry compliance gating, they are gambling with the Importer of Record's (IOR) balance sheet. This chapter delivers the field-tested audit protocols and operational controls required to lock down these target lines and defend against federal targeting algorithms.

## Antidumping & Countervailing Duty (AD/CVD) Hazards

Antidumping Duty (AD) and Countervailing Duty (CVD) enforcement represents the most severe financial hazard in U.S. import compliance. Congress enacted AD/CVD laws under Title VII of the Tariff Act of 1930 to protect domestic industries from foreign goods sold at less than fair value (dumping) or subsidized by foreign governments. While basic customs duties typically range between 0% and 5%, AD/CVD cash deposit rates routinely reach 100% to over 300% of the entered transaction value. More critically, unlike standard entries where duty liability is fixed upon liquidation, AD/CVD entries (Entry Type 03) operate under a retrospective assessment system. The cash deposit paid at the time of entry summary filing is merely an estimate. Final duty rates are fixed years later following administrative reviews by the Department of Commerce. If Commerce determines that the dumping margin increased during the review period, CBP issues a retroactive demand for supplemental duties plus statutory interest.

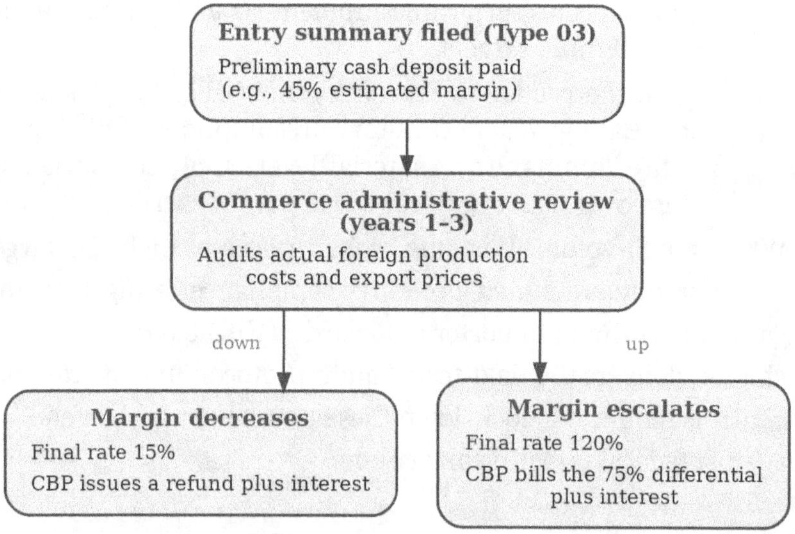

When an entry desk processes AD/CVD lines without strict compliance oversight, three major operational hazards trigger severe financial exposures:

### 1. The Non-Reimbursement Statement Trap (19 CFR § 351.402(f))

One of the most serious administrative traps in AD/CVD enforcement sits inside 19 CFR § 351.402(f). Under Commerce Department regulations, an importer is legally barred from receiving any reimbursement, direct or indirect, from the foreign exporter or producer for antidumping or countervailing duties paid to CBP. To enforce this prohibition, 19 CFR § 351.402(f)(2) mandates that the Importer of Record must file a formal Certificate of Non-Reimbursement with CBP prior to liquidation of the relevant entry summary.

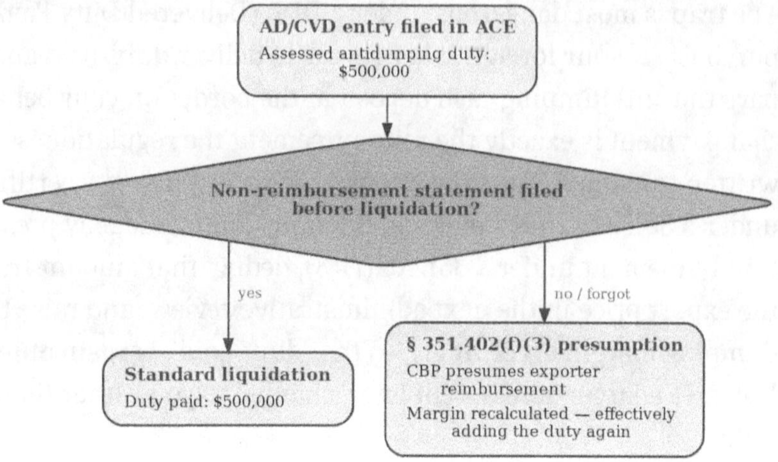


### The Presumption of Reimbursement

If the importer does not file a signed non-reimbursement certificate before the entry liquidates, 19 CFR § 351.402(f)(3) provides that the Secretary "may presume" the exporter or producer paid or reimbursed the antidumping duties.

Note the verb. The presumption is permissive, not automatic: Commerce is not obliged to apply it, and importers do occasionally persuade it not to. In practice, Commerce applies it routinely, and a late certificate is accepted only through protest procedures. Treat "may presume" as "will presume unless you give it a reason not to," and file the certificate.

The consequence, when it applies, is severe. Treating the exporter as having reimbursed the duties, Commerce deducts that amount from export price when it calculates the final dumping margin, which raises the margin and can effectively assess the antidumping duty a second time. An importer that paid $1,000,000 in preliminary AD cash deposits, and whose entry clerk never filed the statement, can face a bill for roughly that amount again at liquidation.

The trap is most dangerous under a DDP (Delivered Duty Paid) purchase. If your foreign seller agrees to deliver duty-paid and pays the antidumping cash deposit at the border on your behalf, that payment is exactly the reimbursement the regulation is written to catch. Unless the importer of record files the certificate under § 351.402(f)(2) before liquidation, Commerce may presume reimbursement under § 351.402(f)(3), deduct that amount from the export price in the next administrative review, and raise the dumping margin accordingly, so the "duty-paid" bargain quietly becomes a larger assessment later, charged to you rather than the seller.

> *Risk and impact. Do not buy antidumping- or countervailing-duty-subject merchandise under DDP or DAP terms. If a vendor insists on delivered pricing, carve customs entry out of the deal: make your own company the importer of record, control the entry, and file the § 351.402(f) non-reimbursement certificate before liquidation. The certificate is a one-page administrative step.*

> *Missing it hands Commerce a presumption that is slow and expensive to unwind.*

## Blanket vs. Line-Item Filings in ACE

Historically, non-reimbursement statements were physical paper certificates attached to entry packets. Under modern ACE business rules, importers can satisfy this requirement electronically via two mechanisms:

1. Line-Item Indicator: The broker toggles the AD/CVD Non-Reimbursement Indicator field ( Y ) directly on the ACE Entry Summary line.
2. ACE Blanket Declaration: The importer creates a centralized Blanket Statement of Non-Reimbursement record inside their ACE Portal account, covering a specific AD/CVD case number, foreign producer, and timeframe (up to 12 months).

## The Broker Audit Protocol for Non-Reimbursement

High-volume brokers frequently omit the line-item Y indicator during fast entry transmission, and they rarely verify whether an importer holds an active Blanket Declaration in ACE. To prevent this presumption from ever triggering, the importer's compliance team must execute a monthly SQL audit across raw ACE ES-002/ES-003 extracts:

```
-- ==================================================================
-- FORENSIC AUDIT: AD/CVD NON-REIMBURSEMENT STATEMENT
   VERIFICATION
-- Identifies any line carrying an AD/CVD case
   number that lacks line-level or blanket
   certification (keyed on the case number, not
   the entry type)
-- ==================================================================

SELECT
    es002.Filer_Code,
    es002.Entry_Number,
    es002.Line_Item_Number,
    es002.ADCVD_Case_Number,
    es002.Entered_Value_USD,
    es002.ADCVD_Duty_Paid_USD,
    es002.Non_Reimbursement_Indicator_ACE,
    es001.Liquidation_Status,
    es001.Scheduled_Liquidation_Date

FROM tbl_ACE_ES002_LineItems es002
```

```
INNER JOIN tbl_ACE_ES001_Headers es001
    ON es002.Filer_Code = es001.Filer_Code
    AND es002.Entry_Number = es001.Entry_Number
WHERE
    es002.ADCVD_Case_Number IS NOT NULL
    AND es001.Liquidation_Status = 'UNLIQUIDATED'
    AND (
        es002.Non_Reimbursement_Indicator_ACE IS NULL
        OR es002.Non_Reimbursement_Indicator_ACE <>
            'Y'
    )
ORDER BY es001.Scheduled_Liquidation_Date ASC;
```

Any open AD/CVD line flagged by this query. That is, any line carrying an AD/CVD case number without a non-reimbursement indicator of Y, whatever its entry type, must immediately trigger the filing of an electronic Blanket Non-Reimbursement Statement in ACE, or a Post-Summary Correction (PSC) to toggle the line-level indicator to Y prior to liquidation. Keying on the case number, not on Entry Type 03, is deliberate: it avoids flagging type-03 lines that carry no AD/CVD (false positives) and catches AD/CVD lines that are not coded 03 (false negatives).

## 2. Case Number Misallocation & Cash Deposit Rate Discrepancies

The second major AD/CVD hazard occurs when entry clerks assign incorrect Commerce case numbers (padding, truncating, or transposing the segments) or select wrong manufacturer-specific company sub-codes ( -001 vs. -000 "All Others").

**Commerce AD/CVD case number — A-570-836-002**

A — antidumping prefix (C = countervailing)

570 — country code (China)

836 — Commerce investigation ID

002 — producer/exporter sub-code (specific factory rate); -000 = the country-wide 'all others' rate

**Factory-Specific Rates vs. Country-Wide "All-Others" Rates**

In non-market economy (NME) investigations (such as China or Vietnam), the Department of Commerce calculates specific, lower dumping margins for foreign factories that demonstrate independence from state control (Separate Rate Applicants). Foreign producers that fail to demonstrate independence receive the heavy Country-Wide Rate.

- Example: For a specific steel commodity, Factory A (A-570-XXX-002) holds an individually investigated cash deposit rate of 8.50%, while the country-wide rate (A-570-XXX-000) sits at 185.00%. (The case number here is an illustrative placeholder; verify the live case number and its rates against the ITA case list and the operative Federal Register notice before relying on either.)

When an entry clerk types an entry summary, if they leave off the specific 3-digit extension ( -002 ) or select the generic -000 extension because the factory details were unclear on the foreign invoice, ACE automatically assesses the 185.00% cash deposit rate. Conversely, if the clerk inputs a low factory rate ( -002 ) without verifying that the physical manufacturer listed on the bill of lading matches the Commerce-approved facility address, CBP will flag the entry for AD/CVD Evasion during a post-entry audit.

**The AD/CVD Scope Determination Defense**

Brokers regularly make assumptions regarding whether a product falls within the physical scope of an active AD/CVD order. If a product description on an invoice contains ambiguous terms, such as "Extruded Aluminum Frame", the broker may assume it is subject to the Aluminum Extrusions AD/CVD order, filing an Entry Type 03 and tying up hundreds of thousands of dollars in cash deposits. Alternatively, the clerk might assume it is exempt under a finished goods exclusion, filing a standard Entry Type 01 without informing the importer. To resolve scope ambiguities, the importer must never rely on a broker's opinion. The importer must:

1. Audit the Commerce ITA Scope Language: Review the narrative scope description published in the Federal Register.
2. Request a Formal Scope Ruling (19 CFR § 351.225): Submit an application to the Department of Commerce for a binding Scope Ruling. If Commerce rules that the product is outside the scope, the ruling binds CBP nationwide and lets the importer clear the goods without the AD/CVD cash deposit going forward, not "duty-free," since ordinary Column 1 duties and any Section 301 tariff still apply; being outside an AD/CVD order only removes that order's duties. Be realistic about recovery, too: a scope ruling's retroactive reach is limited. It generally applies to unliquidated entries and to entries suspended pending the scope inquiry; it does not automatically reopen entries that have already liquidated. Recover the cash deposits on entries within the ruling's reach, and do not assume it claws back everything ever deposited.

## Section 301 Tariff Audits: Transformation, Exclusions, and Duty Recovery

Section 301 of the Trade Act of 1974 authorizes the Executive Branch to impose retaliatory tariffs on foreign imports to address unfair trade practices. Section 301 duties are imposed under a specific set of Chapter 99 headings: 9903.88.01 and .02 (Lists 1 and 2, 25%), 9903.88.03 and .04 (List 3, 25%), 9903.88.09 (List 4A, originally 15%, superseded by .15 effective 14 February 2020), and 9903.88.15 (List 4A, 7.5%). The remainder of the 9903.88 series carries exclusions and transition provisions, not the duties themselves, including .69 and .70, the exclusion headings discussed later in this chapter. The 2024 four-year review added a separate series at 9903.91.01 et seq., with rates running as high as 100% by product, and USTR initiated the second statutory four-year review on 6 May 2026, so the rate structure is under active review as this edition publishes. The current range is 7.5% to 100%, depending on the product. Because Section 301 tariffs represent massive financial costs, importers routinely deploy supply chain restructuring to mitigate duty exposure. However, where importers see legitimate tariff engineering, CBP targeting algorithms see potential trade fraud under 19 U.S.C. § 1592.

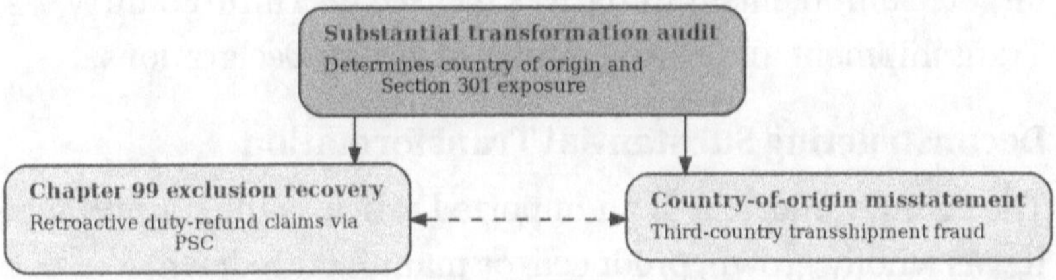


**Section 301 Beyond China: The 2026 Forced-Labor Tariffs**

One 2026 action widened who this section applies to. Effective 24 July 2026, USTR imposed a new set of Section 301 tariffs, under Sections 301(b) and 304(a) of the Trade Act of 1974, on roughly 60 economies it found had failed to prohibit and effectively enforce against the importation of goods made with forced labor (Federal Register document 2026-15181). The rates run from 10 percent to 12.5 percent depending on the economy, and goods already subject to Section 232 are exempted. The practical consequence is that Section 301 is no longer a China question. An importer sourcing from countries nowhere near China can become a Section 301 importer overnight, which means the exclusion tracking, origin discipline, and duty-recovery mechanics in this chapter now reach a far wider set of readers than the original China lists did. Check whether any economy in your supply chain is on the 24 July 2026 list, and confirm the current rate against the operative Federal Register notice: the program is new and will move.

## 1. Substantial Transformation & Third-Country Transshipment

When Section 301 tariffs hit Chinese manufacturing, thousands of importers shifted processing, assembly, or packaging operations to third countries in Southeast Asia, such as Vietnam, Malaysia, Thailand, or Indonesia, to establish a new country of origin and legally bypass Section 301 tariffs. CBP responded by launching targeted enforcement initiatives focused on Third-Country Transshipment and False Country of Origin Declarations.

### Deconstructing Substantial Transformation

The country of origin of an imported article is the country where it was wholly grown, produced, or manufactured; when processing occurs in multiple countries, origin is the country of the last substantial transformation. Substantial transformation occurs when an article emerges from a process with a new name, character, or use distinct from the materials or components that went in, a disjunctive test (a fundamental change in any one can suffice, and in practice the change in character carries the most weight), not a requirement that all three change at once. A note on authority: 19 CFR § 134.1(b) defines "country of origin" for marking purposes as the country of the last substantial transformation; the Section 301 origin determination applies the same common-law substantial-transformation test, but do not treat the marking regulation as the governing rule for the tariff question. Cite it for the definition, and rely on the case law and CBP rulings for the application.

Substantial Transformation Legitimacy Matrix

| MANUFACTURING OPERATION | CBP ORIGIN DETERMINATION | SECTION 301 STATUS |
|---|---|---|
| Simple assembly / screwdriver assembly of Chinese components | NO substantial transformation; origin remains CHINA. | SUBJECT TO SECTION 301 (China tariff applies). |
| Minor surface finishing, | NO substantial | SUBJECT TO SECTION |

| MANUFACTURING OPERATION | CBP ORIGIN DETERMINATION | SECTION 301 STATUS |
|---|---|---|
| cutting to length, or simple packaging | transformation; origin remains CHINA. | 301 (China tariff applies). |
| Complex machining, chemical reaction, or fundamental change in essential character | VALID substantial transformation; origin shifts to VIETNAM/ MALAYSIA. | EXEMPT FROM SECTION 301 (third-country origin). |

### The Broker Transshipment Blind Spot

Entry clerks at brokerage firms process entries based strictly on the country of origin printed on the vendor's invoice. If a Vietnamese exporter prints "Country of Origin: Vietnam" on a commercial invoice, the entry clerk enters VN in ACE without question. If the Vietnamese factory merely performed minor assembly or packaging on Chinese-origin subassemblies without achieving substantial transformation, the entry summary transmitted by the broker contains a materially false statement of origin. When CBP audits the shipment, they execute a Supply Chain Origin Audit, issuing a CBP Form 28 demanding:

- Factory production logs, machine maintenance records, and direct labor timecards from the Vietnamese facility. Bills of materials (BOMs) showing the origin and unit value of every raw material input. Proof that the processing in Vietnam fundamentally altered the essential character of the Chinese components.

If the importer cannot prove substantial transformation, CBP reclassifies the origin to China, assesses retroactive Section 301 tariffs plus interest, and issues a Section 1592 civil penalty for gross negligence or fraud.

These are not hypotheticals. In Royal Brush Manufacturing, Inc. v. United States, 75 F.4th 1250 (Fed. Cir. 2023), CBP found under the Enforce and Protect Act (19 U.S.C. § 1517) that an importer had evaded the antidumping order on cased pencils from China by transshipping Chinese-origin pencils through the Philippines and declaring them of Philippine origin. On appeal the Federal Circuit did not disturb the evasion theory; it faulted CBP for relying on confidential record evidence without disclosing it and sent the case back, a reminder that the government's own procedure is open to challenge, but also that the transshipment itself was the thing that started the fight. EAPA is the mechanism to watch: it lets CBP investigate evasion on a compressed timeline, impose interim measures that hold your entries while it does, and reach an importer who never set foot in the foreign factory.

The civil-fraud exposure has grown teeth of a different kind. On December 18, 2025, the Department of Justice announced that Ceratizit USA LLC agreed to pay $54.4 million to resolve False Claims Act allegations that it had misrepresented the country of origin of Chinese-made tungsten carbide products as Taiwanese to evade Section 301 tariffs, and separately misclassified goods under the wrong tariff codes to lower its duties. Outside counsel described it as believed to be the largest customs-related False Claims Act recovery to that point; DOJ's own release does not make that claim. It was driven by a whistleblower, who received roughly $9.75 million. (U.S. Department of Justice, Office of Public Affairs, press release, dated Thursday, December 18, 2025 on justice.gov; several law-firm client alerts are dated December 19, the day they published their write-ups. Some secondary coverage cites the figure as $5.44 million; the DOJ release states $54.4 million.) The False Claims Act turns a customs misstatement into treble-damages territory and gives an insider, a departing employee, a competitor, a broker who sees the pattern, a direct financial incentive to report you. Between EAPA on the duty side and the False Claims Act on the fraud side, the transshipment shortcut has become one of the most heavily policed moves in trade.

## 2. Validating Section 301 Exclusion Claims and Refund Recovery

Throughout the execution of Section 301 tariffs, the Office of the U.S. Trade Representative (USTR) granted temporary, product-specific tariff exclusions published under Chapter 99 of the HTSUS (currently headings 9903.88.69 and 9903.88.70). Properly managing Section 301 exclusions requires two critical broker oversight mechanisms:

### Mechanism 1: The Exclusion Expiration Cliff

Everything in this section carries a date, because this is the fastest-moving material in the book.

As of this writing, 178 Section 301 exclusions remain in effect, provided for under HTSUS subheadings 9903.88.69 and 9903.88.70. USTR extended them following the November 2025 trade understanding, and they run through 11:59 p.m. on November 9, 2026. (USTR made conforming amendments to the U.S. note text on 2 September 2026 to track USITC statistical-category changes effective 1 July 2026; the count and expiry are unchanged, but the note text has moved. Note also that USTR's own preamble says "November 10" while the operative annex says November 9, the annex date governs.)

That is not a rolling series of individual expirations. It is a single cliff, and every importer relying on any of the 178 hits it on the same night.

Two things follow.

Before the date: know your exposure. Run your ACE ES-002/ES-003 extract for every line claiming 9903.88.69 or 9903.88.70, total the Section 301 duty those exclusions are currently saving you, and put that number in front of your CFO now rather than in December. If USTR extends again, you have lost nothing. If it does not, you have a duty increase you forecast instead of discovered.

After the date: block the habit. The predictable failure is not a policy decision. It is an entry clerk continuing to apply a Chapter 99 heading out of muscle memory or stale software configuration, weeks after it died. If ACE accepts the line, nothing announces the error; CBP finds it in post-liquidation review and issues a rate advance for the unpaid Section 301 duty plus interest. Your broker's platform must enforce an automated block on any Chapter 99 exclusion heading past its expiration date, and that rule needs a calendar entry against November 9, not a hope that someone remembers.

USTR can extend, narrow, or let these lapse at any time, and has done all three before. Confirm the current status on USTR's site before you rely on a claim or plan around a loss.

### Mechanism 2: Retroactive Exclusion Refund Extraction

Conversely, when USTR grants retroactive Section 301 exclusions (or extends previously expired exclusions with retroactive effect), importers are legally entitled to recover 100% of the Section 301 tariffs paid during the retroactive window. To extract these refunds before liquidation or statutory deadlines seal, the importer's compliance team must run an automated extraction query across historical ES-002/ES-003 line-item records:

```
-- ==========================================================
-- FORENSIC AUDIT: SECTION 301 RETROACTIVE REFUND
   RECOVERY EXTRACTOR
-- Identifies entries that paid Section 301 duties
   eligible for exclusion claims
-- ==========================================================

SELECT
    es002.Filer_Code,
    es002.Entry_Number,
    es002.Line_Item_Number,
    es002.HTS_10_Digit,
    es002.Entered_Value_USD,
    es002.Section_301_Duty_Paid_USD,
    es001.Entry_Date,
    es001.Liquidation_Status

FROM tbl_ACE_ES002_LineItems es002

INNER JOIN tbl_ACE_ES001_Headers es001
    ON es002.Filer_Code = es001.Filer_Code
```

```
    AND es002.Entry_Number = es001.Entry_Number
WHERE
    es002.HTS_10_Digit IN ('8471609000',
        '8504409580', '9018907580') -- Targeted
    AND es002.Section_301_Duty_Paid_USD > 0
    AND es001.Entry_Date BETWEEN '2024-01-01' AND
        '2026-06-01' -- Retroactive Exclusion window
    AND es001.Liquidation_Status = 'UNLIQUIDATED'
ORDER BY es002.Section_301_Duty_Paid_USD DESC;
```

Every unliquidated entry flagged by this query must be immediately packaged into a Post-Summary Correction (PSC) amending the entry summary to include the specific Chapter 99 exclusion heading, triggering an automated duty refund check from CBP upon liquidation.

## First Sale: The Legitimate Valuation Lever

Most of this chapter is about hazards. This is the opposite: a lawful way to lower dutiable value that sits squarely inside the valuation discipline the book has been building toward. It is also the single largest duty-reduction lever most mid-market importers never use.

The setup is the multi-tier sale. Your goods pass through a middleman: a foreign manufacturer sells to a trading company or vendor, which sells to you. The ordinary practice is to declare the price you paid the middleman, markup and all. First sale lets you declare the earlier price instead, what the manufacturer charged the middleman, as the transaction value, and leave the middleman's margin out of the dutiable base. The statutory hook is the definition of transaction value in 19 U.S.C. § 1401a: the price "when sold for exportation to the United States." A lower-tier sale can be that sale for export, if it meets the test.

The test comes from Nissho Iwai American Corp. v. United States, 982 F.2d 505 (Fed. Cir. 1992). Start with the threshold the statute imposes: there must be a bona fide sale between the manufacturer and the middleman: a real transfer of title and risk of loss for consideration, not a transfer within one company and not an agency or consignment arrangement. Given a bona fide sale, Nissho Iwai states the manufacturer's price is a viable transaction value when two conditions hold. The goods are clearly destined for export to the United States at the time of that first sale, earmarked for the U.S. rather than sold into general inventory with the destination decided later. And the sale is at arm's length, absent any non-market influence on the price, the condition that does the most work when the manufacturer and the middleman are related. The bona fide sale is the statutory predicate CBP applies alongside those two, not a third holding of the opinion. The Federal Circuit was explicit that this is a case-by-case determination, not a status you qualify for once and keep.

That case-by-case standard is why first sale is a documentation problem before it is a valuation strategy, and why it belongs in a book about records. CBP places the burden on the importer, and its guidance in T.D. 96-87 asks for the complete picture: the manufacturer's invoice showing the first-sale price, evidence of two bona fide sales rather than one sale and a paper markup, proof the goods were destined for the United States at the first sale, and, where the parties are related, support that the price was not distorted by the relationship. Any statutory addition under § 1401a(b), such as an assist or a royalty, has to be carried on the first-sale price, not quietly dropped. This is exactly the per-shipment, source-document capture that the master-data and audit architecture in Chapters 7 through 9 is built to produce, retained for five years under 19 CFR Part 163. An importer that cannot assemble that file for any entry CBP selects does not have a first-sale program. It has an exposure.

First sale is not a loophole and not a scheme. It is a court-sanctioned reading of the valuation statute that CBP continues to apply. A short-lived declaration requirement from the 2008 Farm Bill, importers had to report first-sale use for one year, from 20

August 2008 to 19 August 2009, expired and was not renewed. CBP removed the implementing paragraph, 19 CFR § 141.61(g), by technical correction effective 30 December 2010. The reporting sunset, not the method. One forward-looking caveat belongs on your calendar the way EO 14411 does: S. 3841, the Last Sale Valuation Act of 2026 (Senators Cassidy and Whitehouse), referred to the Senate Finance Committee, would abolish first sale outright by basing transaction value on the last sale before importation. It has not passed, and may not. But build a first-sale program knowing the statute it rests on is under active legislative challenge, and watch the bill. Run as a disciplined, well-documented program rather than an aggressive position, first sale is among the highest-value things a Tier B or C importer can do with records it already has to keep.

## Drawback: Getting Duty Back on What You Export or Destroy

If first sale is the duty you should not have paid, drawback is the duty you can get back. When imported merchandise is later exported or destroyed, 19 U.S.C. § 1313 lets you recover up to 99 percent of the duties, taxes, and fees you paid to bring it in. The one percent CBP keeps is administrative. Everything else is refundable, and for an importer that returns goods, scraps defective inventory, or re-exports, it is often real money sitting uncollected.

There are three main routes. Unused merchandise drawback, under § 1313(j), covers goods exported or destroyed in the same condition they arrived in, (j)(1) where you export the very merchandise you imported, (j)(2) where you export other merchandise classifiable under the same 8-digit HTS subheading. Manufacturing drawback, under § 1313(a) and (b), covers imported inputs consumed in producing something that is then exported. Rejected merchandise drawback, under § 1313(c), covers goods that did not conform to specification, were shipped without your consent, or were defective, and are returned or destroyed. The Trade Facilitation and Trade Enforcement Act rebuilt all of this, effective February 24, 2018: substitution now turns on the 8-digit HTS match rather than the old "commercially interchangeable" test, claims are filed electronically in ACE, and the modernized rules live in 19 CFR Part 190: the mandatory regime for every claim filed on or after 24 February 2019, though the legacy Part 191 still governs claims filed under the transition before that date. The claim deadline is five years from the date of importation, under § 1313(r).

What decides whether the exercise is worth it is which duties are drawback-eligible, and the answer is not uniform. Ordinary Section 301 duties on Chinese-origin goods are eligible, which is what makes drawback worth the effort for many importers. Section 201 safeguard duties are eligible. Section 232 duties on steel and aluminum are not. The no-drawback bar came in Proclamations 9739 and 9740 (April 2018), which amended the original steel and aluminum proclamations, and it carries through today in Proclamations 10895 and 10896 (February 2025). The temporary 10 percent Section 122 surcharge that ran from 24 February to 24 July 2026 is drawback-eligible (CBP CSMS #67844987), with claims filable for five years from importation. Its legal status is contested but was not void for most importers: in Oregon v. United States (Slip Op. 26-47, 7 May 2026) the Court of International Trade held the underlying proclamation ultra vires, but the relief reached only the named plaintiffs: the court did not grant nationwide relief, and the Federal Circuit stayed the ruling on 11 June 2026, finding the government likely to succeed on appeal. Every other importer paid the surcharge through its expiration. One more distinction matters here: CAPE does not reach Section 122 duties (CAPE is IEEPA-specific), so a Section 122 refund is preserved by PSC or protest rather than CAPE, and drawback and a litigation refund are alternative claims on the same dollars, not cumulative. The IEEPA tariffs need a different lens. For the reciprocal tariffs, CBP's CAPE refund process returns the full 100 percent, better than drawback's 99, so CAPE, not a drawback claim, is the route there. The fentanyl and border tariffs on China, Canada, and Mexico are eligible for neither. Because rates and CBP's positions kept moving through 2025 and 2026, do not rely on a general statement about any of these. Check the CSMS message tied to the specific executive order or proclamation in force on your entry date, and confirm eligibility line by line.

Drawback is a recordkeeping payoff, which is why it belongs beside the rest of this book. A claim has to trace a specific exported or destroyed unit back to a specific import entry, its 8-digit classification, and the duty paid, all within the five-year window and all provable in ACE. That is the same transaction-level linkage the master-data and audit machinery in Chapters 7 through 9 already produces. An importer with that architecture in place is most of the way to a drawback claim. An importer without it usually leaves the refund on the table, because it cannot prove the chain.

## UFLPA and Forced-Labor Gating: Raw-Material Supply-Chain Tracing

The most severe operational threat to global supply chains today is the enforcement of the Uyghur Forced Labor Prevention Act (UFLPA) (Public Law 117-78) and Section 307 of the Tariff Act of 1930 (19 U.S.C. § 1307). Under Section 307, importing goods mined, produced, or manufactured wholly or in part in any foreign country by forced labor, convict labor, or indentured labor is strictly prohibited. The UFLPA established what is known as the rebuttable presumption.

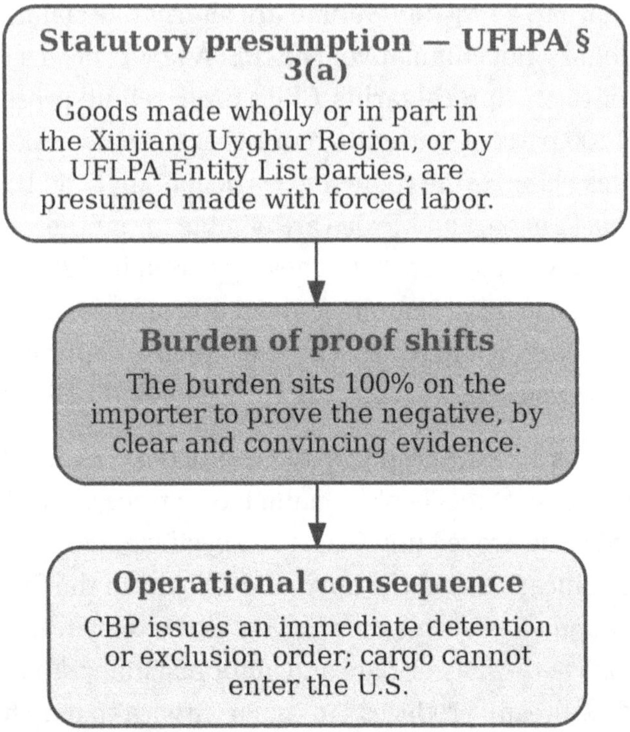


CBP enforces forced labor mandates through a unified enforcement structure, detaining, excluding, or seizing non-compliant merchandise across three distinct enforcement pathways:

1. UFLPA Direct Input & Potential Input Pathways: Covering shipments connected directly or through intermediate inputs to Xinjiang or UFLPA Entity List parties.
2. Withhold Release Orders (WROs) & Formal Findings: Issued under 19 U.S.C. § 1307 targeting specific manufacturers, locations, or commodities.
3. Section 302A of the North Korea Sanctions and Policy Enhancement Act of 2016 (Public Law 114-122), added by § 321(b) of the Countering America's Adversaries Through Sanctions Act (Public Law 115-44) and codified at 22 U.S.C. § 9241a: a rebuttable presumption against goods produced with North Korean labor anywhere in the world.

If a container is detained under the UFLPA, you are in a compressed environment, and the terminology matters, because two different processes get conflated constantly.

An applicability review argues your goods fall outside the statute's scope in the first place. They do not originate in Xinjiang, and no listed entity touched them. An exception request concedes the presumption attaches and seeks to rebut it, which under UFLPA § 3(b) requires you to demonstrate by clear and convincing evidence that the good was not mined, produced, or manufactured wholly or in part by forced labor, and to show you fully complied with the guidance and completely and substantively responded to all CBP inquiries.

These are different arguments with different burdens. Assembling an exception package when you needed an applicability review, or the reverse, wastes the only clock you have.

Submissions go through the CBP Forced Labor Portal, under CBP's Forced Labor Enforcement Operational Guidance for Importers issued in June 2026, which supersedes the 2022 guidance and the document-by-email practice that preceded it.

On the 30 days: the response window stated in a detention notice is CBP operational practice, not a statutory deadline. The statutory backdrop is 19 U.S.C. § 1499(c) and 19 CFR § 151.16, under which merchandise not released within 30 days of presentation for examination is deemed excluded. Treat 30 days as the working assumption and ask for more in writing if the tracing genuinely requires it, but plan on the assumption that you will not get it, because gathering multi-tier factory records from foreign vendors inside a month is the thing that fails.

The Incoterm you buy on decides how exposed you are when this happens. Under EXW or an unverified FOB-origin purchase, physical risk and title pass to you at the foreign dock, but the forced-labor risk lands at the U.S. border, where you, as importer of record, must answer for it. If CBP detains the container, you have 30 days from the detention notice to present clear and convincing evidence tracing the goods through every stage of production back to the raw material, filed through the CBP forced-labor portal. A foreign EXW or FOB seller who will not share sensitive upstream supplier records, whether to protect trade secrets or because it cannot document them, leaves you unable to rebut the presumption. The result is a total loss of a kind few other trade errors produce: you have paid for goods you cannot import, and you absorb the demurrage and the export or destruction costs on top.

> *Risk and impact. For goods in a high-priority forced-labor sector, contract for traceability before you contract for price. Build the tier-by-tier documentation obligation into the purchase order, make it a condition of payment, and verify it before the goods ship. Once the container is detained the 30-day clock is running, and a supplier's silence becomes your loss.*

On scale: CBP's public enforcement dashboard showed more than 18,000 shipments reviewed under the statute, valued at roughly $3.8 billion, as of the 16 January 2026 dashboard update; by mid-2026 the detained value was reported at close to $4 billion. Detention activity has in fact declined markedly since its January 2025 peak, so do not describe the trend as climbing. Re-pull the dashboard and state the figure with its as-of date, and do not mix it with the different cut published in DHS's annual UFLPA strategy.

On brand-name protection: in June 2023 the Forced Labor Enforcement Task Force (FLETF), the DHS-chaired interagency body that maintains the UFLPA Entity List, which CBP then enforces, added Ninestar Corporation, a major Chinese printer and imaging manufacturer, and several subsidiaries to that list.

Ninestar's goods were detained while it challenged the listing at the Court of International Trade. The court denied a preliminary injunction in February 2024; FLETF denied its delisting petition in June 2025; Ninestar has continued to seek removal. It remains on the list, confirmed in the Federal Register notice of 3 August 2026, which added 43 entities and brought the Entity List to 187, and the matter remains open. The lesson for an importer is that a recognizable name upstream is not protection, and that getting off the list is slow, expensive, and not assured.

**High-Priority Sectors and Multi-Tier Supply Chain Tracing**

FLETF and CBP have designated specific High-Priority Enforcement Sectors that receive aggressive automated targeting in ACE:

UFLPA High-Priority Enforcement Sector Matrix

The high-priority list has grown every year, and FLETF counts apparel and cotton as two separate sectors, not one: the 2022 strategy named apparel, cotton, tomatoes, and silica-based products, and their downstream goods (four sectors); aluminum, PVC and seafood were added on 9 July 2024 (seven); and steel, copper, lithium, caustic soda and red dates on 19 August 2025, bringing it to twelve. Treat it as a moving list, not a fixed set, and confirm the current sectors against the latest FLETF strategy update before you scope your program. (DHS's public UFLPA FAQ page has lagged the additions; rely on the FLETF strategy, not the FAQ.)

| Target Sector | Raw Material / Intermediate Input | Downstream Imported Goods |
|---|---|---|
| Cotton | Raw cotton fiber, yarn, thread | Textiles, home furnishings, cotton piece goods |
| Apparel | Unfinished fabric, cut-and-sew components | Garments, footwear, made-up textile articles |
| Tomatoes & Food Products | Fresh tomatoes, tomato paste, seeds, agricultural | Canned foods, sauces, processed foods |

| Target Sector | Raw Material / Intermediate Input | Downstream Imported Goods |
|---|---|---|
| | precursors | |
| Silica-based products & Electronics | Quartz, silicon metal, electronic substrates | Integrated circuits, circuit boards, consumer electronics |
| Aluminum | Bauxite, alumina, unwrought aluminum ingot, cast billets | Extrusions, auto components, beverage cans |
| PVC | Vinyl chloride monomer, PVC resin | Flooring, pipe, packaging, consumer goods |
| Seafood | Wild-caught and processed fish | Frozen and canned seafood |
| Steel | Iron ore, semi-finished steel | Structural steel, fasteners, components |
| Copper | Copper ore, cathode, wire rod | Wire, tube, electrical components |
| Lithium | Lithium ore, refined lithium compounds | Battery materials and cells |
| Caustic soda | Sodium hydroxide | Industrial chemical inputs |
| Red dates (jujube) | Dried and fresh jujube | Dried fruit and processed foods |

### Tracing to the Raw Material Stage

To establish that a shipment is exempt from UFLPA detention (an Applicability Review) or to rebut the statutory presumption (an Exception Review), CBP requires complete, chain-of-custody documentation tracing every component from the raw material origin through every intermediate manufacturing tier down to the finished product. It is not enough to show a bill of lading from a primary supplier in Vietnam or Malaysia. You must map all tiers:

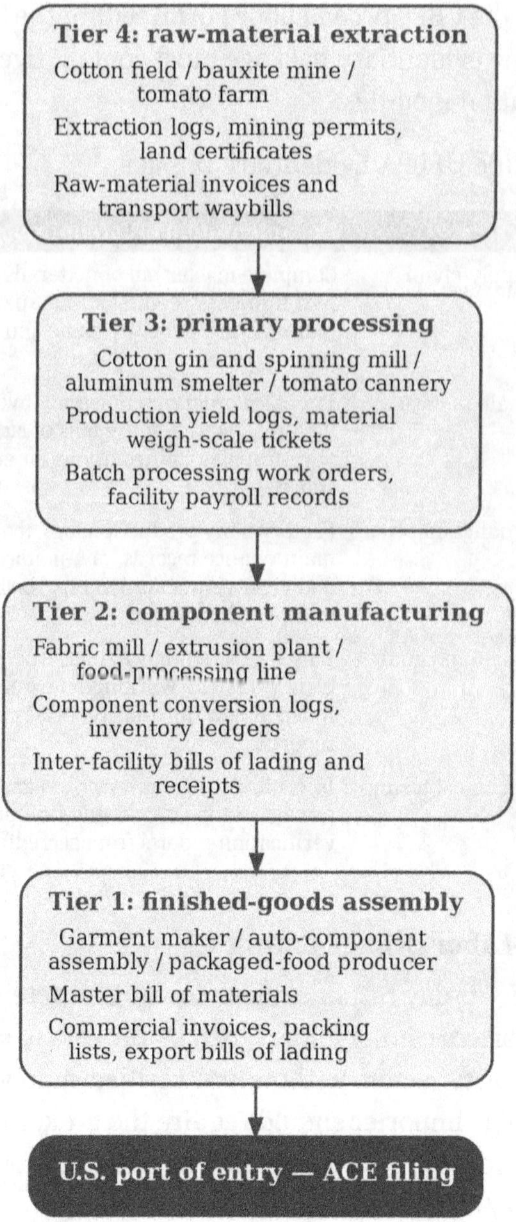


## 2. Constructing the "Audit-Proof" Forced Labor Evidentiary Package

When CBP detains a shipment under UFLPA or a WRO, the importer must submit a structured, fully translated evidentiary dossier via the CBP Forced Labor Portal within the 30-day window. The evidentiary package must contain five distinct documentation modules:

The 5-Module UFLPA Evidentiary Dossier

| Module | Documentation CBP requires |
|---|---|
| Module 1, Supply-chain map | Complete master bill of materials detailing every part number, weight, and the specific manufacturing facility name and address for each tier. |
| Module 2, Chain of custody | Purchase orders, commercial invoices, packing lists, master and house bills of lading, and bank wire-transfer confirmations for every inter-tier transfer. |
| Module 3, Production proof | Factory daily production logs, machine-maintenance records, raw-material weight tickets, and yield-reconciliation reports linking raw input to finished output. |
| Module 4, Labor and audit | Employee attendance timecards, payroll-ledger bank transfers, working-hour records, and independent third-party social-compliance audit reports. |
| Module 5, Technical testing | Isotopic testing analysis (for example, cotton or tomato isotope ratios) and isotopic provenance-verification reports from accredited laboratories. |

### 3. Forced-Labor Broker Gating

Because the 30-day response clock for UFLPA detentions is so short, importers cannot allow Customs Brokers to clear shipments in high-priority sectors without pre-verified supply chain packages. The importer should require the broker to run an automated forced-labor gate inside its entry platform (CargoWise/Descartes):

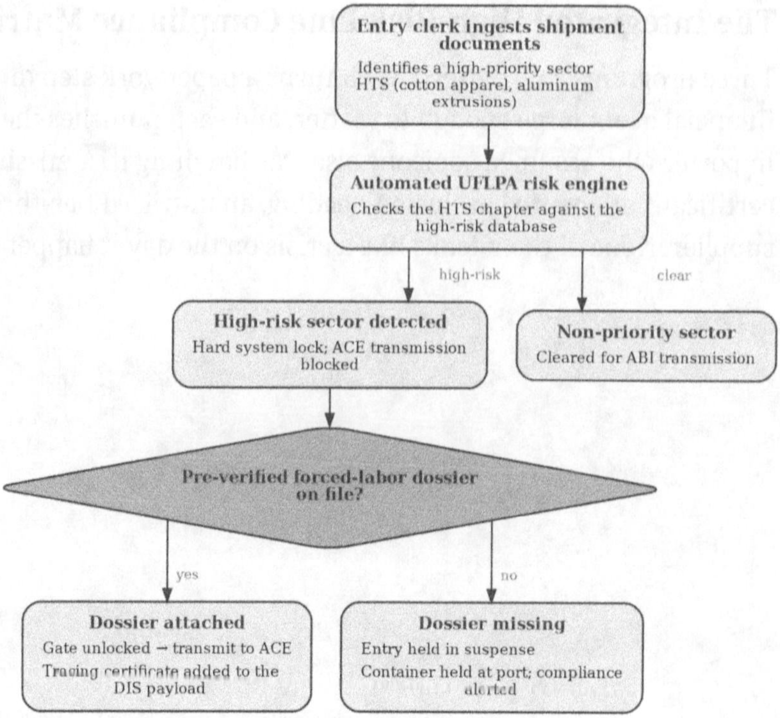


Under this gating protocol:

1. System-Enforced Hold: The broker's software automatically flags any entry containing HTS codes associated with any UFLPA high-priority sector, cotton, apparel, tomatoes, silica-based products, aluminum, PVC, seafood, steel, copper, lithium, caustic soda, and red dates.
2. Compliance release: The entry clerk is barred from transmitting the Entry Type 01 or 03 summary until the importer's supply chain compliance department issues a digital UFLPA Clearance Key.
3. Digital Certificate Injection: The clearance key confirms that the complete 5-module evidentiary package is archived inside the importer's compliance repository, ready for immediate electronic upload to the CBP Forced Labor Portal if a detention notice is served.

## The Integrated High-Risk Line Compliance Matrix

Three programs, one pattern: each turns a paperwork step into a financial event large enough to matter, and each punishes the importer who assumed someone else was handling it. A missing certificate, an expired exclusion heading, an untraced tier-three supplier. None of them looks like a crisis on the day it happens.

# Chapter 12: The CEE Navigation & Escalation Playbook

## Managing CEE Communications Beyond Informal Emails

When U.S. Customs and Border Protection (CBP) fully operationalized the ten national Centers of Excellence and Expertise (CEEs), the structural dynamics of customs enforcement shifted permanently.

Historically, an Importer of Record (IOR) built relationships with local CBP Import Specialists at their primary port of unlading (e.g., the Port of Long Beach or the Port of Newark). When a classification or valuation question arose, the local Customs Broker or importer's compliance manager picked up the telephone, called the local Import Specialist, and discussed the physical characteristics of the goods over a physical sample.

The CEE framework dismantled this localized, human-centric model. Today, trade oversight is divided strictly by industry sector across ten virtualized national centers, ranging from Automotive & Aerospace in Detroit to Electronics in Long Beach and Industrial & Manufacturing Materials in Buffalo.

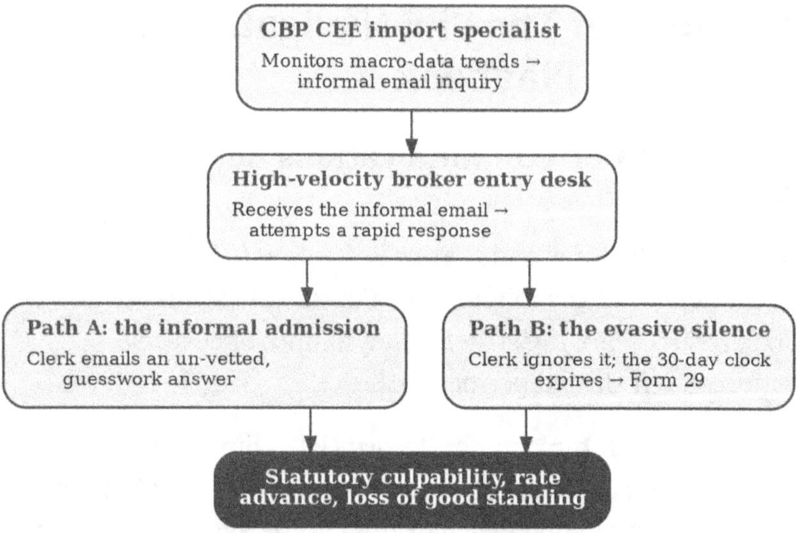


While CEEs were designed to drive nationwide tariff consistency, they created a real compliance vulnerability for importers: the informal CEE communication trap.

Because CEE teams operate through anonymized group email boxes (e.g., CEE-Electronics@cbp.dhs.gov) and national ACE messaging queues, entry clerks at brokerage firms treat CEE inquiries as casual correspondence. When a CEE Import Specialist sends an informal email asking, "Can you clarify the electrical wattage and function of part number X-200 on Entry #123?", the entry clerk often does not escalate the message to the importer's trade compliance director.

Instead, the clerk attempts to clear their processing queue by typing a rapid, un-vetted reply based on guesswork or a superficial web search.

Treat no communication with CBP as truly informal. An email sent by a broker's entry clerk to a CEE inbox is an official statement executed by your authorized agent. If the clerk writes, "This box is used to control power distribution," when the item is legally an automated data processing subassembly, that email is archived in CBP's records.

When CBP subsequently issues a formal CBP Form 28 (Request for Information) or CBP Form 29 (Notice of Action), the CEE can use the clerk's informal email as a party admission to help prove Negligence or Gross Negligence under 19 U.S.C. § 1592, which weakens any later claim to penalty mitigation.

## Informal Email Inquiries vs. Formal CBP Forms 28/29/4647

To manage CEE interactions, establish a communication taxonomy that sorts every incoming regulatory message and dictates how it is handled.

One clarification before the table, because it is widely misunderstood and getting it wrong will cost you. Most of the response windows in customs practice are administrative, not regulatory. The thirty days on a Form 28 is printed on the form; nothing in 19 CFR imposes it. The twenty days associated with a Form 29 is, in the text of the regulation, a limit on how long CBP will withhold liquidation, not a grant of a twenty-day right to respond. This distinction matters in both directions. It means the windows are shorter and softer than a statute would be, and CBP is not obliged to honor them. It also means extensions are available for cause far more readily than people assume, because there is no statute to extend against. Ask.

### CBP Regulatory Communication Taxonomy

| Communication type | Issuance source | Practical response window | Compliance action |
|---|---|---|---|
| Level 1, Informal CEE outreach | Email or ACE messaging queue from a CEE import specialist | No window. Courtesy response in 3–5 business days | Intercept; freeze the broker's reply; draft a formal CEE briefing memo |
| Level 2. CBP Form 28, | CBP's post- | 30 days as printed | Execute the 5-step |

| Communication type | Issuance source | Practical response window | Compliance action |
|---|---|---|---|
| Request for Information | release information request; closest regulatory anchor is 19 CFR § 151.11 (samples and additional examination packages) | on the form. No regulation generally prescribes the CF 28 or its response period; § 151.11 requires prompt compliance and authorizes a bond demand for return of the merchandise if you do not comply | Form 28 audit; submit the evidence package through DIS |
| Level 3. CBP Form 29, Notice of Action | Formal notice of rate advance or reclassification, 19 CFR § 152.2 | 20 days, customary. § 152.2 caps how long CBP will withhold liquidation at 20 days from mailing, absent compelling reasons, and extensions are commonly granted for cause | Executive and legal escalation; rebuttal evidence on a proposed notice; protest on a taken notice |
| Level 4. CBP Form 4647, Notice to Mark and/or Redeliver | Notice under 19 CFR § 134.51 | 30 days from the date of the notice. This one is regulatory, at 19 CFR § 134.54(a), extendable by the Center director for good cause | Mark under CBP supervision or redeliver to CBP custody; execute a physical marking audit |

## Three Notes on the Table

On Form 29, know which box is checked. A proposed notice of action tells you CBP intends to act and invites rebuttal. A taken notice means the decision is made and the entry will liquidate at the higher rate. Once it is taken, your only remedy is a protest under 19 U.S.C. § 1514, filed within 180 days of liquidation. Confusing the two costs you the rebuttal window and pushes a solvable problem into the protest track. Note also that § 152.2 only obliges CBP to issue the notice where the estimated aggregate duty increase exceeds fifteen dollars, so small adjustments arrive without warning.

On Form 4647, the two clocks run in opposite directions. You have thirty days from the notice to mark or redeliver, under § 134.54(a). CBP has its own separate window to issue the demand in the first place: no later than thirty days after release, or thirty days after the end of the conditional release period, whichever is later, under the bond terms at 19 CFR § 113.62(d). If a redelivery demand arrives outside that window, that is a defense, and it is one importers routinely fail to raise. Conditional release periods vary. Textiles run 180 days.

Miss the thirty days and the consequence is not a fine but liquidated damages against your bond equal to the entered value of the goods not marked or redelivered (§ 134.54(a)), or, for general redelivery failures, the value of the merchandise, trebled if the goods are restricted, prohibited, or alcoholic beverages (§ 141.113(i); § 113.62(n)(1)). Relief by petition is available, but under § 134.54(c) it is contingent on depositing the marking duty under 19 U.S.C. § 1304(i) and satisfying the FP&F officer that you acted in good faith and tried by all reasonable means to redeliver. The paper trail your oversight program generates is exactly what that showing requires.

All four now arrive electronically. CBP's modernized ACE CBP Forms application, deployed April 2022, lets trade users view, respond to, and manage electronic Forms 28, 29, and 4647 in the portal. Delivery depends on whether your Trade Account Owner has selected "Portal" as the communication mode. If nobody at your company has, these notices route to your broker and to paper mail, which is how thirty-day clocks quietly expire. Check who your Trade Account Owner is and what mode is selected, and note the mode is two-sided: both your account and the broker's sub-account must be in Portal mode for the electronic courtesy copy to flow. Do it this week. Then add the control most importers miss: since 2 January 2026 you can add 4811 notify parties directly on the Notify Parties tab of your ACE Portal importer sub-account (CSMS #67190197). That tab is a second route, not a replacement. CBP's updated procedures (CSMS #67648307) keep both methods open: email the CBP Form 4811 to your assigned Center, or use the Add Notify Party feature in the portal. Either way the notify party needs a CBP Form 5106 on record. Between the two, these are the single cheapest controls in this book.

### Level 1: Informal CEE Outreach

An informal email from a CEE Import Specialist is an early-warning signal. It indicates that CBP's national targeting algorithms have flagged an anomaly in your ACE ES-002/ES-003 line-item data, but the agency has not yet opened a formal Section 1592 investigation.

### The Broker Communications Intercept Rule

The Service Level Agreement (SLA) should contractually bar the broker from replying directly to any informal CEE inquiry. The broker's sole operational obligation is to forward the email to compliance@importer.com within the twenty-four-hour contractual standard, attaching the full ACE entry summary packet; the four-hour clock is the internal routing target once it reaches your inbox, not a duty imposed on the broker.

### The Formal CEE Response Narrative

All informal email inquiries should be answered by the importer's internal trade compliance team (or designated trade counsel). The response should be structured as a formal PDF memorandum attached to the email, never plain text typed in the email body.

```
=========================================================
FORMAL COMPLIANCE RESPONSE MEMORANDUM
TO: U.S. Customs and Border Protection | Center of
   Excellence and Expertise
FROM: Corporate Trade Compliance Department | Importer of
   Record #: XX-XXXXXXX
```

```
DATE: July 22, 2026
SUBJECT: Clarification Request - ACE Entry Summary #
   XXX-XXXXXXX-X | Line Item 001
=========================================================

1. EXECUTIVE STATEMENT
This memorandum provides the official, vetted response of
Importer of Record ("Company") regarding CEE inquiry
dated July 20, 2026, concerning Part # ELEC-9902.

2. TECHNICAL PRODUCT FUNCTION & SPECIFICATIONS
Part # ELEC-9902 is a monolithic integrated circuit
engineered exclusively for signal processing within
medical imaging hardware... [Attach Engineering
Schematics]

3. TARIFF CLASSIFICATION ANALYSIS & LEGAL JUSTIFICATION
Pursuant to General Rules of Interpretation (GRI) 1 and
6, the subject merchandise is correctly classified under
HTSUS 8542.31.0000 (Duty Free)... [Cite CROSS Rulings]

4. CERTIFICATION OF AUTHORIZED REPRESENTATIVE
I certify that I hold executive authority to represent
Importer of Record in customs matters and that the
technical statements contained herein are true and
correct.

Signature: ______________________________
Title: Director of Global Trade Compliance
```

By converting informal email inquiries into formal legal memorandums, you signal to the CEE that your enterprise exercises rigorous reasonable care, which makes the Import Specialist less likely to escalate the inquiry into a formal CBP Form 28 or penalty proceeding.

### Level 2: CBP Form 28 (Request for Information) Execution

When CBP issues a formal CBP Form 28, the operational clock begins. The form states thirty days from the date of issuance; as set out above, that window is administrative rather than regulatory, which is why extensions for cause are more available than most importers assume, and why you should never let it run out untended.

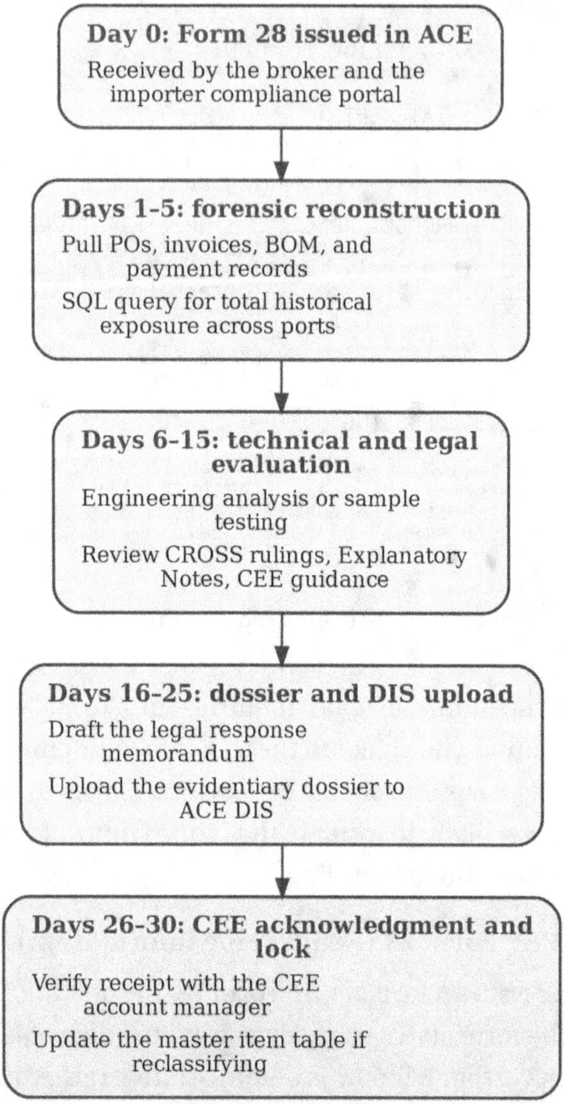


## Level 3: CBP Form 29 (Notice of Action) Escalation

A CBP Form 29 is a formal administrative decision by CBP to reclassify your merchandise, increase entered values, or assess additional duties (Rate Advance). Form 29s are issued in two distinct operational states:

1. Proposed Notice of Action: CBP notifies the importer that it intends to reclassify the goods or assess additional duties. By CBP practice, the importer typically has about 20 calendar days from the date of the notice to submit rebuttal evidence before the action becomes final; this is the customary response window CBP states on the notice, not a fixed statutory deadline, and extensions are commonly granted for cause.
2. Taken Notice of Action: CBP has already executed the reclassification or rate advance on the entry. The decision is finalized, and the entry will liquidate at the higher duty rate unless formally contested.

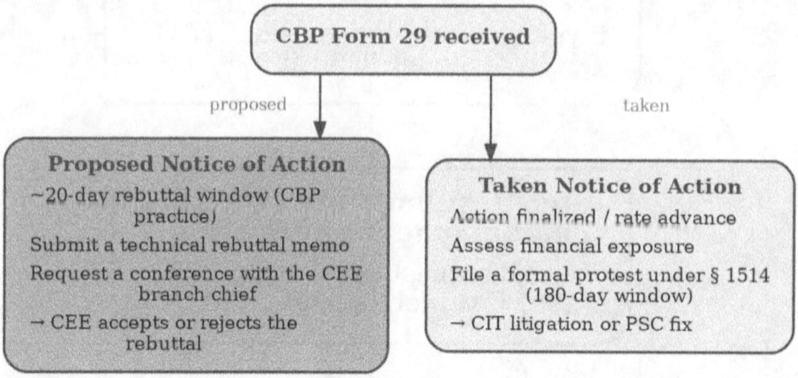


When a Taken Notice of Action is issued, the sole legal remedy to challenge the decision is filing a formal Protest under 19 U.S.C. § 1514 within 180 calendar days of entry liquidation.

## Establishing Direct CEE Account Manager Relationships

The primary mistake importers make when navigating the CEE framework is remaining passive, waiting for the CEE to contact them through generic email boxes.

Under CEE operating guidelines, high-volume importers who demonstrate an active compliance structure can request the assignment of a dedicated CEE Account Manager. A CEE Account

Manager serves as your central point of contact within the sector, bypassing anonymized general queues and allowing pre-emptive resolution of trade disputes.

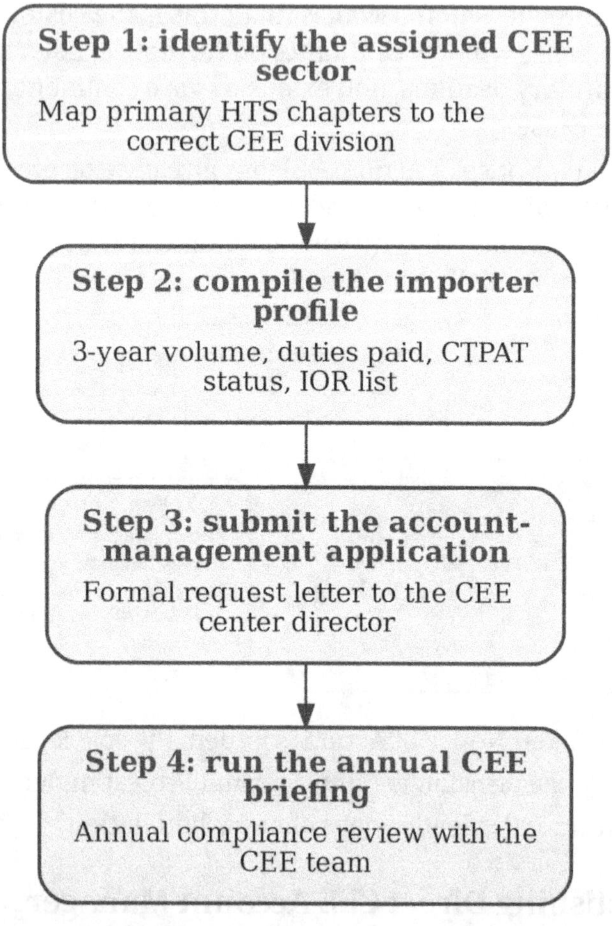


### CEE Engagement, Step by Step

#### 1. Sector Identification

Before you can engage a Center, you need to know which one is yours. Two corrections to the common understanding, both of which trip people up:

You are assigned to one Center, not routed entry by entry. Under 19 CFR § 101.10(b), CBP assigns each importer to an industry category administered by a specific Center, based on the tariff classification in the HTSUS of the predominant number of goods it imports. A company importing across four chapters does not deal with four Centers. It deals with one, and that one handles everything filed under its IOR number, including the commodities that fall outside its sector. CBP can override the default where an importer's business practices, the intended use of the goods, or their relative value warrant it.

There is a second subtlety, and it is where most published summaries overreach. Assignment itself turns on the tariff classification in the HTSUS of the predominant number of goods you import (§ 101.10(b)), with no digit level specified. The four-digit heading level appears in § 101.10(c), in the import data CBP wants when you appeal an assignment, which is a good indication of the granularity CBP thinks in, but it is not the assignment rule. Chapter 85 splits across three Centers; Chapter 84 splits between Machinery and Electronics; Chapter 90 splits between Machinery and Pharmaceuticals, Health & Chemicals. A table organized by chapter is approximate at best.

The current assignments, from 19 CFR § 101.10 and CBP's implementing rule, finalized at 88 FR 69026 (5 October 2023, effective 6 November 2023; the 2016 interim rule was 81 FR 92978):

| CEE sector | Managing city | Principal HTSUS headings |
|---|---|---|
| Agriculture & Prepared Products | Miami, FL | Chapters 1–24 |
| Apparel, Footwear & Textiles | San Francisco, CA | 4015, 4203, 4303–4304, 5001–5007, 5101–5113, 5201–5212, 5301–5303, 5305–5311, 5401–5408, 5501–5516, 5601–5609, 5701–5705, 5801–5811, 5901–5911, 6001–6006, 6101–6117, 6201–6217, 6301–6310, 6401–6406, 6501–6502, 6504–6507 |
| Automotive & Aerospace | Detroit, MI | 4011–4013, 8406–8412, 8511– |

| CEE sector | Managing city | Principal HTSUS headings |
|---|---|---|
| | | 8512, 8601–8609, 8701–8711, 8713–8714, 8716, 8801–8805, 8901–8908 |
| Base Metals | Chicago, IL | 7201–7308, 7312–7318, 7320, 7322, 7324–7413, 7415, 7419–7614, 7616–8113, 8307–8311 |
| Consumer Products & Mass Merchandising | Atlanta, GA | 3303–3307, 3401, 3406, 3605, 3924, 3926, 4201–4202, 4205–4206, 4414, 4419–4421, 4602, 4803, 4817–4818, 4820, 4901–4911, 6601–6603, 6701–6704, 6911–6913, 7113–7118, 7319, 7321, 7323, 7418, 7615, 8210–8215, 8301, 8303–8306, 8469–8470, 8508–8510, 8513, 8516, 8539, 8712, 8715, 9001–9006, 9013, 9101–9114, 9201–9202, 9205–9209, 9401, 9403–9405, 9503–9508, 9601–9619, 9701–9706 |
| Electronics | Long Beach, CA | 3818, 8471, 8473, 8501–8504, 8517–8538, 8540–8548 |
| Industrial & Manufacturing Materials | Buffalo, NY | 2501–2530, 3901–3923, 3925, 4001–4010, 4016–4115, 4301–4302, 4401–4413, 4415–4418, 4501–4601, 4701–4802, 4804–4814, 4816, 4819, 4821–4823, 6801–6910, 6914–7014, 7015–7112, 7309–7311, 9406 |
| Machinery | Laredo, TX | 8201–8209, 8302, 8401–8405, 8413–8468, 8472, 8474–8484, 8486–8487, 8505–8507, 8514–8515, 9007–9008, 9010–9012, 9014–9017, 9020, 9023–9033, 9301–9307 |
| Petroleum, Natural Gas & Minerals | Houston, TX | 2601–2621, 2701–2708, 2709–2716, 3826 |
| Pharmaceuticals, Health & Chemicals | New York, NY | 2801–2935, 2936–2942, 3001–3006, 3101–3302, 3402–3405, 3407–3604, 3606–3817, 3819–3825, 4014, 9018–9019, 9021–9022, 9402 |

Two things to do with this table. First, find your own Center and confirm it, not by reading down the list, but by asking CBP or checking your ACE portal account, since your assignment reflects your predominant imports and may not be what the table suggests. Second, note where your secondary commodities land. When your Machinery-assigned account files an electronics line, the classification expertise sitting behind that review is not necessarily in your Center, and that is worth knowing before you argue a position.

CBP revises these assignments as it reorganizes. Confirm against the current § 101.10 text and the operative Federal Register notice before relying on any specific heading.

## 2. Submitting the Account Management Application

Draft a formal engagement letter addressed to the CEE Center Director. The application should prove that your enterprise represents significant commercial volume and maintains an active compliance infrastructure.

```
==============================================================
FORMAL APPLICATION FOR CEE ACCOUNT MANAGEMENT ASSIGNMENT
TO: Center Director | Center of Excellence and Expertise
   - Electronics
LOCATION: 301 E. Ocean Blvd, Suite 1400, Long Beach, CA
   90802
DATE: July 22, 2026
==============================================================

1. APPLICANT IDENTIFICATION
Importer of Record Name: Global Tech Industries LLC
Primary IOR Number: 12-3456789-00 | Secondary IORs:
   98-7654321-00
CTPAT Tier Status: Tier 2 Validated Partner (Account #
   99021)

2. COMMERCIAL IMPORT VOLUME & DUTY CONTRIBUTION
Annual Entered Value (FY2025): $145,000,000.00
Annual Total Duties, Taxes, & Fees Paid to CBP:
   $18,200,000.00
Primary Ports of Unlading: Port of Long Beach (2704),
   Port of Newark (1001)

3. TRADE COMPLIANCE INFRASTRUCTURE
Company maintains an internal Trade Compliance Department
headed by a Licensed Customs Broker, deploys real-time
system-to-system master data synchronization, and
executes weekly SQL forensic data mining across raw ACE
ES-002/ES-003 extracts.
```

```
4. FORMAL REQUEST
We formally request the assignment of a dedicated CEE
Account Manager to serve as our primary operational
liaison for classification, valuation, and partnership
matters, ensuring national tariff consistency across all
entry ports.

Submitted by: ______________________________
Vice President, Global Supply Chain & Legal
```

Once assigned, host an Annual CEE Briefing Conference (remote or in-person). Present your upcoming product pipeline, explain your internal master data gating rules, and review open PSC filings.

Establishing this direct executive relationship raises the odds that when an entry clerk makes a data-entry mistake, the CEE Account Manager calls your compliance director before issuing an adverse Form 29 Rate Advance.

# PART V: INSTITUTIONALIZING THE BROKER MANAGEMENT SYSTEM (BMS)

# Chapter 13: Conducting the Annual Broker Audit

## The On-Site / Remote Broker Audit: 19 CFR § 111.28 and Recordkeeping

In the post-2026 customs enforcement landscape, the annual audit of your Customs Broker is not a casual vendor review meeting over coffee. It is a formal, forensic investigation into your agent's operational execution, internal controls, and statutory compliance. Most Importers of Record (IOR) fall into the Vendor Soft-Audit Trap. They send their broker a generic 10-question questionnaire asking: "Do you exercise Reasonable Care? Do you have licensed Customs Brokers on staff? Are your servers secure?" The broker's corporate compliance officer checks "Yes" to every box, attaches a marketing brochure, and returns the form. The importer files the PDF in a folder and tells their Board of Directors that they maintain "broker oversight." When CBP's Trade Regulatory Audit directorate initiates a Focused Assessment, a Quick Response Audit, or a Risk Analysis and Survey Assessment under 19 U.S.C. § 1509, subsection (b) of which entitles you to an entry conference, an estimate of the audit's duration, a closing conference, and a written report within 90 days of that conference, that 10-question questionnaire is utterly worthless. (Importer Self-Assessment, the old standalone program, has been folded into CTPAT Trade Compliance and no longer exists.) CBP auditors will ask a single devastating question:

- "Show us the raw data, workstation logs, classification workpapers, and physical evidence where you audited your broker's exercise of Responsible Supervision and Control under 19 CFR § 111.28."

If you cannot produce independent audit workpapers, line-item discrepancy logs, and proof of physical or remote workstation inspections, CBP treats your broker relationship as un-monitored, exposing your firm to the un-mitigated 50% penalty floors the 2026 executive order directs CBP to adopt.

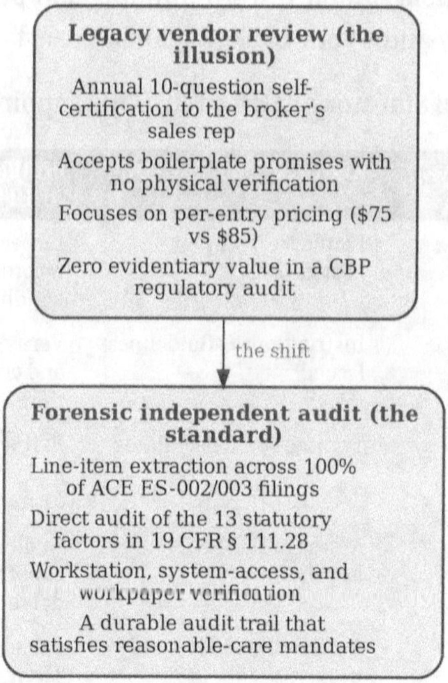


## Deconstructing 19 CFR § 111.28: The Regulatory Audit Standard

To conduct a disinterested broker audit, your audit protocol must be anchored directly in 19 CFR § 111.28: the federal regulation governing Responsible Supervision and Control. When CBP evaluates whether a Customs Broker has maintained responsible supervision over its employees and entry operations, 19 CFR § 111.28(a) sets out 13 non-exclusive regulatory factors CBP may consider in its discretion (the list is illustrative, not exhaustive). The table below maps the eight of the thirteen most susceptible to outside verification: the ones a client can actually test from ACE data and the broker's own records. The remaining five, including factor (13), internal communications within the brokerage (arguably the most telling one for a client auditing escalation behavior), turn on records you cannot readily inspect from outside; note that your table covers eight of the thirteen, and ask the broker to attest to the rest rather than treating an eight-factor pass as the whole standard. Your annual audit protocol should systematically audit your broker against these factors:

19 CFR § 111.28 Statutory AUDIT FACTOR Mapping

| CFR FACTOR | REGULATORY FACTOR | FORENSIC IMPORTER AUDIT |
|---|---|---|
| 111.28(a)(1) | Employee Training Provided | Inspect the actual training records for the clerks handling your account. |
| 111.28(a)(2) | Instructions & Guidelines Issued | Verify the presence of SOPs and client-profile rules in the broker's system. |
| 111.28(a)(4) | Transaction Reject Rates | Extract the ACE edit-reject and warning-override history. |
| 111.28(a)(5) | Access to HTSUS & Regulations | Audit software subscriptions and ruling-database integration. |
| 111.28(a)(6) | Availability of Licensed Brokers | Calculate the ratio of Licensed Customs Brokers (LCBs) to entry volume as an internal benchmark. Section 111.28(a)(6) requires only "a sufficient number of individually licensed brokers" and CBP has never fixed a numeric ratio, so treat any threshold you set as your own risk tolerance, not a regulatory mandate a broker has failed. |
| 111.28(a)(8) | Internal Audit Frequency | Review the broker's internal-control audit logs for your account. |
| 111.28(a)(11) | Timeliness of Entry & Duty Payment | Audit ACH payment timing, entry dates, and late-filing history. |
| 111.28(a)(12) | Responsiveness to CBP Notices | Measure timestamp velocity on Form 28/29/4647 escalations. |

### The Audit, Step by Step

The annual broker audit is executed across four distinct operational phases over a 30-day window.

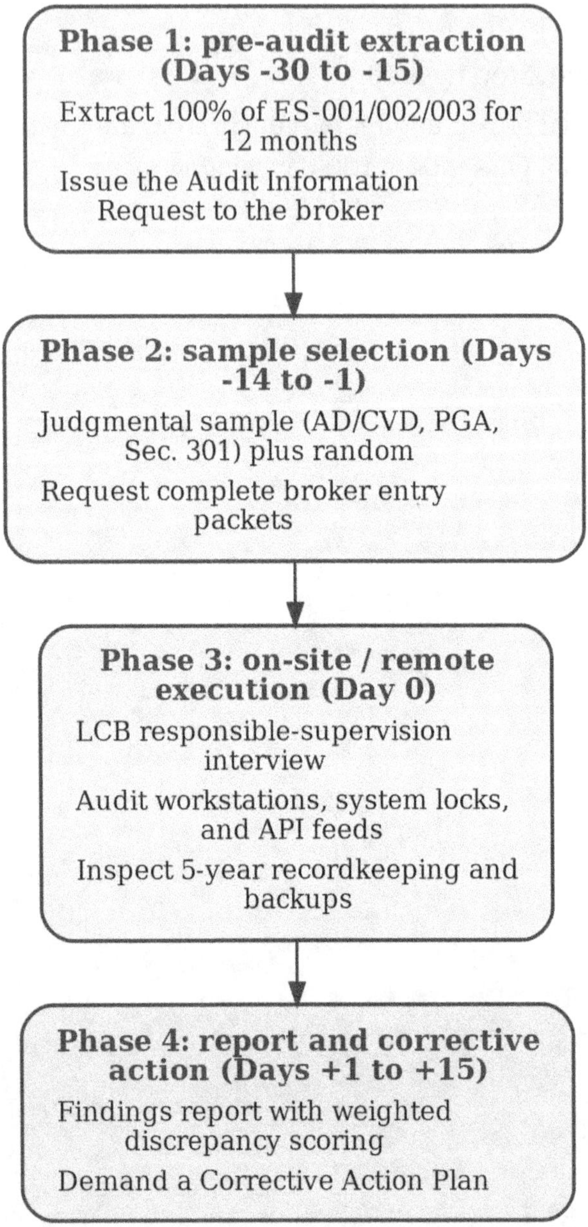


**Phase 1: The Pre-Audit Information Request (AIR)**

Thirty days prior to the audit date, the importer serves the broker's corporate compliance officer with a formal Audit Information Request (AIR). One point to be honest with yourself about before you send it: § 111.28 imposes these duties on the broker as obligations owed to *CBP*, not to you. No regulation entitles you to a broker's internal audit reports, employee training files, or system logs. You get them only if your services agreement says so, which means your SLA (Tool B) needs an explicit audit-rights and records-access clause, and the AIR should be framed as a request under that clause ("Agent shall provide, under § _ of the SLA..."), not as "the broker must provide" as though a regulation compelled it. Add the clause to the SLA; then the broker shall provide documentary proof for the following seven operational domains:

1. Organizational Chart & License Roster: Complete org chart of the entry processing unit handling the importer's account, detailing the full names, CBP-issued individual broker license numbers, physical office locations, and the name of the licensed individual broker qualifying the permit under which your entries are filed, for all Licensed Customs Brokers (LCBs) exercising supervision over non-licensed entry clerks. (Do not ask for Social Security numbers. No broker will or should provide them, and receiving them creates a data-protection liability with no compliance benefit. The license number is the identifier that lets you verify the license.)
2. National Permit & Employee Reporting Proof: Copies of the broker's active National Permit and written verification of compliance with 19 CFR § 111.28(b) employee reporting submissions to CBP via the ACE Portal.
3. Written Standard Operating Procedures (SOPs): Current, dated copies of internal operating manuals, classification decision trees, and software user guides provided to entry clerks handling the importer's commodities.
4. Internal Quality Control Audit Logs: Copies of all internal audit reports executed by the broker's LCBs under 19 CFR § 111.28(a)(8) covering the importer's entry summaries during the prior 12 months.

5. Training & Continuing Education Records: Proof that entry clerks assigned to the account have completed mandatory training on recent regulatory updates, including CEE trade notices, Section 301 changes, and UFLPA detention protocols.
6. ACE Edit Rejection & Error Logs: System-generated logs showing all ABI transmission edits, rejects, and census warnings generated during entry summary transmissions for the importer's account.
7. Record Retention Infrastructure Proof: Disaster recovery plans, SOC 2 Type II compliance certificates, and digital architecture diagrams detailing how transaction records are archived for the mandatory 5-year period under 19 CFR Part 163.

**Phase 2: Transactional Forensic Sample Selection**

Simultaneously, the importer's compliance team extracts 100% of the raw ACE ES-002/ES-003 line-item records filed by the broker over the preceding 12 months. From this master dataset, the auditor constructs a two-tier audit sample:

Forensic Transaction Sample Selection

| SAMPLE TIER | SAMPLE SIZE | SELECTION CRITERIA & TARGET HIGH-RISK LINES |
|---|---|---|
| Tier 1: Judgmental Sample (High-Risk Lines) | 30 to 50 specific entry summaries | All Entry Type 03 (AD/CVD) lines; lines applying Section 301 exclusions; lines flagged for PGA agency clearance; lines with entered value over $250,000; lines using a generic fallback HTS code. |
| Tier 2: Statistical Sample (Routine Lines) | 50 to 100 random entry summaries | Stratified random sample generated using NEWID() queries across standard consumption entries to evaluate baseline error rates. |

The importer demands that the broker provide the complete Internal Broker File for every sampled entry summary. The internal broker file must contain:

- The original commercial invoice, packing list, and bill of lading received from the forwarder/vendor. The exact XML/EDI transmission payload generated by the entry clerk. The ACE Entry Summary Acceptance Notice (CBP Form 7501). All internal email threads, chat logs, and clerk notes associated with line-item classification, valuation, or PGA decisions.

**Phase 3: On-Site / Remote Operational Audit Execution**

On the audit day, the importer's audit team interviews the designated Licensed Customs Broker qualifying the national permit and conducts a forensic inspection of entry clerk workstations.

Workstation Forensic Audit Checklist

| AUDIT DOMAIN | WORKSTATION FORENSIC VERIFICATION MANDATE |
|---|---|
| 1. LCB supervision ratio | Check the ratio of non-licensed entry clerks to Licensed Customs Brokers against the 10:1 benchmark, and verify that an LCB reviews high-risk entries before ABI transmission. The 10:1 figure is this book's benchmark, not a CBP rule, § 111.28(a)(6) requires only "a sufficient number" of licensed brokers and fixes no numeric ratio, so treat it as your own risk tolerance, not a standard the broker has failed. |
| 2. Master-data profile hard-lock | Have the broker's own Licensed Customs Broker attempt, on a test record in the broker's training/test ABI environment against your account, to modify a locked 10-digit HTS or PGA indicator, and produce the resulting system log confirming the "No-Default" restriction blocked it. Do this on a test environment, never a live production filing, and never on a workstation displaying other clients' entry data, which 19 CFR § 111.24 makes confidential. Your team observes; your people do not touch a production filing workstation. |
| 3. Tariff & regulation access | Confirm entry clerks have real-time digital access to the current HTSUS, 19 CFR, Explanatory Notes, and the CBP rulings |

| AUDIT DOMAIN | WORKSTATION FORENSIC VERIFICATION MANDATE |
|---|---|
| | database directly from their entry screen. |
| 4. Recordkeeping & archival stress test | Request retrieval of an entry-summary packet from years prior; measure retrieval speed and verify the completeness of archived correspondence. |
| 5. CBP Form 28/29 log audit | Inspect the broker's master ACE Form 28/ 29 tracking log and verify that zero pending inquiries are unaddressed or hidden from the importer. |

## Scoring Broker Performance: Designing the Quarterly "Broker Scorecard"

An annual audit provides a deep structural review, but managing a Customs Broker on a daily operational level requires an ongoing, metrics-driven governance framework. High-performing importers deploy a Quarterly Broker Scorecard. The quarterly scorecard aggregates data from weekly ACE ES-002/ES-003 extractions, accounts payable duty reconciliations, and compliance escalation logs into a mathematically weighted performance score. If a broker drops below pre-defined performance thresholds, financial SLA offsets trigger automatically, and the broker enters a defined cure process.

Quarterly Broker Scorecard: Weighting

| DOMAIN METRIC CATEGORY | SCORE WEIGHT (%) | TARGET COMPLIANCE PERFORMANCE |
|---|---|---|
| 1. Classification & Data Accuracy | 35% | ≥ 99.5% match against the master HTS table |
| 2. High-Risk Operational Control | 25% | 100% compliance on AD/CVD, PGA, and UFLPA gating |
| 3. Filing Velocity & Timeliness | 20% | 100% filed within 5 days of release |
| 4. Regulatory Responsiveness | 10% | 100% of CBP notices escalated within 24 hours |

| DOMAIN METRIC CATEGORY | SCORE WEIGHT (%) | TARGET COMPLIANCE PERFORMANCE |
|---|---|---|
| 5. System Integration & Billing | 10% | 100% electronic invoice/data accuracy |

## The Weighted Scoring Method

The Broker Scorecard calculates a final Composite Performance Score (S_Comp), from 0.0 to 100.0 points, as the weighted sum of five category scores (C1 through C5):

```
S_Comp = (C1 x 0.35) + (C2 x 0.25) + (C3 x 0.20) + (C4 x
    0.10) + (C5 x 0.10)

C1  Classification & Data Accuracy (35%)
    C1 = ( 1 - (E_HTS + E_Val + E_MID + E_Qty) / T_Lines )
        x 100
      E_HTS = lines with unauthorized HTS modifications
      E_Val = lines with valuation slippage > 1%
      E_MID = lines with transposed or generic MIDs
      E_Qty = lines with unit-of-measure conversion errors
      T_Lines = total lines transmitted in ACE during the
          quarter

C2  High-Risk Operational Control (25%)
    C2 = ( 1 - (E_ADCVD + E_PGA + E_301 + E_UFLPA) /
        T_HighRiskLines ) x 100
      Note: a missed AD/CVD Non-Reimbursement Statement
          or an unauthorized PGA disclaimer is a
      high-risk failure. A first, isolated miss caps C2
          at 50 for the quarter and triggers a written
      corrective-action notice and a 30-day cure. A repeat
          within four quarters, or an uncured miss,
      drops C2 to zero. Reserve the zero for a pattern,
          not a single slip.

C3  Filing Velocity & Timeliness (20%)
    C3 = ( N_OnTimeSummaries / T_Summaries ) x 100
      N_OnTimeSummaries = entry summaries transmitted and
          duty-scheduled
                                within 5 business days of cargo
                                    release

C4  Regulatory Responsiveness (10%)
    C4 = ( N_CompliantNotices / T_NoticesReceived ) x 100
      N_CompliantNotices = CBP Forms 28/29/4647 forwarded
          to importer
                                 within 24 hours of receipt

C5  System Integration & Billing Health (10%)
    C5 = ( 1 - (E_BillingErrors + E_APIFailures) /
        T_Invoices ) x 100
```

### Scorecard Performance Tiers and Actions

Scorecard Performance Tier Action Matrix

| COMPOSITE SCORE | PERFORMANCE TIER | CONTRACTUAL & OPERATIONAL ACTION |
|---|---|---|
| 95.0 – 100.0 | Tier 1: Premier Compliance | Account in full compliance. Standard volume. Preferred status for new lane expansions. |
| 90.0 – 94.9 | Tier 2: Acceptable Risk | Minor operational deficiencies. Broker issues Notice of Discrepancy. Monthly monitoring required. |
| 80.0 – 89.9 | Tier 3: Conditional Warning | Severe performance deterioration. 25% SLA fee credit applied to quarterly invoices. Corrective Action Plan (CAP) mandated within 10 business days. |
| Below 80.0 | Tier 4: Unacceptable Breach | Material contract breach. 50% SLA fee credit and immediate freeze on new entry volume. Where the breach is a first, isolated high-risk miss, run the 30-day cure before offboarding. Reserve offboarding for an uncured or repeated breach, then initiate it with the RFP process. |

## Broker Vetting and the RFP: Rebuilding the Selection Process

The ultimate root cause of broken broker oversight is the traditional corporate procurement Request for Proposal (RFP) process. When corporate procurement departments run a Customs Broker RFP, they treat brokerage services like a raw commodity, such as cardboard boxes or office supplies. They send out a spreadsheet asking three basic questions:

1. What is your clearance fee per entry? ($50 vs $75 vs $100)
2. What is your ISF filing fee? ($25 vs $35)
3. What is your continuous bond markup?

Logistics providers eager to win freight volume engage in a Race-to-the-Bottom Pricing War. They quote $45 per entry summary. At $45 per entry summary, the broker cannot afford to assign experienced Licensed Customs Brokers to your account. They cannot afford to build direct API data integrations, and they cannot afford to give entry clerks the minutes a complex entry actually needs. To make a profit at $45, they must deploy high-velocity entry processing factories, outsource data entry offshore, default to generic catch-all HTS codes, and rely on automated PGA disclaimers.

To break this cycle, importers must strip procurement of sole decision-making authority and use a technical-compliance RFP.

### The Technical Compliance RFP Questionnaire

Your broker RFP questionnaire must force bidding brokers to disclose their operational reality across 10 technical domains:

Technical Compliance RFP Evaluation Domains

| TECHNICAL EVALUATION DOMAIN | MANDATORY BIDDER DISCLOSURE |
|---|---|
| 1. LCB-to-clerk operational ratio | Disclose the exact ratio of Licensed Customs Brokers to entry clerks in the specific branch that would handle the account. |
| 2. API & ERP integration capability | Provide technical architecture diagrams for REST integration into CargoWise eAdapter or Descartes. |
| 3. "No-Default" software gating locks | Certify willingness to activate hard system locks on manual HTS overrides and default PGA disclaimers. |
| 4. 19 CFR § 111.39 reporting policy | Disclose the written internal policy governing error notifications and reporting-escalation procedures. |
| 5. High-risk sector experience (AD/CVD & UFLPA) | Provide case studies proving experience with AD/CVD handling and UFLPA raw-material supply-chain tracing. |
| 6. POA addendum acceptance | Formally accept the importer's overriding POA Addendum and its carve-outs for gross negligence. |

### The Technical Interview & Live System Demonstration

Never award a brokerage contract based on written RFP responses alone. Bidding brokers must undergo a rigorous, two-hour Live Technical Demonstration before an evaluation committee composed of your Trade Compliance Director, Customs Auditor, and IT Logistics Lead. During the live demonstration, the evaluation team subjects the broker to three live operational stress tests:

System Demonstration Stress Tests (Test Environment Only)

| STRESS TEST | METHOD | PASS CRITERIA |
|---|---|---|
| 1. HTS override attempt (test environment) | In the broker's training/ test ABI environment, against synthetic data on a test record, hand the broker's Licensed Customs Broker an ambiguous invoice for a complex electronic device and have them attempt to force a generic fallback HTS code (.9000). Never direct a broker to stage a code the parties agree is wrong on a live entry. That implicates 19 CFR § 111.39 and, if transmitted, § 1592. | The test system blocks it, or the broker refuses the override and insists on technical schematics per SOP. |
| 2. AD/CVD & PGA disclaimer test | Input a line carrying an active AD/CVD flag and a TSCA chemical indicator; observe whether the software prompts for Commerce case numbers and forces a line-level non-reimbursement selection. | The software blocks transmission until the non-reimbursement statement and chemical certification are attached. |
| 3. 15-minute archive retrieval | For an incumbent, name one of your own entry summaries from four years prior and demand the complete packet: invoice, 7501, and underlying correspondence. For a bidder with no history on your account, ask them to demonstrate the retrieval workflow on their own internal test or training records and to state, in writing, their retrieval service level and retention architecture. Do not ask a broker to produce another client's file: 19 CFR § 111.24 makes those records | The complete packet is retrieved and displayed in under 15 minutes (or, for a bidder, the workflow and service level are demonstrated and documented). |

| STRESS TEST | METHOD | PASS CRITERIA |
|---|---|---|
| | confidential, and a broker who hands them over has told you how yours will be treated. | |

Ask yourself one question before your next broker review: if CBP asked tomorrow how you know your broker is doing this correctly, what would you hand them? If the honest answer is a questionnaire the broker filled out about itself, you have your agenda.

# Chapter 14: Building the Internal Broker Oversight Manual (BOM)

## Drafting the Broker Oversight Manual

In the final analysis of federal trade compliance, an enterprise's defense against aggressive enforcement algorithms does not rest on good intentions, informal verbal understandings, or high-level corporate mission statements. It rests entirely on the presence of a durable, institutionalized Broker Oversight Manual (BOM). When CBP's Trade Regulatory Audit (TRA) directorate initiates a Focused Assessment, or when the Department of Justice initiates a civil inquiry under the False Claims Act (31 U.S.C. § 3729) for systemic duty underpayment, government auditors do not evaluate what your executives intended to do. They look for a centralized, written governance manual that proves the corporation exercises active, continuous, and systematic control over its third-party Customs Brokers. If your broker management policies are scattered across un-indexed internal emails, legacy PDF memos, or personal desktop folders held by individual compliance managers, the law treats your governance structure as non-existent. Section 1484 imposes the entry duty and the reasonable-care standard; the negligence liability itself arises under § 1592(a), with the standard defined in 19 CFR Part 171, Appendix B. No statute declares passive reliance on an un-monitored broker to be negligence as such. The courts reach that result on the facts, as Golden Ship Trading and Horizon Products show. But the practical lesson those cases teach is the same: unmonitored reliance is where negligence findings come from, and a documented oversight program is the record that answers them. The Broker Oversight Manual is the master operational blueprint of your enterprise. It bridges the gap between high-level legal mandates (Reasonable Care, 19 CFR Part 111 Modernization, Executive Order directives) and daily supply chain execution.

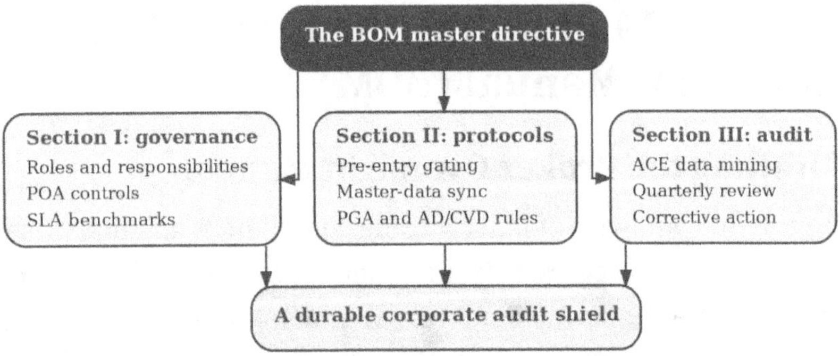


## 1. Deconstructing the Statutory Reasonable Care Standard

To survive a CBP Trade Regulatory Audit or Focused Assessment, the BOM must explicitly address and satisfy the core questions outlined in CBP's official Reasonable Care Informed Compliance Publication (ICP). An ICP is agency guidance, not statute, and it is not a checklist auditors are bound to score you against, but it is the framework CBP works from, and the questions it asks are the questions you should be able to answer. When CBP auditors inspect an Importer of Record (IOR), they evaluate the BOM against the questions CBP's own guidance says it asks:

1. Written Compliance Instructions: Does the importer provide clear, written instructions to its Customs Brokers regarding classification, valuation, and partner government agency (PGA) filings?
2. Expert Consultation & Review: Does the importer employ qualified internal trade compliance professionals or engage licensed Customs Brokers/trade attorneys to establish product classifications and valuation rules?
3. Systematic Data Verification: Does the importer maintain an ongoing, written process to verify the accuracy of entry summaries (CBP Form 7501) filed by its brokers against internal purchase orders, commercial invoices, and master item tables?
4. Error Remediation & Disclosure: Does the importer possess a documented protocol for executing Post-Summary

Corrections (PSCs) or filing Prior Disclosures under 19 U.S.C. § 1592(c) when entry errors are identified?

If your Broker Oversight Manual answers all four of those questions in writing, and your operations actually match what it says, you have accomplished something specific. It is worth being precise about what.

You have not created a safe harbor. There is none to create: no statute, regulation, or case establishes a presumption of reasonable care that a compliance manual can trigger, and any book that tells you otherwise is selling something. Reasonable care is judged on the totality of the circumstances, every time, on the facts in front of the officer or the judge. A manual does not shift that burden.

What a manual does is change what you can show.

Reasonable care is not a state of mind. It is a course of conduct, and conduct has to be proved from records made at the time. When a CBP auditor asks how your classifications were established, there are two possible answers. One is a dated procedure, the workpapers behind the decision, the audit that checked it, and the correction log showing what happened when something slipped. The other is a compliance manager's sincere recollection.

Both may describe a company that genuinely tried. Only one of them survives the file review.

That distinction runs through everything in this book. The Power of Attorney addendum in Chapter 4 does not prevent a broker error; it determines who pays for one. The ACE audit in Chapter 7 does not stop a clerk from typing the wrong code; it finds the code while the correction is still free. The Post-Summary Correction in Chapter 10 does not erase the mistake; it puts your initiative in the record ahead of CBP's discovery. In each case the machinery generates evidence, and the evidence is the point.

So be honest with yourself about the limits. A documented program will not immunize you against a penalty. An isolated typographical error by your agent is still an error made under your number, and you will answer for it. What the program does is make your answer a good one. That the error was caught by a control you built, corrected on a schedule you set, and prevented from recurring by a change you can date.

That is what reasonable care actually looks like when someone examines it from the outside. Not perfection. A practice, running, with a paper trail.

## 2. The Structure of the Manual

An audit-proof Broker Oversight Manual must be constructed as a standing corporate policy document, approved by the Board of Directors, signed by the Chief Executive Officer, and embedded directly into the Enterprise Resource Planning (ERP) platform (SAP GTS, Oracle GTM, NetSuite). The manual is organized into six modules:

Broker Oversight Manual (BOM) Module Taxonomy

| MODULE | TITLE & DOMAIN FOCUS | MANDATORY OPERATIONAL CONTROLS |
|---|---|---|
| Module 1 | Corporate Authority & Governance Architecture | Executive reasonable-care mandate; organizational reporting hierarchy. |
| Module 2 | Power of Attorney and Contractual Controls | POA addendum text; broker liability carve-outs. |
| Module 3 | Master Data Synchronization & Pre-Entry Gating | API mapping specs; "No-Default" rules; locked HTS and PGA classifications. |
| Module 4 | High-Risk Operations & Targeting Controls | AD/CVD non-reimbursement protocol; Section 301 transformation rules; UFLPA due diligence. |

| MODULE | TITLE & DOMAIN FOCUS | MANDATORY OPERATIONAL CONTROLS |
|---|---|---|
| Module 5 | Forensic Data Mining & ACE Portal Exploitation | Weekly ES-001/ES-002/ES-003 extraction; SQL fat-finger audit queries. |
| Module 6 | Annual Audit, Scorecarding & Corrective Action | Annual audit protocol; scorecard engine; broker offboarding. |

## 3. Module-by-Module Technical Drafting Guidelines

### Module 1: Corporate Authority and Governance

This section establishes the legal scope and organizational authority of the trade compliance department.

- Executive Reasonable Care Statement: A signed statement from the CEO establishing that compliance with U.S. customs laws takes precedence over transportation speed or freight cost minimization.
- Organizational Hierarchy & Authority Matrix: Defines explicit roles and decision-making limits. Specifies who holds authority to execute Power of Attorney agreements, approve 10-digit HTS classifications, authorize duty payments via ACH, and correspond with CBP officials.
- Recordkeeping Policy (19 CFR Part 163): Mandates a strict 5-year record retention rule for all customs business documents (entry summaries, invoices, packing lists, bills of lading, classification workpapers, and email logs) stored in a SOC 2 Type II certified digital archive.

### Module 2: Power of Attorney and Contractual Controls

Codifies the legal and contractual constraints imposed on third-party brokers.

- POA addendum: Incorporates the complete, overriding text of the Customs Power of Attorney Addendum, stripping the broker liability cap, restricting sub-agency assignments, enforcing 19 CFR § 111.36 direct communication rules, and carving out liability for gross negligence.

- Service Level Agreement (SLA) Benchmarks: Details the KPIs governing broker performance, including the 5-day entry summary filing window, 99.5% master data match rates, and 24-hour escalation windows for CBP Forms 28, 29, and 4647.
- Fee Offset & SLA Penalty Schedule: Outlines the automatic financial credits applied to broker invoices when operational SLA benchmarks are breached.

**Module 3: Master Data Synchronization & Pre-Entry Gating**

Establishes system-to-system integrations and software-enforced workflow gates.

- API / XML Integration Specifications: Technical parameters for pushing pre-vetted compliance payloads (Part Number, 10-digit HTS, MID, SPI, PGA data) directly into broker platforms (CargoWise, Descartes, BluJay).
- "No-Default" Workflow Rules: System configurations blocking entry clerks from manually editing locked HTS fields or selecting generic fallback provisions ( .90 / .9000 catch-all subheadings).
- Automated Exception Workflows: Protocols for handling new, un-matched Part Numbers through an internal compliance review portal prior to cargo departure.

**Module 4: High-Risk Operations & Targeting Controls**

Deep operational mechanics for managing severe regulatory liabilities.

- Antidumping and countervailing duty (AD/CVD) rules: Procedures for verifying Commerce Department case numbers, applying manufacturer-specific cash deposit rates, and executing electronic Non-Reimbursement Statements (19 CFR § 351.402(f)) prior to entry liquidation.
- Section 301 and country-of-origin rules: For auditing substantial transformation in third countries (e.g., Vietnam, Malaysia), tracking Chapter 99 exclusions, and executing refund recovery via PSCs.

- Uyghur Forced Labor Prevention Act (UFLPA) rules: Raw-material supply-chain tracing requiring full 5-module evidentiary packages (Tier-1 through Tier-4 mapping) for the UFLPA high-priority sectors (cotton, apparel, tomatoes, silica-based products, aluminum, PVC, seafood, steel, copper, lithium, caustic soda, and red dates) prior to port arrival.

**Module 5: Forensic Data Mining & ACE Portal Exploitation**

Instructions for continuous, automated post-entry auditing.

- Automated Extraction Pipeline: Parameters for scheduling recurring ACE Reports runs (ES-001 Header, ES-002 Line, ES-003 Tariff-Line, plus the Cargo Release and Manifest universes) with e-mail delivery or export to CSV/Excel and a shared internal folder. Note: there is no SFTP or FTP delivery path for trade users. CBP disabled the BI Inbox after the BusinessObjects 4.3 upgrade (CSMS #60527352), and restored scheduled runs with e-mail delivery for multi-account users on 4 December 2024 (CSMS #63362323).
- SQL Audit Script Engine: Production-ready SQL query library used to cross-reference raw ACE line items against ERP accounts payable ledgers and master item tables.
- 300-Day PSC Window Playbook: Standardized workflows for drafting, narrative writing, and electronically transmitting Post-Summary Corrections (PSCs) in ACE to remedy identified filing errors before liquidation.
- IEEPA Refund Playbook (use CAPE, not a PSC): The workflow for recovering IEEPA tariffs, a separate instrument on a separate clock, covered below.

#### The Third Clock: IEEPA Refunds and CAPE

There is a third recovery clock running right now that has nothing to do with the 300-day PSC window, and for many importers it is the largest single dollar figure on the desk. On February 20, 2026, the Supreme Court held in *Learning Resources, Inc. v. Trump* that the International Emergency Economic Powers Act (IEEPA) does not authorize the President to impose tariffs, and the United States terminated the IEEPA-based tariffs at 12:00 a.m. ET on February 24, 2026. Duties paid under those tariffs are refundable, and the refundable set is broader than the two headline actions: it spans every IEEPA tariff CBP collected, each with its own start date: the China "fentanyl"/trafficking tariffs from February 4, 2025 (EO 14195); the Canada and Mexico trafficking tariffs (EOs 14193 and 14194); the "reciprocal" tariffs from April 5, 2025 (EO 14257); and later country-specific actions such as the Brazil tariff from August 6, 2025 (EO 14323) and the Russia-related measure on India from August 27, 2025 (EO 14329), all running through the February 24, 2026 termination. Scope a CAPE claim against CBP's IEEPA duty-refunds guidance, which publishes the per-order start dates, not from the two headline dates alone, or you will under-claim on the very entries this section calls the largest refund on the desk.

The instrument is not a PSC. CBP stood up **CAPE** (Consolidated Administration and Processing of Entries) in ACE to consolidate these refunds, Phase 1 on April 20, 2026, Phase 2 on June 29, 2026, and CBP has said plainly that filers "are prohibited from initiating an IEEPA duty refund request by filing a PSC." If you route an IEEPA refund through the 300-day PSC playbook above, you are using the wrong tool; use CAPE. Any *non-IEEPA* PSC on the same entry should be filed before you submit the CAPE declaration.

If you would rather litigate than take the administrative refund, that route has its own clock: a residual-jurisdiction action at the Court of International Trade under 28 U.S.C. § 1581(i) carries a two-year limitations period under 28 U.S.C. § 2636(i), measured from each entry's date of deposit. Be precise about that citation, because it is easy to get wrong: § 1581 only grants the court jurisdiction and contains no limitations period, and the two-year clock is the residual rule for § 1581(i) suits. Other CIT actions run shorter (a denied protest under § 1581(a) must be challenged within 180 days under § 2636(a)), so confirm which jurisdictional basis your claim rests on before you rely on the two years. Assuming the § 1581(i) route, the earliest claims begin to expire around February 4, 2027 (fentanyl) and April 5, 2027 (reciprocal); because the clock runs per entry, later entries roll forward from there. Confirm the current CAPE phase, coverage, and any liquidation constraints against CBP's IEEPA duty-refunds guidance before you build the workflow. This is a fast-moving area.

**Module 6: Annual Audit, Scorecarding & Corrective Action**

Framework for continuous broker evaluation, offboarding, and legal remediation.

- Annual Broker Audit Protocol: Step-by-step checklist for auditing a broker's physical/remote workstations, recordkeeping infrastructure, and 13 regulatory factors under 19 CFR § 111.28.
- Quarterly Weighted Scorecard Engine: Mathematical scoring formulas for evaluating brokers across Classification Accuracy (35%), High-Risk Control (25%), Timeliness (20%), Responsiveness (10%), and Billing/API Health (10%).
- Prior Disclosure (19 U.S.C. § 1592(c)) Protocol: step-by-step instructions for executing two-stage prior disclosures (initial blanket filing plus perfected tender) to freeze penalty clocks when systemic historical broker errors are uncovered.

## Cross-Functional Governance: Bridging Logistics, Legal, Procurement, and Accounting

Customs compliance failure is rarely caused by a lack of technical knowledge within the trade compliance team. It is caused by siloed corporate operations. In most corporations, procurement negotiates vendor contracts without consulting trade compliance; logistics selects freight forwarders based strictly on transit speed; accounting pays Customs Broker invoices without auditing line-item duty charges; and legal only gets involved after CBP issues a formal penalty notice under 19 U.S.C. § 1592. To build a resilient Broker Management System, the BOM must establish a Cross-Functional Governance Framework that binds Logistics, Legal, Procurement, and Accounting into an integrated compliance chain.

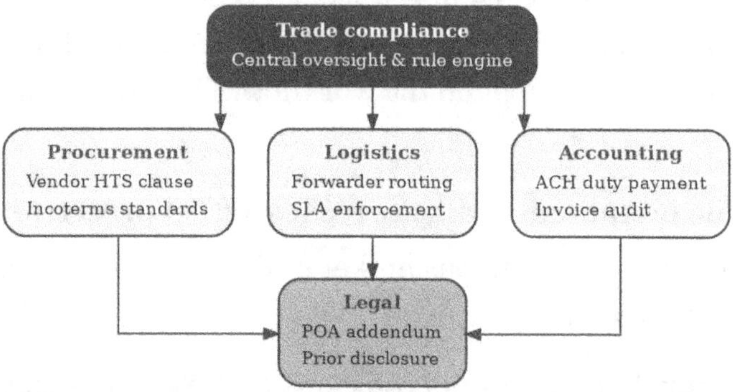


## 1. Inter-Departmental Governance

### Procurement Integration Mandates

- Contract clauses: Procurement is barred from issuing purchase orders or executing vendor master agreements that lack the standard Corporate Trade Compliance Clause. Foreign vendors must agree to provide 10-digit HTSUS classifications, bills of materials, and raw material origin tracing data 30 days prior to cargo shipment.
- Incoterms Standardization: Procurement must enforce FCA (Free Carrier) terms for routed exports and DDP/DAP restrictions to ensure the corporation maintains complete control over the Importer of Record designation and filing broker selection. Uncontrolled DDP (Delivered Duty Paid) shipments from foreign vendors are prohibited because foreign sellers frequently use shell IORs and fraudulent low valuations, exposing the U.S. buyer to joint liability.

### Logistics & Supply Chain Integration Mandates

- Forwarder Instruction Lock: Logistics coordinators are prohibited from authorizing a freight forwarder to handle customs entry. Customs clearance authority rests exclusively with pre-vetted brokers operating under approved POAs and SLAs.

- Pre-Alert Data Transmission: Logistics must transmit electronic pre-alerts (commercial invoice, packing list, bill of lading) to the compliance portal at least 72 hours prior to vessel departure at the foreign port, allowing automated pre-entry gating engines to validate records.

### Accounting & Finance Integration Mandates

- ACH Payment Enforcement: Accounting must execute all customs duty payments directly to CBP via the corporation's Automated Clearing House (ACH) Payer Account. Broker invoices requesting duty reimbursement via manual checks are automatically blocked by accounting software to eliminate broker duty-float schemes and fee markups.
- Post-Entry Invoice Auditing: Accounts Payable cannot process a broker's transactional fee invoice until the broker provides the matching ACE Entry Summary Acceptance Notice (CBP Form 7501) and the line items pass automated SQL reconciliation against the ERP purchase order.

### Legal Department Integration Mandates

- POA Execution Lockout: Only the Legal Department, in direct coordination with the Trade Compliance Director, holds authority to sign Customs Powers of Attorney. Signing un-amended broker POAs or freight forwarder boilerplate agreements is classified as a material breach of corporate policy.
- CBP Inquiry Escalation: Any CBP communication involving a CBP Form 28, Form 29, Form 4647, or grand jury subpoena must be escalated to the Legal Department and Trade Compliance Director within 4 hours of receipt.

## 2. The Cross-Functional Operational Workflow

To ensure seamless execution, the BOM details how these four departments interact across the lifespan of a single import transaction:

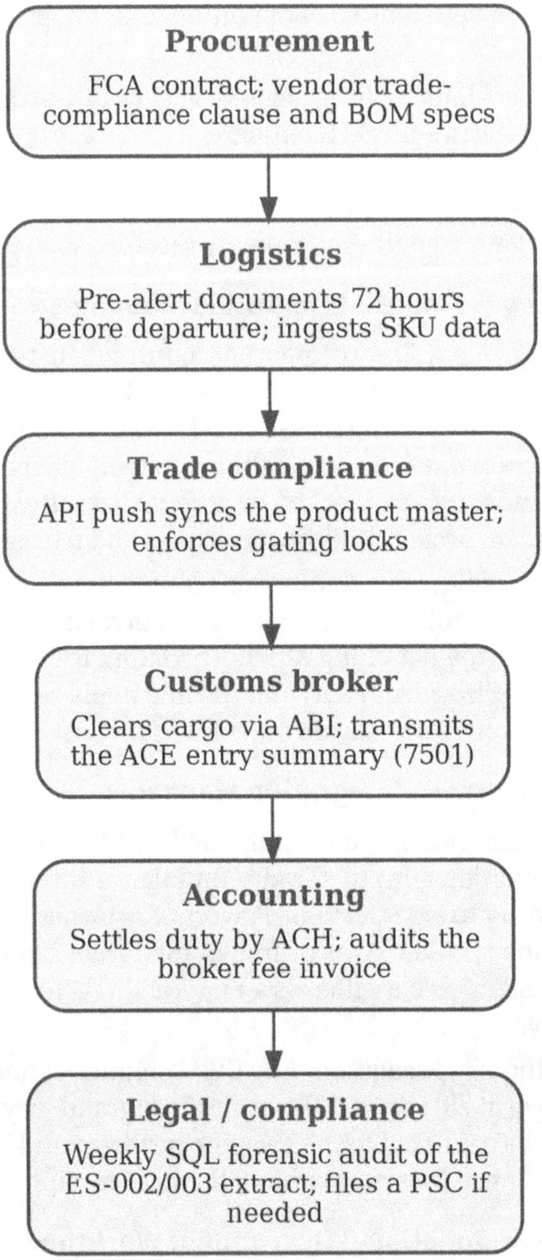


## Reporting to the C-Suite and the Board

The final element of the program is the board report. C-suite executives (CEOs, CFOs, General Counsels) and Board Audit

Committees often view trade compliance as a minor operational detail, until a CBP penalty notice or forced labor detention halts operations and threatens corporate earnings. Under post-2026 enforcement rules, corporate officers can face personal administrative liability and reputational destruction if their enterprise is barred from importing due to loss of "Good Standing" status on CBP registries. To maintain executive alignment and secure necessary compliance resources, the Trade Compliance Director must deliver a Quarterly Executive Compliance Dashboard to the Board Audit Committee.

Quarterly Executive Compliance Dashboard KPI Matrix

| EXECUTIVE METRIC | TARGET STATUS | ENTERPRISE RISK IMPACT / EXPOSURE |
|---|---|---|
| 1. CBP "Good Standing" Status | 100% ACTIVE | Loss of Good Standing = total import shutdown |
| 2. Composite Broker Scorecard | ≥ 95.0 Points | Score below 90 triggers SLA offsets |
| 3. Un-Mitigated Penalty Exposure | $0.00 | Measures potential 50% penalty-floor exposure |
| 4. UFLPA Supply Chain Tracing | 100% Archived | Un-traced lines = port detention risk |
| 5. Duty Overpayment Recovery | $ Active Tracked | Net cash recovered via PSC filings |

## 1. The Executive Dashboard, Module by Module

The quarterly executive presentation must summarize complex customs operations into concise, risk-quantified metrics across three primary reporting modules:

### Module A: Enterprise Risk Exposure & Good Standing Status

- IOR Registry Standing: [Forward-looking. CBP has not yet defined good standing or stood up a registry; the 180-day deadline is 30 November 2026. Until it publishes, report this line as "not yet applicable, monitoring," and use the affiliate IOR map from Chapter 3 as the substitute metric.] Once the registry exists, this line verifies that all corporate IOR numbers maintain active good-standing status.

- Open CBP Inquiry Count: Displays the status of all active CBP Forms 28, 29, and 4647 across all U.S. ports. Confirms that zero notices remain open past 15 calendar days.
- Continuous Bond Health: Monitors bond utilization metrics against current Section 301 and AD/CVD duty exposure, certifying that continuous customs bonds are fully backed and free of surety claims.

**Module B: Broker Performance & SLA Accountability**

- Composite Scorecard Results: Displays the quarterly weighted scores (SComp ) for all primary and secondary Customs Brokers.
- Discrepancy & Error Metrics: Quantifies broker-caused error rates (classification mismatches, valuation slippage, MID swaps) extracted from raw ACE ES-002/ES-003 data.
- SLA Financial Recovery: Reports total dollar amounts recovered from underperforming brokers via contractual fee offsets, invoice discounts, and administrative penalty claims.

**Module C: Strategic Duty Engineering & Cash Recovery**

- Free Trade Agreement Savings: Quantifies total duties saved through USMCA, GSP, and regional trade preferences.
- Retroactive Exclusion Refunds: Reports cash recovered from CBP via Post-Summary Corrections applying retroactive Section 301 exclusions.
- Duty Drawback Recovery: Tracks duty recovery claims filed under 19 U.S.C. § 1313 for re-exported merchandise.

## 2. The Board Presentation Narrative Template

To ensure C-suite executives grasp the financial and operational impact of trade compliance, the Trade Compliance Director uses a structured executive narrative script during quarterly board meetings:

- "Executive Summary: During Q2 2026, the Enterprise tracked good-standing readiness across all active Importer of Record numbers. CBP has not yet stood up the good-standing registry (the rule is due 30 November 2026), so this line is reported as 'not yet applicable, monitoring,' with the affiliate IOR map from Chapter 3 as the working substitute. Through automated system-to-system integration and pre-entry gating protocols, our primary Customs Broker achieved a 99.7% Master Data Match Rate across 4,200 entry lines. Our weekly ACE ES-002/ES-003 forensic data mining engine identified 14 broker typing errors within the 300-day window, allowing us to execute Post-Summary Corrections (PSCs) that recovered $185,000 in overpaid duties. A PSC is not itself a penalty safe harbor; what protects us is that each error was found and corrected on our own initiative ahead of any CBP inquiry, with a prior disclosure filed where an error was material enough to warrant one. All high-risk target lines, including Antidumping duties and UFLPA supply chain tracing for our electronics division, remain 100% pre-verified and archived in our compliance repository. Total un-mitigated penalty exposure across all import operations remains at exactly $0.00."

## A Worked Example: One Importer, End to End

The chapters in this book each solve one problem. This is what they look like working together, on a single importer, over a single year. The company below is a composite, drawn to illustrate the program rather than to describe a real client, but every step traces to a chapter you have already read.

Northwind Components imports industrial motor assemblies from three factories in Asia, roughly two thousand entries a year, with one compliance manager and a broker it inherited from its freight forwarder. It sits squarely in Tier B.

It starts with the Power of Attorney. Northwind's counsel adapts the addendum from Chapter 4, removing the liability cap for the broker's own gross negligence, restricting sub-agency, and requiring that CBP Forms 28 and 29 reach Northwind's compliance inbox within one business day. The broker signs it, grudgingly. Nothing has been filed yet, but the leverage has already shifted.

Next comes the Service Level Agreement from Chapter 5. Northwind sets a 99.5% classification-match benchmark, a 24-hour notification standard on CBP inquiries with a 48-hour breach threshold, and a fee offset when the broker misses. It is not an ultimatum; it is the standard the good broker on the account was already meeting and can now prove.

Then the data. Northwind's IT team stands up the master-data synchronization from Chapters 8 and 9, pushing vetted tariff codes, manufacturer identification codes, and country-of-origin data straight into the broker's platform, and turning on the No-Default rules so an entry clerk can no longer type over a locked field. The monthly ACE spot-audit from Chapter 7 runs every Monday against the ES-002/ES-003 extract.

In March, the audit catches one. A clerk, working a rush shipment before the feed had updated, hand-keyed a motor assembly under a generic "other" subheading carrying a 2.7% rate plus a 25% Section 301 tariff, when the correct classification was duty-free. The financial impact flagged in the scorecard is $46,000 across the month's entries. Under the old arrangement Northwind would never have seen it; it would have surfaced, if at all, two years later in a CBP audit letter.

Instead, Northwind files a Post-Summary Correction under Chapter 10, well inside the 300-day window, with a clean narrative and the supporting documentation uploaded to the Document Image System at the moment of transmission. The correction processes without a Form 28. The refund arrives at liquidation. There is no penalty, because there is nothing to penalize: the error was found and fixed on the importer's own initiative, which is the entire meaning of reasonable care.

At year end, the caught error becomes a single row in the annual scorecard from Chapter 13: one classification discrepancy, corrected, exposure neutralized. The broker's overall score is strong. Northwind renews the relationship, now on its own terms, and the good broker keeps an account that no longer competes on price alone.

That is the whole program in one year: the POA that rebalanced the risk, the SLA that set the standard, the data pipeline that prevented most errors, the audit that caught the one that slipped through, the correction that fixed it for free, and the scorecard that turned it all into a record CBP would respect. None of the steps is heroic. Together they are the difference between an importer who is exercising reasonable care and one who is merely hoping.

## Conclusion: Reasonable Care Is a Practice, Not a Purchase

The argument of this book fits in a sentence: the liability is yours, so the oversight has to be yours too. Everything between the covers, the case law, the model contracts, the SQL, the scorecards, exists to close the distance between that legal fact and the way most importers actually operate.

If you set the book down now and do only three things, do these. Fix your Power of Attorney, because it is a one-time legal task with a permanent payoff. See what is actually filed under your number, because a monthly look at your own ACE data will surface most broker errors while they are still free to fix. And know your clocks: the 300-day PSC correction window and the days-long response window on a CBP inquiry, and, while it is live, the IEEPA refund clock that runs through CAPE rather than a PSC (Chapter 14), because missing any of them turns a fixable problem, or a seven-figure entitlement, into a loss. Everything else in this book makes those three moves faster, more automated, and more defensible. But those three, alone, prevent most of the damage.

The point is not adversarial. A broker who does the work well has nothing to fear from a client who can finally see it, and everything to gain from competing on that rather than on price.

A word on timing, because this book was written on a moving target. Much of its urgency traces to Executive Order 14411 and the enforcement regime it sets in motion, and as of this writing that regime still depends on rulemaking that CBP and the Department of Homeland Security have been directed to complete. The direction is not in doubt: the penalty floors, the repeat-offender bar, and the good-standing registry are coming. The specific numbers and deadlines may shift as the final rules publish. Treat every specific mechanic in these pages as something to confirm against the primary source before you rely on it, and expect this book to need a second edition as the rules settle. As those rulemakings finalize, the current rule numbers and effective dates will be posted on the companion page for this book at Trade Underground Press.

The customs system will not get simpler, and the cost of treating it as someone else's problem will not get smaller. But the importer who reads its own entries, holds its broker to a written standard, and can show CBP a record of diligence is playing a different game than the one who signs whatever comes back. Reasonable care is not a product you buy. It is a practice you keep. Start with the three things, and build from there.

# APPENDIX / TOOLKIT: MASTER COMPLIANCE INSTRUMENTS

> *A note before you use these instruments, because they are not all the same kind of thing. Two of them are contract language: the model Power-of-Attorney addendum (Tool A) and the model Service Level Agreement (Tool B), which carries the indemnity and liquidated-damages terms. These are illustrative drafting starting points, not execution-ready documents, and they have real legal consequences. Do not sign, send, or file either as written. Take them to your own qualified customs or trade-law counsel to adapt to your contracts, your jurisdiction, and your facts first. The other three are operational tools, not legal instruments: the SQL audit library (Tool C), the pre-entry checklist (Tool D), and the annual broker scorecard (Tool E). Use those as starting templates and adapt them to your own data and workflow. They do not need a lawyer. All of this material is educational and is not legal advice. See the full notice at the front of the book.*

## Tool A: Model Overriding Customs Power of Attorney Addendum

> *Educational drafting example, not legal advice, and not ready to sign. The clauses below illustrate how an importer might rebalance a standard broker Power of Attorney. Contract language must be adapted to your facts and reviewed by your own qualified counsel before use.*

```
=================================================================
OVERRIDING CUSTOMS POWER OF ATTORNEY ADDENDUM
INDEPENDENT LEGAL ATTACHMENT: SUPERSEDES ALL BROKER
STANDARD TERMS & CONDITIONS
=================================================================

THIS POWER OF ATTORNEY ADDENDUM ("Addendum") is executed
on this _____ day of _______________, 20___, by and
between ____________________________________ ("Principal /
```

Importer of Record"), holding IRS/IOR Number
____________________, and
____________________ ("Agent / Customs Broker"), holding National Broker Permit Number
_______________.

1. OVERRIDE AND LEGAL PRECEDENCE
This Addendum explicitly amends, controls, and legally supersedes any standard power of attorney form, credit application, service agreement, or boilerplate terms and conditions executed between Principal and Agent (including, but not limited to, NCBFAA model terms). In the event of any conflict, ambiguity, or inconsistency between the terms of this Addendum and any agreement provided by Agent, the terms of this Addendum shall strictly govern and control.

2. CARVE-OUT FOR GROSS NEGLIGENCE AND STATUTORY LIABILITIES
Notwithstanding any clause in Agent's standard terms capping liability (whether at $100.00, $50.00, the brokerage fee, or any other amount) or excluding consequential damages, such limitation of liability shall NOT apply to any loss, fee, liquidated damage, civil penalty, interest, or court cost incurred by Principal arising out of or resulting from Agent's gross negligence, willful misconduct, intentional violation of law, or failure to follow explicit, written master data classification and entry instructions provided by Principal. Agent shall hold harmless and indemnify Principal for direct financial losses, including interest, liquidated damages, statutory penalties under 19 U.S.C. § 1592 or 19 U.S.C. § 1641, and the reasonable professional and administrative costs of correction, caused directly by Agent's gross negligence or failure to exercise Responsible Supervision and Control under 19 CFR Part 111. This indemnity does not extend to the underlying duties, taxes, and fees themselves, which Principal owes to CBP by statute regardless of fault.

3. NOTICE OF CLAIM AND LIMITATION OF ACTIONS
Any contractual claim-notice or limitation-of-actions period in Agent's standard terms is superseded to the extent it is shorter than the following: Principal must give Agent written notice of a claim within thirty (30) days of Principal's discovery of the underlying error, and may commence suit within two (2) years of that discovery. A failure by Agent to raise a shorter contractual period as to any claim governed by this Addendum shall not be a defense.

4. RESTRICTION ON SUB-AGENCY DELEGATION
Agent's authority to appoint sub-agents under this Power of Attorney is strictly restricted. Agent shall not delegate, assign, or transfer customs business authority to any third-party Customs Broker, sub-agent, or independent contractor without securing the prior written consent of Principal's Corporate Compliance Officer. Agent remains fully, jointly, and severally liable for all acts, omissions, and entries filed by any approved sub-agent.

5. DATA SOVEREIGNTY AND CONFIDENTIALITY
All commercial data, technical specifications, product descriptions, HTS classification databases, vendor identities, unit pricing, purchase orders, and ACE entry

summary data provided by Principal or generated by Agent shall remain the exclusive intellectual property and confidential information of Principal. Agent is prohibited from selling, sharing, mining, aggregating, or disclosing Principal's data to any third party, affiliate, freight forwarding division, or commercial entity for any commercial purpose. This prohibition does not restrict disclosures the law requires or expressly permits: transmission to CBP and partner government agencies to execute entries; production of records under 19 CFR § 111.23 and 19 CFR Part 163; disclosure to the surety on a particular entry as permitted by 19 CFR § 111.24; response to a subpoena, court order, or other compelled legal process; and transmission to Agent's own ABI software and ACE service providers bound by equivalent confidentiality obligations.

6. DIRECT COMMUNICATION AND IMMEDIATE REGULATORY ESCALATION
Agent acknowledges its regulatory obligations under 19 CFR § 111.36 and agrees to maintain direct communication with Principal's compliance team. Agent shall transmit copies of all ACE entry summary data (CBP Form 7501) directly to Principal's portal (compliance@importer.com). Agent shall immediately, and in no event later than twenty-four (24) hours from receipt, forward to Principal any CBP Form 28, Form 29, Form 4647, or formal inquiry received from CBP or any Partner Government Agency (PGA). Agent shall not take a substantive position, or submit substantive responsive content, to CBP or any PGA in Principal's name without prior written authorization from Principal. This does not bar Agent from acknowledging receipt, confirming factual matters within Agent's own knowledge, or requesting an extension. If Principal does not respond within a reasonable period before the applicable CBP deadline, Agent may respond as necessary to preserve compliance, with contemporaneous notice to Principal and a copy of anything filed; nothing in this Addendum requires Agent to withhold information CBP is entitled to or to file a document Agent knows to be false.

7. MUTUAL EXECUTION AND CONSIDERATION
This Addendum imposes obligations on Agent and is therefore effective only upon execution by an authorized officer of Agent below. The parties acknowledge mutual consideration, including Agent's continued engagement and fees and Principal's grant of authority. An Addendum returned unsigned by Agent has no effect.

IN WITNESS WHEREOF, the parties have executed this Overriding Addendum as of the date first written above.

PRINCIPAL / IMPORTER OF RECORD:
By: ______________________________
Name: ____________________________
Title: ___________________________
Date: ____________________________

AGENT / LICENSED CUSTOMS BROKER:
By: ______________________________
Name: ____________________________
Title: ___________________________
Date: ____________________________

## Tool B: Model Broker Service Level Agreement (SLA) Contract

> *Educational drafting example, not legal advice, and not ready to sign. The benchmarks, remedies, and gating language below illustrate how an oversight-minded SLA can be structured. Adapt every term to your commercial arrangement and have your own qualified counsel review it before use.*

```
============================================================
Customs Broker SERVICE LEVEL AGREEMENT (SLA) &
PERFORMANCE CONTRACT
MANDATORY OPERATIONAL KEY PERFORMANCE INDICATORS (KPIs)
AND SLA OFFSETS
============================================================

1. PURPOSE & SCOPE
This Service Level Agreement ("SLA") defines the
operational performance benchmarks, entry gating
controls, and financial remedies governing customs entry
summary execution provided by Customs Broker ("Agent") to
Importer of Record ("Principal").

2. MANDATORY OPERATIONAL BENCHMARKS
Agent shall satisfy the following quantifiable Key
Performance Indicators (KPIs):

   a. Entry Summary Filing Velocity: 100% of standard
      consumption entries (Type 01) and AD/CVD entries
      (Type 03) must be fully transmitted, validated, and
      duty-scheduled in ACE within five (5) business days
      of cargo release.
   b. Master Data Classification Match Rate: Transmitted
      HTS codes, values, MIDs, and quantities must
      achieve a 99.5% exact match rate against
      Principal's synchronized Master Item Database.
   c. Regulatory Inquiry Escalation: 100% of CBP Forms
      28, 29, 4647, and informal CEE communications must
      be forwarded to Principal within 24 hours of
      receipt.
   d. Post-Summary Correction (PSC) Execution: Requested
      PSCs must be executed and transmitted in ACE within
      ten (10) business days of written request.

3. MANDATORY ENTRY GATING PROTOCOLS
Agent's software platform must enforce hard system blocks
preventing ABI entry summary transmission for:

   a. Any line item containing an active AD/CVD flag
      without attached written AD/CVD Pre-Clearance
      Authorization and signed Non-Reimbursement
      Statement.
   b. Any line item associated with high-risk
      forced-labor sectors (cotton, apparel, tomatoes,
      silica-based products, aluminum, PVC, seafood,
      steel, copper, lithium, caustic soda, red dates)
      without attached UFLPA Clearance Key.
   c. Any line item where the entry clerk manually alters
      a locked 10-digit HTS code or selects a generic
```

fallback code (.90 / .9000).

4. FINANCIAL REMEDIES & SLA OFFSETS
In the event Agent fails to meet agreed performance benchmarks, the following financial remedies shall automatically apply as fee credits against Agent's monthly service invoices:

a. Late Filing / Liquidated Damages: If Agent fails to transmit an entry summary within the regulatory 10-working-day window, resulting in CBP Liquidated Damages, Agent shall pay 100% of the assessed damages, issue a 100% entry fee credit, and pay Principal a flat $500.00 administrative fee per incident.
b. Accuracy Threshold Offsets: If Agent's monthly Classification Match Rate drops below 99.5%, Agent shall apply a 25% service credit across all processing invoice fees for that month. If the match rate drops below 98.0%, the credit increases to 50%. (99.5% is a negotiated commercial target; no CBP or industry standard fixes a broker match rate.)
c. Discrepancy Audit Costs: If Agent commits a fat-finger valuation or HTS typing error resulting in a CBP rate advance, Agent shall reimburse Principal for interest, penalties, and the internal legal and audit costs incurred to file corrective PSCs or Prior Disclosures. This does not extend to the underlying duties, which Principal owes regardless of fault.
d. Filing-Velocity Service Credit: If Agent files an entry summary after the five (5)-business-day standard in Section 2(a) but within the regulatory window, a service credit set by the parties (for example, a fixed per-entry credit) shall apply. Price this credit, or the five-day standard is aspirational rather than enforceable.
e. Remedy Election and Character of Credits: The credits above are agreed price adjustments applied to the next invoice, not a self-help withholding (which is contestable and can trigger Agent's lien). For any single breach, Principal shall elect either the service credit or actual damages, not both; the credits do not operate as a ceiling on Principal's right to actual damages for gross negligence or willful misconduct.

5. RECORDS ACCESS AND AUDIT RIGHTS
Upon reasonable notice, Agent shall provide Principal or Principal's designated auditor access to the records and system logs relating to Principal's account that are necessary to verify Agent's performance under this SLA, including entry-level filing data, classification workpapers for Principal's entries, ACE reject logs, and evidence of the entry-gating controls in Section 3. These audit rights are created by this Agreement: 19 CFR Part 111 imposes duties on Agent owed to CBP, not to Principal, so Principal's right to these materials arises from this contract, not from the regulation.

EXECUTED AND AGREED:

PRINCIPAL COMPLIANCE DIRECTOR:
Signature: ______________________________

```
Date: ________________________________

BROKER CORPORATE OFFICER / LCB:
Signature: ___________________________
Date: ________________________________
```

## Tool C: Master ACE ES-002/ES-003 Line-Item Audit SQL Engine

```
-- ==========================================================
-- MASTER FORENSIC AUDIT SCRIPT
-- Executes Complete Transactional Reconciliation Across
   ACE ES-001 / ES-002 / ES-003
-- Targets: Valuation Slippage, HTS Overrides, AD/CVD
   Omissions, MID Errors
-- Note: tbl_ACE_ES002_LineItems is a flattened ES-002 +
   ES-003 line view (joined on filer, entry, line),
--      so HTS and AD/CVD tariff-line fields resolve
   here. Unmatched ERP rows are caught via IS NULL.
-- ==========================================================

WITH MasterAuditExtract AS (
    SELECT
       es001.Filer_Code,
       es001.Entry_Number,
       es001.Entry_Type,
       es001.Entry_Date,
       es001.Import_Date,
       es001.Summary_Date,
       es001.Liquidation_Status,
       es002.Line_Item_Number,
       xwalk.Commercial_Invoice_Number,
       es002.HTS_10_Digit AS ACE_Transmitted_HTS,
       erp.Master_HTS AS ERP_Approved_HTS,
       es002.Entered_Value_USD AS ACE_Entered_Value,
       erp.Expected_Value_USD AS ERP_Expected_Value,
       es002.Transmitted_MID_Code AS ACE_Transmitted_MID,
       erp.Approved_MID_Code AS ERP_Approved_MID,
       es002.ADCVD_Case_Number,
       es002.Non_Reimbursement_Indicator_ACE,
       es002.Special_Program_Indicator,

      -- Calculated Audit Flags
      CASE
          WHEN erp.Master_HTS IS NULL THEN 0
          WHEN es002.HTS_10_Digit <> erp.Master_HTS THEN 1
              ELSE 0
      END AS Flag_HTS_Mismatch,

      CASE
          WHEN erp.Master_HTS IS NULL THEN 1 ELSE 0
      END AS Flag_No_ERP_Match,

      CASE
          WHEN erp.Expected_Value_USD > 0
               AND ABS(es002.Entered_Value_USD -
                   erp.Expected_Value_USD) /
                   erp.Expected_Value_USD > 0.05
          THEN 1 ELSE 0
      END AS Flag_Valuation_Slippage,
```

```
        CASE
            WHEN es002.Transmitted_MID_Code <>
                erp.Approved_MID_Code THEN 1 ELSE 0
        END AS Flag_MID_Mismatch,

        CASE
            WHEN es002.ADCVD_Case_Number IS NOT NULL
                 AND (es002.Non_Reimbursement_Indicator_ACE
                     IS NULL OR
                     es002.Non_Reimbursement_Indicator_ACE <>
                     'Y')
            THEN 1 ELSE 0
        END AS Flag_ADCVD_Reimbursement_Missing

    FROM tbl_ACE_ES002_LineItems es002

    INNER JOIN tbl_ACE_ES001_Headers es001
        ON es002.Filer_Code = es001.Filer_Code
        AND es002.Entry_Number = es001.Entry_Number

    LEFT JOIN tbl_Broker_Line_Crosswalk xwalk
        ON es002.Entry_Number = xwalk.Entry_Number
        AND es002.Line_Item_Number =
            xwalk.Entry_Summary_Line
    LEFT JOIN tbl_ERP_Master_Catalog erp
        ON xwalk.ERP_Item_Key = erp.ERP_Item_Key

    WHERE es001.Entry_Date >= DATEADD(month, -12,
        GETDATE())
)
 SELECT
    Filer_Code,
    Entry_Number,
    Entry_Date,
    Line_Item_Number,
    Commercial_Invoice_Number,
    ACE_Transmitted_HTS,
    ERP_Approved_HTS,
    ACE_Entered_Value,
    ERP_Expected_Value,
    ACE_Transmitted_MID,
    ERP_Approved_MID,

    -- Consolidated Audit Risk Status
    CASE
        WHEN Flag_No_ERP_Match = 1 THEN
            'VERIFY: NO ERP MATCH'
        WHEN Flag_ADCVD_Reimbursement_Missing = 1 THEN
        'CRITICAL: AD/CVD REIMBURSEMENT STATEMENT MISSING'
        WHEN Flag_HTS_Mismatch = 1 THEN
            'HIGH: UNAUTHORIZED HTS CODE OVERRIDE'
        WHEN Flag_Valuation_Slippage = 1 THEN
            'HIGH: VALUATION SLIPPAGE > 5%'
        WHEN Flag_MID_Mismatch = 1 THEN
            'MEDIUM: INVALID MID CODE TRANSMITTED'
        ELSE 'COMPLIANT'
    END AS Forensic_Audit_Status

FROM MasterAuditExtract
WHERE Flag_HTS_Mismatch = 1
   OR Flag_No_ERP_Match = 1
   OR Flag_Valuation_Slippage = 1
   OR Flag_MID_Mismatch = 1
   OR Flag_ADCVD_Reimbursement_Missing = 1
```

```
ORDER BY Entry_Date DESC, Entry_Number ASC;
```

## Tool D: Pre-Entry High-Risk Verification Checklist

```
=========================================================
PRE-ENTRY HIGH-RISK CLEARANCE CHECKLIST (AD/CVD, SECTION
301, UFLPA)
MANDATORY PRE-TRANSMISSION GATING VERIFICATION FOR ENTRY
CLERKS
=========================================================

ENTRY SUMMARY REFERENCE DATA:
Importer of Record (IOR) #: ______________________
Filer Code / Entry #: ____________________________
Commercial Invoice #: ____________________________
Vessel / Flight #: _______________________________
Estimated Entry Date: ____________________________
Port of Entry: ___________________________________

---------------------------------------------------------
CHECKLIST GATE 1: ANTIDUMPING & COUNTERVAILING DUTY
(AD/CVD) VERIFICATION
---------------------------------------------------------
[ ] 1a. Does the tariff code carry an active AD/CVD flag
        in HTSUS?
    [ ] YES (Proceed to 1b)    [ ] NO (Gate Cleared)
[ ] 1b. Is the shipment entered as Entry Type 03?
[ ] 1c. Verified full Commerce Case # (with company/rate
        suffix): _______________
[ ] 1d. Verified Cash Deposit Rate: ________% (Matches
        factory rate, not country-wide)
[ ] 1e. Non-Reimbursement Statement signed and toggled
        'Y' in ACE payload.
[ ] 1f. Signed AD/CVD Pre-Clearance Authorization on file
        from Importer Compliance.

---------------------------------------------------------
CHECKLIST GATE 2: SECTION 301 TARIFF & ORIGIN
VERIFICATION
---------------------------------------------------------
[ ] 2a. Is the merchandise produced in China, or does it
        contain Chinese components?
    [ ] YES (Proceed to 2b)    [ ] NO (Gate Cleared)
[ ] 2b. Applied Chapter 99 Section 301 Heading:
        _______________
[ ] 2c. If third-country processing occurred
        (Vietnam/Malaysia/Thailand), is a formal
        Substantial Transformation Legal Opinion
        attached?
[ ] 2d. If Chapter 99 Exclusion is claimed, is the
        exclusion active in ACE?

---------------------------------------------------------
CHECKLIST GATE 3: UFLPA & FORCED LABOR SUPPLY CHAIN
TRACING
---------------------------------------------------------
[ ] 3a. Does cargo contain UFLPA high-priority sector
        inputs (cotton/apparel, tomatoes, silica-based
        products, aluminum, PVC, seafood, steel, copper,
        lithium, caustic soda, red dates)?
    [ ] YES (Proceed to 3b)    [ ] NO (Gate Cleared)
[ ] 3b. Is a pre-verified 5-Module UFLPA Evidentiary
        Package archived in portal?
```

```
[ ] 3c. Tier-1 through Tier-4 raw material supply chain
        map verified to raw origin.
[ ] 3d. Digital UFLPA Clearance Key issued by Importer
        Compliance Director:
        Key #: _______________________

ENTRY CLEARANCE AUTHORIZATION:
I certify that all high-risk pre-entry gating protocols
above have been verified against physical shipping
documents and electronic master data records.

Filing Entry Clerk Signature: ______________________
Date: ____________________________

Licensed Broker Supervisor Signature: ______________
Date: ____________________________
```

## Tool E: Annual Customs Broker Scorecard & Audit Evaluation Sheet

### Broker & Evaluation Details

| FIELD | ENTRY |
|---|---|
| Broker corporate name | __________________ |
| National permit # | __________ |
| Primary processing branch | __________ |
| Designated qualifying LCB | __________________ |
| Period covered | Q1 2026 – Q4 2026 |
| Evaluation date | __________ |

### Category Evaluation Breakdown

| CATEGORY (WEIGHT) | METRICS | SCORE |
|---|---|---|
| 1. Classification & data accuracy (35%) | Lines audited ___; discrepancy lines ___; master HTS match ___ %; valuation match ___% | ___ / 35.0 |
| 2. High-risk operational control (25%) | AD/CVD non-reimbursement [ ] PASS [ ] FAIL; PGA/TSCA disclaimer [ ] PASS [ ] FAIL; UFLPA gating [ ] PASS [ ] FAIL | ___ / 25.0 |
| 3. Filing velocity & timeliness (20%) | Entries released ___; summaries transmitted under 5 days ___; timeliness ___% | ___ / 20.0 |
| 4. Regulatory responsiveness (10%) | Notices received (28/29/4647) ___; escalated under 24 hours ___; | ___ / 10.0 |

| CATEGORY (WEIGHT) | METRICS | SCORE |
|---|---|---|
| | responsiveness ___% | |
| 5. System integration & billing health (10%) | API product-master sync ___%; billing invoice accuracy ___% | ___ / 10.0 |

**Composite Score & Performance Tier**

**Final composite score: ___ / 100.0 points.**

| TIER | RANGE | ACTION |
|---|---|---|
| [ ] Tier 1: Premier Compliance | 95.0 – 100.0 | Account approved |
| [ ] Tier 2: Acceptable Risk | 90.0 – 94.9 | Notice of Discrepancy issued |
| [ ] Tier 3: Conditional Warning | 80.0 – 89.9 | 25% SLA fee offset plus CAP |
| [ ] Tier 4: Unacceptable Breach | Below 80.0 | 50% SLA offset plus offboarding |

These instruments are starting points, not answers. Take them to your counsel, adapt them to your facts, and, this is the part that actually matters, use them. A model agreement in a drawer protects no one.

# Primary Sources and Where to Verify

This book cites statutes, regulations, cases, and agency guidance throughout. When a number or a rule matters to a decision you are about to make, go to the primary source rather than to this book. The following are the ones this book leans on most, and where to find them.

Statutes, in the United States Code. 19 U.S.C. § 1484 (entry and reasonable care), § 1592 (penalties), § 1504 (liquidation), § 1517 (the Enforce and Protect Act), and § 1307 (forced labor). Read them at the Office of the Law Revision Counsel (uscode.house.gov) or Cornell's Legal Information Institute (law.cornell.edu).

Regulations, in the Code of Federal Regulations. 19 CFR Part 111 (Customs Brokers), Parts 141 and 142 (entry), Part 163 (recordkeeping), and 19 CFR § 351.402(f) (antidumping and countervailing duty reimbursement). The current text is on eCFR (ecfr.gov), which shows the version in force today.

Executive Order 14411, "Strengthening Customs Enforcement," and its implementing rules. The order is in the Federal Register (federalregister.gov); watch the same source for the CBP and DHS rulemakings it directs.

Court decisions. The Court of International Trade (cit.uscourts.gov) and the Court of Appeals for the Federal Circuit (cafc.uscourts.gov) publish their opinions. The cases cited here, Golden Ship Trading, Horizon Products, Trek Leather, and Royal Brush, are available there and through free services such as CourtListener and Justia.

CBP guidance and rulings. CBP's Informed Compliance Publications (cbp.gov) explain the agency's expectations in plain language; the CROSS database (rulings.cbp.gov) holds binding classification and origin rulings; and CBP's UFLPA statistics dashboard and forced-labor guidance (cbp.gov) track that program.

Enforcement actions. Department of Justice press releases (justice.gov) announce customs False Claims Act settlements and judgments, including the Ceratizit settlement discussed in Chapter 11.

Treat this as a starting map, not a complete bibliography. The point of it is the habit: when the stakes are real, read the source.

# Glossary of Key Terms and Acronyms

A quick reference for the abbreviations used throughout this book. Where a term carries a specific regulatory meaning, the chapter that covers it gives the full treatment.

| Term | Meaning |
|---|---|
| ABI | Automated Broker Interface, the electronic channel brokers and filers use to transmit entry data into ACE. |
| ACE | Automated Commercial Environment. CBP's primary electronic system for processing imports and generating trade data. |
| AD/CVD | Antidumping and Countervailing Duty, additional duties offsetting unfairly low-priced or subsidized imports; cash-deposit rates can reach several hundred percent. |
| BMS | Broker Management System, the overall governance system an importer builds to control its brokers (Part V). The BOM is the written manual at its core. |
| BOM | Broker Oversight Manual, the internal governance document proposed in Chapter 14 that anchors the BMS (distinct from a bill of materials). |
| CBP | U.S. Customs and Border Protection, the agency that administers and enforces import law at the border. |
| CEE | Center of Excellence and Expertise, one of CBP's ten industry-sector trade centers that handle entry review nationally. |
| CTPAT | Customs Trade Partnership Against Terrorism. CBP's voluntary supply-chain security program. |
| DIS | Document Image System, the ACE facility for uploading supporting documents tied to an entry. |
| EAPA | Enforce and Protect Act, the CBP process for investigating AD/CVD duty evasion. |
| ERP | Enterprise Resource Planning system (for example SAP, Oracle, NetSuite), the importer's system of record for parts, values, and origins. |
| FP&F | Fines, Penalties, and Forfeitures, the CBP office that assesses and mitigates civil penalties. |
| GTM / GTS | Global Trade Management / Global Trade Services, trade-compliance modules that sit on top of an ERP. |
| HTS / HTSUS | Harmonized Tariff Schedule (of the United States), the classification system that sets each product's duty rate. |
| IOR | Importer of Record, the party legally responsible for the entry, the |

| Term | Meaning |
|---|---|
| | duties, and reasonable care. |
| LCB | Licensed Customs Broker, an individual or firm licensed by CBP to conduct customs business for others. |
| MID | Manufacturer Identification code, a coded identifier for the foreign producer, built from its name and address. |
| NCBFAA | National Customs Brokers and Forwarders Association of America, the trade association whose standardized Terms and Conditions of Service, incorporated by reference into broker POA packages, carry the liability cap and one-sided indemnity the book analyzes. NCBFAA also publishes standardized power-of-attorney forms. |
| PGA | Partner Government Agency, another federal agency (FDA, EPA, APHIS, and others) whose data an entry may require. The FCC is not among them; it left the entry process when Form 740 was eliminated in 2017. |
| PMS | Periodic Monthly Statement. CBP's consolidated monthly duty-payment mechanism. |
| POA | Power of Attorney, the instrument by which an importer authorizes a broker to act on its behalf. |
| PSC | Post-Summary Correction, the electronic mechanism to correct an accepted entry summary before liquidation, generally within 300 days of entry. |
| SLA | Service Level Agreement, the performance contract governing the broker's obligations, developed in Chapter 5. |
| SPI | Special Program Indicator, the code claiming a preferential-duty program such as USMCA or GSP. |
| UFLPA | Uyghur Forced Labor Prevention Act, the law creating a rebuttable presumption that certain goods are made with forced labor. |
| USTR | Office of the U.S. Trade Representative, the office that administers Section 301 tariffs and exclusions. |
| WRO | Withhold Release Order, a CBP order detaining goods suspected of being made with forced labor. |

## About the Author

James R. Ferry II, CCS, CES, CIT, is a trade-compliance practitioner and the founder of Ferry Trade Group (FTG), a consultancy that helps importers build Customs Broker oversight programs, audit their ACE data, and hold their filings to a defensible standard of reasonable care. He holds the Certified Customs Specialist (CCS), Certified Export Specialist (CES), and Certificate in International Trade (CIT) designations.

He writes from The Trade Underground, where the ideas in this book took shape, and publishes through Trade Underground Press. Reasonable Care is his field manual for the importer who has understood a single, uncomfortable fact: the customs liability filed under your number is yours, and the oversight has to be yours too.

Ferry Trade Group advises importers who want to put the program in this book to work. The author can be reached at james@ferrytrade.com or ferrytrade.com.

## Keep This Book Current

This book was written into a live rulemaking. Executive Order 14411 directs a new customs-enforcement regime: a directed penalty floor of not less than 50 percent, a bar on mitigation for repeat offenders, and new "good standing" and importer-registry requirements, but these are directed revisions, not rules in force: the implementing rules from CBP and DHS take their final form, subject to the Administrative Procedure Act, only when those agencies publish them. When they do, I will revise this book to match the final rule text and release it as an updated edition.

If you bought this paperback, that update is yours at no charge. Scan the code below, enter the coupon, and download the current digital edition, the PDF and the EPUB, free. You will also be on the update list, so when the post-rulemaking edition ships, you receive it the same way: free, through the same link. Buy the book once, and stay current as the rules settle.

**Coupon code: TURCV2**

Or go to payhip.com/b/HO2kF and enter the code at checkout. This offer is for paperback owners. The digital editions read on any device.

Educational material, not legal advice. Before you rely on a specific rule, deadline, or number, confirm it against the primary source. This page will point you to the current edition whenever the rules change.

# Index of Authorities

Page numbers refer to the 6×9 print edition.

### Statutes



### Regulations (Title 19, Code of Federal Regulations)

**Cases**

**CBP forms, executive orders, and proclamations**